W9-BEO-652

# LEADING

*Alex. Ferguson*

hachette
BOOKS

# LEADING

## Learning from Life and My Years at Manchester United

## ALEX FERGUSON

### AND MICHAEL MORITZ

hachette
BOOKS

NEW YORK   BOSTON

Copyright © 2015 by Sir Alex Ferguson and Sir Michael Moritz
Epilogue copyright © 2015 by Sir Michael Moritz
Archive material copyright details: Letter to Eric Cantona from Alex Ferguson © Sir Alex
Ferguson and Manchester United Football Club PLC 1997; Letter from Ian McLeod to
Alex Ferguson © Ian McLeod and Celtic Football Club 2002; Manchester United
bonus structure document © Manchester United Football Club PLC; Letter from
Kenny Dalglish to Alex Ferguson © Kenny Dalglish and Liverpool Football Club 1989;
Manchester United board meeting document © Manchester United Football Club PLC;
Extract from the United Review © United Review 2009; Letter from Ian Settle to
Alex Ferguson © Ian Settle 2013.
All rights reserved. In accordance with the U.S. Copyright Act of 1976, the scanning,
uploading, and electronic sharing of any part of this book without the permission of the
publisher constitute unlawful piracy and theft of the author's intellectual property.
If you would like to use material from the book (other than for review purposes),
prior written permission must be obtained by contacting the publisher at
permissions@hbgusa.com. Thank you for your support of the author's rights.

Hachette Books
Hachette Book Group
1290 Avenue of the Americas
New York, NY 10104
HachetteBookGroup.com

Printed in the United States of America

RRD-C

First published in Great Britain in 2015 by Hodder & Stoughton

First U.S. Edition: October 2015
10  9  8  7  6  5  4  3  2  1

Hachette Books is a division of Hachette Book Group, Inc.
The Hachette Books name and logo are trademarks of Hachette Book Group, Inc.

The Hachette Speakers Bureau provides a wide range of authors for speaking events.
To find out more, go to www.hachettespeakersbureau.com or call (866) 376-6591.

The publisher is not responsible for websites (or their content)
that are not owned by the publisher.

ISBN: 978-0-316-26808-0

For my family

I have had a privileged life after being brought up in Govan, a working-class area of Glasgow, where my parents Alex and Lizzie gave me a foundation that has stayed with me to this day. My brother Martin has always been a loyal and great friend, following the same path that was laid out by our parents.

I had the good fortune to meet a wonderful girl who has been my rock for almost 50 years. Cathy has presented me with three great sons who have inherited our work ethic and are a credit to both of us. Those three sons have given us more joy than we could ever have imagined, 11 grandchildren ranging in age from five to 21.

It has been an interesting journey as we have watched their development through the years and it is amazing to see the traits I expect from our family within them. I hope that their futures are lined with the same success that I have been fortunate enough to enjoy. Good luck to all of them.

*Alex Ferguson*


For the winning teams of Sequoia Capital – with thanks.

*Michael Moritz*

# CONTENTS

**INTRODUCTION 1**

**1. BECOMING YOURSELF 9**
Listening 11 / Watching 17 / Reading 21

**2. RECOGNISING HUNGER 25**
Discipline 27 / Work Rate 37 / Drive 46 /
Conviction 49

**3. ASSEMBLING THE PIECES 59**
Organisation 61 / Preparation 62 / Pipeline 75

**4. ENGAGING OTHERS 85**
Teamwork 87 / Captains 102

**5. SETTING STANDARDS 109**
Excellence 111 / Inspiring 118 / Complacency 132

**6. MEASURING PEOPLE 141**
Job Hunting 143 / Networking 148 / Firing 155

**7. FOCUS 161**
Time 163 / Distractions 167 / Failing 178 /
Criticism 191

8. **OWNING THE MESSAGE  197**
   Speaking 199 / Writing 211 / Answering 213

9. **LEADING NOT MANAGING  223**
   Owners 225 / Control 235 / Delegation 238 / Decision-making 242

10. **THE BOTTOM LINE  249**
    Buying 251 / Frugality 255 / Compensation 263 / Negotiation 271 / Brokers 276

11. **BUSINESS DEVELOPMENT  283**
    Innovation 285 / Data Overload 291 / Confidentiality 297

12. **THE RELEVANCE OF OTHERS  303**
    Rivalries 305 / Global Markets 310

13. **TRANSITIONS  321**
    Arriving 323 / Leaving 328 / Fresh Challenges 338

**EPILOGUE  345**
**ACKNOWLEDGEMENTS  387**
**PICTURE ACKNOWLEDGEMENTS  388**
**THE DATA ROOM**
**THE ARCHIVE**

# INTRODUCTION

When I left Govan High School in Glasgow at the age of 16 to begin my apprenticeship as a tool-maker at Remington Rand and start my life in football at Queen's Park, I could never have imagined that, 55 years later, I would be standing at the front of a lecture theatre at the Harvard Business School, talking to a class of MBA students about myself.

The first class I taught in October 2012 was jammed to the rafters. From my position in the pit at the front of the lecture hall, I could see the students waiting patiently in their tiered rows of seats – each with their own name card in front of them – and yet more crammed in the aisles. It was an intimidating scene, but also a tribute to the fascination exerted by Manchester United. Our club was in very good company, because among the organisations studied during the Strategic Marketing in Creative Industries course at the Business School are Burberry, the fashion retailer; Comcast, the giant American cable television operator; Marvel Enterprises, the Hollywood studio behind the *Spider-Man* and *Iron Man* comic and film franchises; and, of all things, the business activities of the music superstars Beyoncé and Lady Gaga.

When I looked at the students gathered in one of Aldrich Hall's lecture rooms, I was struck by their cosmopolitan nature, age and intelligence. There were as many nationalities represented in the room as there are on the books of any Premier League squad. The students were all extremely well schooled, and would either work, or had already worked, for some of the most successful companies in the world. All were at the point where they could look forward to the best years of their lives. I could not help but think that the quieter ones, who seemed to be absorbing everything, were the people who would become the most successful.

I found myself on the campus of Harvard University in October of 2012 thanks to a collision of circumstances. A year or so previously I had received an approach from Anita Elberse, a professor at Harvard Business School. She had been curious about the way I managed United and the success that the club had enjoyed, and this resulted in a Harvard case study, *Sir Alex Ferguson: Managing Manchester United*, which was written following Anita spending a few days shadowing me at our training ground in the mornings and interviewing me in the afternoons. Around the same time, she invited me to come and speak to her class at their campus in Boston. I was intrigued, if a little daunted, and accepted the invitation.

Looking back, it's easy to see that this lecture marked the start of a transitional phase in my career. Although I didn't know it at the time, we were just a few weeks into what would turn out to be my final season in charge at Old Trafford, and there was a lot on my mind. We had lost the title in the previous season on goal difference to our local rivals, Manchester City, but were determined to bounce back. And we had started the new season strongly. Two days before I flew to Boston, we had come away from St James' Park with a 3–0 win over Newcastle United. It was our fifth victory in seven games and took us to second place in the Premier League, four points behind Chelsea.

We had also made a 100 per cent start to our Champions League campaign, UEFA's premier club competition, formerly known as the European Cup.

But for the time being, as I stood at the front of the classroom in Harvard, I put the Premier League and Champions League campaigns to one side and focused on sharing some of the secrets behind Manchester United's recent success.

The class began with Professor Elberse providing an overview of the different constituents I dealt with as manager of Manchester United – the players and the staff, the fans and the media, the board and our owners. I followed this by giving the students my thoughts on the principal elements of leadership. I then took questions from the students. This was the most enjoyable part of the day and it raised topics that I found myself thinking about in the days that followed. The students were all curious about how I became a leader, the individuals who had a major influence on my approach to life, the way I dealt with absurdly gifted and highly paid young men, the manner in which United maintained a thirst for excellence – and a raft of other topics. Understandably they also wanted to know about the daily habits of household names like Cristiano Ronaldo and David Beckham.

It took me a bit of time to adjust to standing in front of a blackboard rather than sitting in a football dugout, but I gradually began to realise that teaching bears some similarities to football management. Perhaps the most important element of each activity is to inspire a group of people to perform at their very best. The best teachers are the unsung heroes and heroines of any society, and in that classroom I could not help but think of Elizabeth Thomson, a teacher at Broomloan Road Primary School, who encouraged me to take my school work seriously and who helped me gain admission to Govan High School.

I have spent much of my life trying to coax the best out of young people and the Harvard classroom presented another such opportunity. As the years have gone by, I have found that my appetite for, and appreciation of, youthful enthusiasm has only grown. Young people will always manage to achieve the impossible – whether that is on the football field or inside a company or other big organisation. If I were running a company, I would always want to listen to the thoughts of its most talented youngsters, because they are the people most in touch with the realities of today and the prospects for tomorrow.

The books I have previously written about my addiction to football are full of details about competitions, games and the composition of teams that I played in and managed. The first, *A Light in the North: Seven Years with Aberdeen*, appeared in 1985, two years after Aberdeen's European Cup Winners' Cup victory. In 1999, after Manchester United won the Treble – the Premier League, the FA Cup and the UEFA Champions League – I published *Managing My Life*, and a few months after my retirement in 2013, *My Autobiography* was released.

This book is different. It's my attempt to sum up what I learned from my life in general and my time as a manager – first in Scotland for 12 years with East Stirlingshire, St Mirren and Aberdeen, and then, south of the border, for 26 years with Manchester United. I have also included some interesting data covering my time in management and some archival material that has not been seen before as a way to illustrate a few of the topics being addressed. The data and archive material can be found at the back of the book.

Figuring out what it takes to win trophies with a round ball differs from the challenges facing the leaders of companies like BP, Marks & Spencer, Vodafone, Toyota or Apple, or the people who run large hospitals, universities or global charities. Yet there are traits that apply to all winners, and to organisations whose leaders aspire to win. This is my attempt to explain how I built, led and managed the organisation at Manchester United, and the sorts of things that worked for me. I don't pretend for a moment that they can be easily transplanted elsewhere, but I hope that readers will find some ideas or suggestions that can be emulated or modified for their own use.

I am not a management expert or business guru, and have little interest in pounding the lecture circuit repeating a canned pitch. So don't expect any academic jargon or formulaic prose. Don't ask me to explain double-entry book-keeping, how to hire 500 people in six months, the challenges of matrix management, the way to get a manufacturing line to churn out 100,000 smartphones a day, or the best approach to developing software. I don't have a clue. That expertise belongs to others because my whole life has revolved around football. This book contains the lessons and observations about how I pursued excellence on and off the football pitch.

Unlike the great American basketball coach John Wooden, whose 'Pyramid of Success' accompanied him throughout most of his career from 1928 to 1975, I never employed a one-page diagram or a massive guide that would be handed out to players at the start of each season and viewed as gospel. Nor did I favour minute instructions written on 3- x 5-inch cards, or copious notes compiled over the years. My approach to leadership and management evolved as the seasons went by. This is my attempt to sum up what I learned and distil it on paper.

This book came to life after I was approached by Michael Moritz, Chairman of Sequoia Capital, the US headquartered private investment firm best known for helping to shape and organise companies such as Apple, Cisco Systems, Google,

PayPal and YouTube and, more recently, WhatsApp and Airbnb. We had first talked about collaborating on a book several years before my retirement, but the timing was not right for either of us. Happily, in the past couple of years, we both had the time to devote our energy towards putting words on paper. It turned out that Michael, who led Sequoia Capital between the mid-1990s and 2012, had always wondered how Manchester United had maintained a high level of performance over several decades. As we talked, it was obvious that Michael's interest stemmed from his desire to ensure that Sequoia Capital did the same. As you might know, Sequoia Capital has been able to collect more than its fair share of silverware. Michael has contributed an epilogue to the book which, though it makes me blush from time to time, explains more fully why and how our paths came to cross.

*Leading* is the result of many conversations between Michael and me that cover a range of topics – some of which I hadn't pondered previously. The conversations allowed me to collect my thoughts about issues that confront any leader but which, because of the pressure of their daily obligations, I never had time to gather. I hope you find some of them useful.

Alex Ferguson
Manchester
August 2015

# 1

---

# BECOMING YOURSELF

## Listening

How does someone become their true self? When I was young I never gave the topic much thought but, as a player and particularly as a manager, I became increasingly interested in the subject. If you are leading people, it helps to have a sense of who they are – the circumstances in which they were raised, the actions that will draw out the best in them, and the remarks that will cause them to be spooked. The only way to figure this out is by two underrated activities: listening and watching.

Most people don't use their eyes and ears effectively. They aren't very observant and they fail to listen intently. As a result, they miss half of what is going on around them. I can think of some managers who could talk under water. I don't think it helps them. There's a reason that God gave us two ears, two eyes and one mouth. It's so you can listen and watch twice as much as you talk. Best of all, listening costs you nothing.

Two of the best listeners I have met were television interviewers. Before his death in 2013, David Frost had spent nearly five decades interviewing people, including, most famously, the former US president Richard Nixon. I first met Frost in 2005 when we were both investors in a property fund manager. A few years later, after he'd left the BBC, he interviewed me for Sky Sports.

Unlike most television interviewers, David did not feel the need to prove he was smarter than his guest. He did not keep snapping at their heels, or interrupting, but he was definitely no pushover – as he demonstrated with the 28 hours and 45 minutes of conversations he taped with Richard Nixon in 1977. Some of this was because of the format of his shows. He was not doing post-match, 90-second interviews with a producer yelling into his earpiece demanding a sound-bite. And he wasn't swivelling his head, mid-interview, as he tried to catch the eye of his next unsuspecting target. David would look you in the eyes, lock out the rest of the world and demonstrate great interest. He had time on his side – 30 or 60 minutes (an eternity in today's world of instant messaging and Twitter) to gradually make his guest feel at ease. David's greatest gift was his ability to get a guest to relax, and that always seemed to allow him to extract more from an interview. It's little wonder that his nick-name was 'The Grand Inquisitor'.

Charlie Rose, the American television interviewer, is similar. I don't know Charlie as well as I knew David, but a couple of years ago I was invited to appear on his show. I was a little apprehensive about appearing on American television, which isn't as familiar to me as all the British talk shows. The day before I went on Charlie's show, he invited me for a drink at Harry Cipriani, an Italian restaurant on Fifth Avenue in New York. Charlie is a big man and has hands the size of dinner plates, so I wondered whether he was going to clamp me in a vice. His opening line was, 'You know I'm half Scottish', and after that, I knew all would be well. Charlie had cleverly put me at my ease and given us something familiar to talk about.

On the following day the taping went fine, with Charlie listening just as intently as David, even though I suspect his producer was wondering about whether she would have to use subtitles to make my Scottish accent comprehensible to viewers in Mississippi and Kansas.

I have never been a television host but I've always valued listening. This doesn't mean I was in the habit of phoning people to ask them what I should do in a particular situation. On the whole I liked to work things out for myself. But I do remember seeking help when, in 1984, I was offered the manager's position at Glasgow Rangers by John Paton, who was one of the club's largest shareholders. It was the second time that there had been overtures from Rangers, so I called Scot Symon, who had managed the club for 13 years, and sought his advice. I already had my doubts about going to Rangers. If I was going to leave Aberdeen I was unsure about going to another Scottish club. When Scot discovered that I had not talked to the ultimate authority at Rangers, vice-chairman Willie Waddell, he urged me to decline the offer, since he felt it was more of a fishing expedition and probably hadn't been officially sanctioned by the board. I did, and I've never regretted that decision.

Many people cannot stop long enough to listen – especially when they become successful and all the people around them are being obsequious and pretending to hang on their every word. They launch into monologues as if suddenly they know everything. Putting these megalomaniacs to one side, it always pays to listen to others. It's like enrolling in a continuous, lifelong free education, with the added benefit that there are no examinations and you can always discard useless comments. A few examples come to mind:

Years ago somebody gave me a set of tapes containing conversations with Bill Shankly, the Liverpool manager between 1959 and 1974. They were reminiscences, and were not designed for broadcast, but I listened to them several times while driving. They contained all sorts of anecdotes, but the inescapable truth of those tapes was the degree of Shankly's complete obsession with football, which must have been in his bone marrow. Even if Shankly verged on the extreme, it reinforced to me the dedication required to succeed.

On another occasion, after a game against Leeds United in 1992, I was in the team bath with the players – which was highly unusual for me – listening to their analysis of the match. Steve Bruce and Gary Pallister were raving about Eric Cantona, the French striker Leeds had signed from Nîmes. Steve Bruce, who was then United's captain, was particularly complimentary about Cantona's abilities. Somehow, those comments planted a seed, which soon afterwards led to us buying Cantona.

Even as we signed Eric Cantona, I sought advice from people I trusted. I chatted with both Gérard Houllier, the French manager, and the French sports journalist, Erik Bielderman, in an attempt to better understand the player I was buying. I also spoke to Michel Platini who said, 'You should sign him, his character is underestimated, he just needs a bit of understanding.' They all provided tips about the best way to handle Eric, who arrived at United with a reputation – which was unfair – for being unmanageable. It proved to be a pivotal decision for United that season – arguably for the whole decade. In the six games we played before Eric arrived we had scored four goals. In the six games following his arrival, we scored 14.

The comment that led us to Cantona was unusual but I made it a practice to listen intently to how the players would predict the probable line-up of our opponents. It was always a guessing game until we got handed the team-sheet and our opponents' line-up could have a big influence on our tactics. During the week before a game, players often talk to their pals around the League, particularly their former team-mates, so they sometimes pick up clues about which players they would be facing in the tunnel. We used to have little competitions to see whether we could guess the line-up. No matter how hard I listened, I could never fully anticipate the 11 characters we would be up against. As the squads expanded, it became even harder to do. Inevitably, after we eventually had the information, the line-up would differ from what I had expected and the players would rib me by saying, 'You're right again, Boss.'

After United got beaten at Norwich in November 2012, out of courtesy I had to show my face in their manager's room. Chris Hughton was gracious enough, but the room was packed with people celebrating their win. I did not want to show any weakness, so I put on a good face and listened to what they had to say – particularly about the players they were singling out for praise. I just remembered all their names and made a mental note to put everyone on our radar screen.

Looking back further, I remember another critical piece of advice. In 1983, when Aberdeen – the team I managed between 1978 and 1986 – were due to play Real Madrid in the final of the European Cup Winners' Cup in Gothenburg, I invited Jock Stein to accompany us. Jock was one of my heroes and was the first British manager to win the European Cup in 1967, when Celtic beat Inter Milan. Jock said two things that I have never forgotten. First, he told me, 'Make sure you are the second team on the ground for training on the day before the game because then your opponents will think you are watching them while they work.' He also advised me to take along a bottle of Macallan whisky for Real Madrid's manager, the great Alfredo

Di Stéfano. When I gave Di Stéfano that bottle, he was really taken aback. It made him think that we were in awe of him – that he was the big guy and that little Aberdeen felt they were beaten already. I'm glad I listened to Jock because both his tips helped.

Later, when I worked for Jock as assistant manager of Scotland, I used to pepper him with questions about tactics and dealing with management issues. He was as close to a managerial mentor as I ever had, and I would soak up almost everything he had to say. Jock used to advise me never to lose my temper with players straight after the game. He kept saying, 'Wait till Monday, when things have calmed down.' It was sound advice; it just didn't happen to suit my style. Nonetheless, it is no coincidence that in my office in Wilmslow the largest photograph on the wall is of Jock Stein and me, before the Wales v Scotland game on 10 September 1985 – the night he died.

There is one final example that comes to mind: Jimmy Sirrel, who was manager of Notts County and an instructor on a coaching course I attended in 1973 at Lilleshall, one of the United Kingdom's National Sports Centres, taught me a crucial lesson. He told me never to let all the players' contracts expire around the same time because it allows them to collude against the manager and the club. I'd never thought about that before Jimmy mentioned it to me but, afterwards, I paid very close attention to making sure we staggered the contracts. I bet Jimmy's advice took him less than a minute to convey, but the benefit of listening to him lasted me a lifetime. It just shows that advice often comes when you least expect it, and listening, which costs nothing, is one of the most valuable things you can do.

# Watching

Watching is the other underrated activity, and again, it costs nothing. For me there are two forms of observation: the first is on the detail and the second is on the big picture. Until I was managing Aberdeen and hired Archie Knox as my assistant manager, I had not appreciated the difference between watching for the tiny particulars while also trying to understand the broader landscape. Shortly after he arrived at Aberdeen, Archie sat me down and asked me why I had hired him. The question perplexed me, until he explained that he had nothing to do since I insisted on doing everything. He was very insistent, and was egged on by Teddy Scott, Aberdeen's general factotum, who agreed with him. Archie told me that I shouldn't be conducting the training sessions but, instead, should be on the sidelines watching and supervising. I wasn't sure that I should follow this advice because I thought it would hamper my control of the sessions. But when I told Archie I wanted to mull over his advice, he was insistent. So, somewhat reluctantly, I bowed to his wishes and, though it took me a bit of time to understand you can see a lot more when you are not in the thick of things, it was the most important decision I ever made about the way I managed and led. When you are a step removed from the fray, you see things that come as surprises – and it is important to allow yourself to be surprised. If you are in the middle of a training session with a whistle in your mouth, your entire focus is on the ball. When I stepped back and watched from the sidelines, my field of view was widened and I could absorb the whole session, as well as pick up on players' moods, energy and habits. This was one of the most valuable lessons of my career and I'm glad that I received it more than 30 years ago. Archie's observation was the making of me.

As a player I had tried to do both – paying attention to the ball at my feet whilst being aware of what was happening else-where on the field. But until Archie gave me a finger wagging, I had not really understood that, as a manager, I was in danger of losing myself to the details. It only took me a handful of days to understand the merit of Archie's point, and from that moment I was always in a position to be able to zoom in to see the detail and zoom out to see the whole picture.

As a manager you are always watching out for particular things. You might be monitoring a player in training to see if he has shaken off a thigh injury; appraising a promising 12 year old in the youth academy; looking at a hot prospect in a night game at some stadium in Germany; examining the demeanour of a player or coach at the lunch table. You could also be searching for patterns and clues in a video analysis reel, the body language during a negotiation, or the length of the grass on a pitch. Then, on Saturday afternoons or Wednesday evenings, there would be the need for the other, wider lens – the one capable of taking in the whole picture.

It sounds simple to say you should believe what your eyes tell you, but it is very hard to do. It is astonishing how many biases and preconceived notions we carry around, and these influence what we see, or, more precisely, what we think we see. If I was told by a scout that a player had a good left foot, it would be hard for me to forget that observation when I went to watch him in action – and in doing so it would be easy to overlook another quality or, much more painfully, ignore a major fault. I was certainly interested in what other people had to say, but I always wanted to watch with my own eyes without having my judgement swayed by the filters of others.

Here is one observation from which I benefited for decades. In 1969 West Germany were training at Rugby Park in Kilmarnock and I asked Karl-Heinz Heddergot, of the German FA, for permission to watch the practice. The only people in the ground were the German players and staff, a few groundsmen, and me. I watched the training for around an hour and a half. The German squad played without goalkeepers, and just concentrated on possession of the ball, which was unusual during a period when coaches used to emphasise training sessions composed of long-distance running. That one encounter made an enormous impression on me, and thereafter I started to emphasise the importance of possession. As soon as I became a coach at St Mirren, I started doing 'boxes' – where we'd pit four players against two in a confined amount of space. We started with boxes that were 25 yards by 25 yards, which forced the players to perform in a confined space and improve their ball skills. As players' skills improved, we tightened the boxes. It helped with everything: awareness, angles, touch on the ball, and eventually it led to being able to play one-touch football. It was a coaching technique I used right up until my last training session at United on 18 May 2013. Watching that practice for 90 minutes in Kilmarnock back in 1969 furnished me with a lesson I used for half a century.

Observation – sizing up others and measuring situations – is an essential part of preparation, and, at United, we made it a habit to carefully watch opponents before going up against them in big games. This was even more important in the era prior to sophisticated video analysis, when the best we could do was fast forward or rewind through a videotape. One example of this paying off was in United's 1991 European Cup Winners' Cup final against Barcelona. It was the first European final to be played by an English team following the ban from European competition after the Heysel disaster of 1985. I had attended Barcelona's semi-final first leg against Juventus with Steve Archibald, a former Aberdeen player, during which their main striker, Hristo Stoichkov, was hugely impressive and scored two goals. In the second leg in Turin he suffered a hamstring injury that ruled him out of the final. It played havoc with their normal formation. During the final they relied on Michael Laudrup to be their chief offensive weapon, driving forward from midfield which, thanks to watching Barcelona previously, we had anticipated. We had already adjusted our tactics, steadfastly refused to be lured too far forward by Laudrup, and eventually won 2–1.

There were also plenty of times when I saw a player out of the corner of my eye who came as a complete, but pleasant, surprise. In 2003 I had gone to watch a young Petr Čech play in France. Didier Drogba, whom I had not heard of, was playing in the same game. He was a dynamo – a strong, explosive striker with a true instinct for goal – though he ultimately slipped through our fingers. That didn't happen with Ji-sung Park. I had gone to get the measure of Lyon's Michael Essien in the Champions League in 2005 during their quarter-final ties with PSV Eindhoven, and saw this ceaseless bundle of energy buzz about the field like a cocker spaniel. It was Ji-sung Park. The following week I sent my brother, Martin, who was a scout for United, to watch him, to see what his eyes told him. They told him the same thing and we signed him. Ji-sung was one of those rare players who could always create space for himself.

These were very special moments. I always enjoyed stumbling across a new talent when I was least expecting it. Very rarely do you see something so astonishing that you sense it arrived from another world (though Eric Cantona, at his very best, could have done so). These moments – and players – are the reward for a lifetime of careful watching. None of them suddenly dropped into our lap; they were the result of keeping our radar operating 24 hours a day.

# Reading

I have picked up a lot from reading books over the years. As a boy I disappointed my parents by not working hard enough at school (largely because I was already besotted by football), so my formal education ended when I was 16. But I've always liked reading. In fact I was in the library in Glasgow on 6 February 1958 when I heard about the Munich air disaster. I've subscribed for many years to the *Daily Express* during the week and the Scottish *Sunday Mail* and *Sunday Post*, the *Sunday Express* and *Independent* on the weekends. I've also been partial to the *Racing Post*, which keeps me up to date on horse racing. But, more importantly, I've always liked books.

My interest in books stretches far beyond football. One of the coaches I read about came from a sport about which I know nothing. He was the great UCLA basketball coach John Wooden, who led his team to ten national championship titles in 12 seasons. He was probably stronger as an inspirational coach than as a master of tactics, but there was no misunderstanding about who was boss. He would not tolerate any waywardness or people straying from the path he mapped out. I also read up on Vince Lombardi, who was a household name in the United States during the time he was the coach of the Green Bay Packers. He was as obsessed about American football as I was about English football. I found him easy to identify with and love his quote, 'We didn't lose the game; we just ran out of time.'

I have dipped into other books about management and leadership but, maybe because I was always so preoccupied with my own job, I never found one that spoke to me. The same goes for sports books and players' biographies. For the most part, a United player's autobiography was an account, albeit from a different angle, of something I had already lived through. I just found I preferred reading books that had little to do with my daily work. From time to time I tripped across other football books such as David Peace's novel, *The Damned Utd*, a fictionalised account of Brian Clough's 44-day spell as manager of Leeds United in 1974, but cannot say I found it captivating. However, I was taken by *Farewell but not Goodbye*, the autobiography of Bobby Robson, a man whom I admired greatly, who started his life down a coal-mine and who, after being fired as England manager after being one step short of the 1990 World Cup final, showed great courage by picking himself up and going to the Netherlands to manage PSV Eindhoven before later heading to Porto and Barcelona and, eventually returning to his hometown, Newcastle. Of the players' autobiographies, the one I would single out is Gary Neville's *Red*, which was published in 2011. It's a thoughtful book and helps the reader understand the pressure on players and their need to succeed.

I don't want to overplay this, but I found some observations in books about military history relevant to football. Every general has to learn the best time to attack and when it is better to be conservative. Oddly, this was reiterated by a training course I attended with the SAS, who explained how they mounted attacks by outflanking and diverting the enemy on either side and then launching a deadly assault down the middle. One year we took the whole United squad to the SAS training grounds in Herefordshire for a couple of days during a break in the season. They gave us a taste of everything – winching descents from helicopters, the shooting range, and simulated break-ups of hostage situations. The players loved it. One lesson I took from the SAS was the effectiveness of a battle formation, where troops attacking on the flanks create softness in the central defences. I took that lesson right to the training pitch where we worked on it for a week before a Liverpool game. I had players attacking the back post and the front post and then Gary Pallister came from right outside the centre of the box to score. In fact Pallister scored twice using precisely the same ploy. It could have been a re-enactment of a battle plan – except none of the TV commentators picked up on that.

I've always been interested in American history – both military and political – and I've read a fair amount about Abraham Lincoln and JFK, especially the value of taking your time before making decisions. I found Doris Kearns Goodwin's book *Team of Rivals: the Political Genius of Abraham Lincoln* absorbing, while JFK's careful approach during the Cuban Missile Crisis of 1962 is as fine an example of deliberate decision-making as you will find. I certainly found more virtue in patiently working towards the right decision as I got older. In my early days as a manager I could be impetuous – always in a hurry to get things done and stamp my authority on a situation. It takes courage to say, 'Let me think about it.' When you're young you want to fly to the moon and you want to get there quickly. I think it's usually enthusiasm that causes this. As you get older you temper your enthusiasm with experience.

I realise that we're shaped by lots of other forces beyond just watching, listening and reading. We're all accidental victims of our parents' DNA; we are shaped by the luck of the draw, the circumstances in which we grew up and the education we received. But we all have two sets of very powerful tools that we completely control: our eyes and our ears. Watching others, listening to their advice and reading about people are three of the best things I ever did.

# 2

## RECOGNISING HUNGER

# Discipline

Discipline was drummed into me from an early age. My father was a real disciplinarian. He worked in ship-building, which was a hard and cruel business. He didn't talk much. He could be stubborn and was a man of few words but he was very intelligent. He was self-educated, left school at 14, but read all the time. He wanted my brother and me to be trained in a craft and refused to let me become a professional footballer until after I had finished my apprenticeship as a tool-maker. He drummed discipline into us from an early age. On schooldays he would always shake my leg promptly at 6 a.m. He would also be out of the house at 6.45 a.m. on the dot because he liked to be at the yard when the gates opened. Maybe that's why, a couple of decades later as a manager, I got into the habit of appearing for work before the milkman arrived. After I started being paid for playing football, I used to go out on Saturday nights. My father didn't like that. He thought I was living life too well. I went about six months without talking to him. The two of us were too alike.

When I was 14 I started playing for Drumchapel Amateurs, which was the biggest amateur team in Scotland. It was run by Douglas Smith, a relatively wealthy man whose family owned a shipbreaking yard. He had an arrangement with Reid's Tea Rooms in the centre of Glasgow so that boys could get a free lunch. He ran five teams – Under-18s, Under-17s, Under-16s, Under-15s and Under-14s. Every weekend he would take us down to his estate in Dunbartonshire, just outside Glasgow, walk us through his piggery and then make us play five-a-side games on his bowling green. He tensed up when one of his teams lost and would start sweating and get visibly angry. He had a great sense of discipline and a deep desire to win.

Discipline had been an issue from day one at St Mirren, which I managed between 1974 and 1978. When I first arrived, the local paper, the *Paisley Daily Express,* sent a photographer out to take a picture of the team with their new manager. The next morning I saw the photograph in the paper with Ian Reid, the player who had been the team captain, standing behind me with his fingers making a set of rabbit ears. After we lost our first game to Cowdenbeath, I called Reid into my office on the Monday morning. He said that his rabbit ears were only a joke and I told him, 'It's not the kind of joke I like.' John Mowat was a good, young player who started answering back when I gave him instructions during a game. I put both Reid and Mowat in my black book. There was another player who told me that he couldn't attend a training session because he and his girlfriend had tickets for a pop concert. I asked him whether the concerts were on every night of the year. When he said that wasn't the case, I told him, 'If you want to go to the concert, fine, but don't come back.' I just wanted to make it very clear to all the players that I did not want to be messed about with. They got the message.

When I became a manager, one of my duties was to instil discipline. At St Mirren, the team was composed of part-time players but, nonetheless, we all travelled on the same bus to away games. One player decided to drive himself to East Fife one Saturday. I tore into him in the dressing room before the game for being too big for his boots and I told him he wouldn't be part of the team that day. Then I realised I didn't have a spare player to replace him with, so that piece of discipline went out the window.

When I got to Aberdeen, which is a more sedate place than Glasgow, I realised that I would need to inject a bit of Glaswegian ferocity and discipline into the team. I didn't spare the horses. I was aggressive and demanding and I suspect not everyone enjoyed it, but it made the players into men and increased their profiles.

At Aberdeen there were three players who, in my opinion, were a nuisance. They just did not take training seriously enough. So I would make them work out again each afternoon, dumped them into the reserve team and sent them to play in freezing places like Peterhead on Tuesday and Wednesday nights. Eventually, I just got rid of them all.

Discipline might also have been instilled, decades ago, by the fact that teams rarely seemed to change. It's hard to believe (especially when you see the seven substitutes sitting on the bench during Premier League games) that substitutes were only first allowed in the mid-1960s. When I was a boy a team barely changed for the entire season, and even now I can name the Raith Rovers team from the early 1950s. There was also a large element of economic necessity about staying in the team to ensure you got your bonus money.

From time to time, in my younger days, I was too much of a disciplinarian and did things that I regretted. For example, after Aberdeen returned home from Sweden with the European Cup Winners' Cup in 1983, we had a parade which ended at our stadium, Pittodrie, which was packed to the gills. All the fans wanted to see the players carry the trophy around the field and Mark McGhee, Aberdeen's centre-forward, was eager to show them the trophy. However, I thought he had been celebrating too much and so I tore into him and forbade him from carrying the trophy. Then his mother arrived in the dressing room and, of course, that made me feel rotten. So the next morning I phoned McGhee and apologised and asked him to accompany me down to the harbour where he and I showed the trophy to the fans who had travelled by boat back from Gothenburg. I was not eager to repeat incidents like that.

The issue of discipline accompanied me throughout my career. In the conversations I had with Martin Edwards before accepting Manchester United's offer to join them in November 1986, he alluded to the habit of some of the players to drink too much. He mentioned that one of the reasons United had been interested in me was that I had built a reputation as a manager who was known for maintaining discipline and not tolerating poor behaviour.

When I got to United there was a lax attitude towards lots of things, including the clothes the players wore when travelling to games. They used to wear the tracksuits of whatever clothing company was sponsoring them – Reebok, Puma, adidas. It was a royal mess. I immediately insisted that they travel in flannels, the club blazer and tie. When Fabien Barthez joined us in 2000 as a goalkeeper from Monaco, he had to adjust to our clothing regimen. He did this by changing clothes on the bus on the way to games. After the game he would return his jacket, trousers, shirt and tie to Albert Morgan, our kit man, who would take care of them until Fabien was required to again appear as a representative of our club. Eric Cantona breached the dress code on one occasion when there was a big civic reception in the town hall for the team and he appeared wearing a suede jacket which had long fringes and a picture of an American Indian chief on the back. The next day he swore to me – and I believed him – that he had thought it was going to be a casual occasion, which is how it would have been treated in France.

Players give a manager plenty of opportunities to crack the whip, so it's best to pick and choose the moments. You don't have to mete out punishment very often for everyone to get the message. For example, I never thought it useful to fine players if they were late for training. Around Manchester, especially in the winter, the roads quickly get clogged if there is an accident or maintenance works. Players would sometimes get stuck in traffic jams and arrive late. If it happened once or twice I didn't care. However, if someone was a repeated late offender, I'd suggest to him that he leave his house ten minutes earlier and would point out to him that, by being late, he was letting his team-mates down. No team player wants to do that. I only remember fining one player for tardy appearances at the training ground and that was the goalkeeper, Mark Bosnich, who was repeatedly late.

I wasn't afraid of crossing into what some of the players might have considered their private territory – hairstyles and jewellery. I never understood why players would want to have long hair when they spend so much effort trying to be as fit and quick as possible. Anything, even a few extra locks of hair, just didn't seem sensible. I had my first issue with a player on this topic when Karel Poborský came to Manchester from Slavia Prague in 1996, looking as though he was going to play for Led Zeppelin rather than United. I did manage to persuade him to trim his locks but, even so, they were always too long for my taste. There were other players who would be wearing necklaces carrying crosses that seemed heavier than those the pilgrims carry up the Via Dolorosa in Jerusalem. I banned all those. However, there wasn't much I could do about tattoos since it was hard – even for me – to argue that they added any weight. Eric Cantona started that particular craze when he arrived one morning with the head of an American Indian chief stencilled on to his left breast. Since Eric was venerated by his team-mates, several other players followed suit. I was always struck by the fact that Cristiano Ronaldo never chose to deface his body. It said a lot about his self-discipline.

Leaders can also hand down different sentences. Inexperienced, or insecure, leaders are often tempted to make any infraction a capital offence. That is all well and good except, once you have hung the person, you are plumb out of options. I gradually began to understand the wisdom behind the phrase, 'Let the punishment fit the crime' and, as judge, jury and chief executioner, I had plenty of sentences at my disposal. A simple yet deadly one was silence, and I used it often. It did not require any public humiliation or tongue-lashing, yet because everyone likes to be acknowledged, the recipient of my silent treatment knew that he was in the woodshed. I doled out lots of fines to players as a way to rap their knuckles and try to keep them focused on the team. They would usually be handed out after bookings or red cards received for stupid behaviour, like dissent shown towards the referee or a wild tackle or unsuitable behaviour off the pitch. These numbers grew more consequential in absolute size as pay ballooned in the Premier League, but the nature of the fine – a week's or two weeks' wages – remained constant. After a disastrous Christmas party in 2007, I fined the first and the reserve team a week's wages.

For the youngsters who were hoping to make the squad, I could set their heads spinning by just refusing to let them travel with the first team. For the squad members there were a couple of other ways I used to drive home the price of infractions. One was to leave a player out of the side, but the more severe was to make him sit in the stands dressed in his civvies. That is a footballer's equivalent of a public hanging. Nobody was immune from this.

Finally, there were the severest penalties of all – a suspension and a transfer. You might think that the second was the toughest, but that was not the way I looked at it. Once we had decided a player was going to be transferred, it was because he either no longer fitted into what we needed at United or, in a few cases, like Cristiano Ronaldo, we were honouring promises. From my point of view, the suspension was by far the most painful because the penalty was borne by both the player *and* the club. That happened in January 1995 when Eric Cantona was suspended for the final four months of the season by United and a further four months by the FA.

Every player dislikes being omitted from the first team, and that sense of disappointment only grows as players age and start to come to grips with the fact that their best playing days are behind them. However, I never let sentiment interfere with my team selections and that was particularly true for big games. In 1994 I dropped Bryan Robson from the squad for the FA Cup final. Bryan was at the end of his distinguished 13-year stay at United and I had underestimated how important it was to him to have a crack at winning his fourth FA Cup medal. In retrospect, I would have kept him in the squad and perhaps played him for the last part of the game

Even though, as my players knew too well, I had a tendency to explode, my temper usually did not have a destructive effect. That was not the case for players who abandoned their self-control and self-discipline on the field. If they got a string of yellow cards or, worse still, a red card as a result of some rush of blood to the head, it could have bitter consequences for the team. Not only did we have to play with ten men but we also lost the services of the player while he was suspended. Peter Schmeichel, Paul Ince, Bryan Robson, Roy Keane, Mark Hughes and Eric Cantona could all start a fight in an empty house. That did not help our cause one bit, and I made no secret about my displeasure when they got sent off for committing some act of folly.

There are some people who just seem to be immune to discipline. Juan Sebastián Verón, the Argentinian midfielder, was like that. Try as I might, I could not get him to fit into our system. He was a fantastic player with tremendous ability, but he was just a wild card. If I played him centre midfield he would end up wide right. If I played him wide right, he would wind up wide left. He simply did not have the necessary self-discipline and so we traded him after two years and 82 appearances. You cannot build a team with blithe free spirits.

There are also some players who will follow instructions to the letter. Ji-sung Park, our South Korean midfielder, was one of those. If I gave him an instruction he was like a dog with a bone – he just would not let go. When we played AC Milan in the Champions League in 2010, I asked Ji-sung Park to mark Andrea Pirlo, their midfielder and creative force. Pirlo was used to running the show for Milan but Ji-sung effectively suffocated him.

I placed discipline above all else and it might have cost us several titles. If I had to repeat things, I'd do precisely the same, because once you bid farewell to discipline you say goodbye to success and set the stage for anarchy. Shortly after Christmas in 2011, I discovered that three United players had gone out on the town on Boxing Day and were the worse for wear when they showed up for training the following morning. So I ordered all of them to do extra training, and dropped the three of them from the team we fielded for the following game against Blackburn Rovers. We already had a large number of injuries, and although this decision weakened us further, I felt this was the correct thing to do. We lost the game to Blackburn 3–2, which cost us a precious three points, and eventually we lost the League to Manchester City on goal difference. Many years earlier, in 1995, our decision to suspend Eric Cantona for the remainder of the season, following his fight with a fan after he got sent off at Crystal Palace, cost us both the League and FA Cup. At the time we suspended Eric (a suspension that, subsequently, was made even more severe by the FA) we were just a point off the top of the table and, had he played for the remainder of the season, I am positive we would have won by about ten points, instead of being pipped at the post by one point by Blackburn Rovers. In the long run principles are just more important than expediency.

If you can assemble a team of 11 talented players who concentrate intently during training sessions, take care of their diet and bodies, get enough sleep and show up on time, then you are almost halfway to winning a trophy. It is always astonishing how many clubs are incapable of doing this.

Before we beat Liverpool 1–0 in the 1996 FA Cup final, I sensed we would win the game by the way our opponents appeared for their pre-match inspection of the pitch. The entire Liverpool team, with the exception of the manager and his assistant, appeared in white suits supplied by a fashion designer. For me it signalled a breakdown in discipline and showed that the team was distracted by a frivolous sideshow. I mentioned this to my kit manager, Norman Davies, and the forecast proved correct when Eric Cantona scored a few minutes from the final whistle. A different example occurred years earlier when in September 1985 Aberdeen beat Rangers 3–0 at Ibrox Park after two of our opponents got sent off during the first half. Rangers had just tried to bully us and, with the crowd going nuts, lost control of their senses. It was complete pandemonium and we had to scuttle to the dressing room for safety for a period during the second half while the police cleared the pitch of marauding fans. This was one of those classic cases where our opponents destroyed themselves.

I always felt that our triumphs were an expression of the consistent application of discipline. It may surprise some to learn that much of the success comes from not getting carried away or trying to do the impossible and taking too many risks. I had a habit of sitting down in January and looking at the fixtures for the remainder of the season for both United and our principal opponents, and would tot up the points that I thought each club would obtain. I was never too far off and the exercise helped illuminate how important it was to grind out the unglamorous 1–0 results. During these sorts of games, we would concentrate on maintaining a compact midfield and yielding nothing. One particular game sticks in my mind: in

March 2007 we went to Middlesbrough during a three-month period when we had the Swedish striker, Henrik Larsson, on loan from Helsingborgs. I could not have asked more from him when, under real pressure, he abandoned his attacking position and fell back into midfield just to help dig out the result. When Henrik appeared in the dressing room at the end of the game, all the players and staff stood up and spontaneously broke into applause for the immense effort he had made in his unaccustomed role. At the end of the season we requested an extra Premier League winners' medal for Henrik, even though he had not played the ten games that at the time were required to obtain the award.

## Work Rate

My parents always worked. My father worked in the Glasgow shipyards while my mother first worked in a wire factory and then in one that made parts for aeroplanes. My father often worked 60 hours a week and his was a tough, cold, dangerous existence. Glasgow is at about the same latitude as Moscow, so when the winter winds swept up the Clyde, the shipyards were brutal places. He would usually take two weeks off a year. In 1955 he worked 64 hours a week for pay of £7 and 15 shillings, or about £189 in today's money. After he died from cancer in 1979, my mother cleaned houses. My parents' devotion to work was probably accentuated by the fact that there wasn't much of a social safety net. Safety standards were appalling, health benefits were negligible, and the industry of lawyers who specialise in making ridiculous claims for the thinnest of reasons didn't exist. I never knew a time when my parents were not working. For a holiday in the summer we used to take a bus to Saltcoats, where all my brother and I did was play football or draughts or chess.

Since both my parents worked their fingers to the bone, I somehow just absorbed the idea that the only way I was going to improve my life was to work very hard. It was baked into my marrow. I was incapable of coasting and I have always been irritated by people who frittered away natural talents because they were not prepared to put in the hours. There's a lot of satisfaction that comes from knowing you're doing your best, and there's even more that comes when it begins to pay off. I suppose that explains why I played in games on the day that I got married and on the day my first son was born. I only missed three United games out of 1,500 – the first to be in Glasgow with my brother following the death of his wife in 1998, then because of my eldest son's wedding in South Africa in 2000 and finally to scout David de Gea in 2010.

At St Mirren and Aberdeen I used to watch as many games a week as possible. I usually did this with Archie Knox, who was Aberdeen's assistant manager. Archie's parents were farmers and he grew up on a farm outside Dundee. So he had always worked farmers' hours and shared my sort of work ethic. The two of us would travel to the games together and, if we were going to Glasgow, Archie would drive down there and I would sleep, and on the way back I'd do the driving and Archie would be snoring away. The round trip could take six hours. Whenever we got tempted to skip a game and take the night off, we'd always say to each other, 'If we miss one game in Glasgow, we'll miss two.'

In most football clubs, managers work much harder than people imagine. Within the Premier League there is unrelenting pressure, and outside the Premier League there isn't enough money around for managers to employ big staffs. That was certainly true when I was starting out. At St Mirren I had a staff of four, which included the assistant manager, a reserve team coach, the physio and a part-time kit manager. At Aberdeen Teddy Scott was the kit man, coach of the reserves and general oiler of any squeaky wheels. He also did all the laundry and ironed the kits. Occasionally he'd sleep on the snooker table because he'd missed the last bus. Even at United, when I started, we only had a staff of eight.

A few times at Aberdeen the entire staff, the apprentices and even the chairman would be up at six o'clock in the morning to go and clear snow from the ground. In March 1980 we started our run towards my first League championship on a day when we had cleared seven or eight inches of snow off the field. We beat Morton 1–0. It was the only game played that day in Scotland.

All the top managers, Carlo Ancelotti, José Mourinho and Arsène Wenger have a formidable work ethic. But it is the unsung heroes who I always admired the most – the sort of managers who would never give up, even though life and luck had not given them one of the top teams. In Scotland I used to run into Alex Smith and Jim McLean in all sorts of godforsaken places, on nights when the rain was hammering down and it would have been much nicer to be sitting in front of the television. Alex managed clubs north of the border for almost 40 years, and Jim was the manager of Dundee United for 22 seasons. Lennie Lawrence and John Rudge are two men whose names most people outside football probably don't even know but Lennie is one of the few people who has managed over 1,000 games for clubs like Charlton Athletic, Bradford City, Luton Town and Grimsby Town, while John managed Port Vale for 16 seasons before spending another 14 years or so as the director of football at

Stoke City. Neither of them ever gave up. Football consumed them. I would often see them watching our reserve team play in front of a handful of fans.

The relentless perseverance of these men was matched by some players on the pitch. Three for whom I developed great admiration were Tony Adams of Arsenal, Gianfranco Zola when he played for Chelsea and Jamie Carragher of Liverpool. I always thought Adams was a United player in the wrong shirt. Alcohol has ruined the careers and lives of many footballers, and at United the sad legacy of George Best will always loom large in our collective memories, so Tony's brave confrontation with his demons at the end of the 1990s was, in itself, extraordinary. But it was what he made himself on the field that captured my attention. What he lacked in talent and pace, he more than compensated for in attitude. He was an average player who transformed himself into an outstanding leader through sheer hard work and application. He always had a winning attitude, and handsomely repaid both George Graham's and Arsène Wenger's faith in him.

I thought Zola was a fantastic example of workmanship. He always gave us trouble but he just never gave up. Even though he is a small man, he could more than hold his own with defenders who were eight or ten inches taller and far stronger. He was full of guile, inordinately creative and completely relentless. His approach to the game dovetailed with mine.

Jamie Carragher trained with United as a youngster. When he was with us he was a midfielder and a mundane, run-of-the-mill player. After he signed for Liverpool, he somehow transformed himself into the heart and soul of the team and its controlling force. In my last season he came on as a substitute in a game that we controlled and I whispered to him, 'Just a wee word, stop kicking our boys.' He responded, 'I'm going to kick every one of them.' I have spent some time with him since I retired and have been really impressed. I wouldn't be surprised if he becomes Liverpool's manager at some point in the future, but first he has to decide if he wants to leave the TV studio and get back into a more challenging role in football.

At United we have been blessed with many players who have this sort of winning attitude. When winning becomes a way of life, true winners are relentless. Corny though it sounds, the very best footballers were competing against themselves to become as good as they could be. It was no accident that players like Ronaldo, Beckham, the Neville brothers, Cantona, Scholes, Giggs and Rooney would all have to be dragged off the training ground. They all just had a built-in desire to excel and improve. Gary Neville, for example, pushed himself harder because he knew that he did not possess the natural talent of some of his team-mates. I never used to worry about what he was up to on a Friday night because, certainly in his younger years, he would always be in bed by 9.30 p.m.

David Beckham was also extraordinary. When he came to us he lived in digs, and would not just train in the mornings and afternoons, but would then show up in the evening to train with the schoolboys. When, at the start of the season, we gave players what in England is called the 'bleep test', to get a sense of their level of aerobic fitness, Beckham would always be off the scales. The same goes for Ronaldo. He had this desire to become the greatest player in the world and was determined to do so. He also paid tremendous attention to nutrition, which pre-dated his move to England. These days he is religious about taking ice baths after every game so that he can continue to play at the level he demands of himself. He does not touch alcohol, and keeps himself at about three kilograms below his natural weight because, now in his thirties, he has found this helps him maintain his pace.

In a perfect world I would have filled every team-sheet with 11 men who had as much determination as talent. But life is not like that, and if I had to choose between someone who had great talent but was short on grit and desire, and another player who was good but had great determination and drive, I would always prefer the latter. The former might work well for a brief period, but they never have the staying power that gives a great club stability and consistency.

The work ethic I have just described of a handful of managers and players is true of the very best athletes in any sport. They have a formidable appetite for work and extraordinary self-discipline. Look at A. P. McCoy, the jockey who won more than 4,000 races and who, over the course of his career, broke every single rib and numerous other bones. His natural weight is about 75 kg, but for about 25 years he has kept himself at about 63 kg. When he announced his retirement, his wife said she would finally have to learn how to cook potatoes. Novak Djokovic, the tennis champion who is a friend of United's long-time defender, Nemanja Vidić, has a similar intensity. You can only marvel when you hear about his fitness routine and dietary regimen.

The world's best footballers are just as disciplined, even though the occasional photograph of them sunning themselves in Dubai or at a nightclub with a young lady may suggest otherwise. They need to work relentlessly, not just because that's what is required to get to the top, but because there is always someone eager to take their place in the squad. It also explains why almost all football players have working-class roots.

Understandably, middle-class parents want to make sure

their boys go to college or acquire skills which means football never gets as much attention in those households. Around the world, football attracts boys for whom further education is unlikely and who have no choice but to work very hard on acquiring and improving their footballing skills as the path towards a better life. Today the phrase 'working class' does not carry the same connotations as it did decades ago, but most of United's players came from what nowadays are called 'lower-income households'. I don't want to sound like an old fogey, but the overall rise in the standard of living means that today's players grew up with hot water, television, telephones, computers, cars and budget airlines, and in physical surroundings that are far more comfortable than those in which I grew up. I've long had a soft spot for people from a working-class background, because I think it prepares them for the hardness of life.

For almost all the British players who played for me, football was their ticket out of miserable circumstances. Ryan Giggs had a tough start. He was born in Cardiff to a mother who was just 17 and, because his paternal grandfather was from Sierra Leone, Ryan had to deal with racial taunts as a child. As a small boy he was uprooted from Wales when his father, Danny Wilson, left rugby union to become a professional rugby league player in the north of England. His father left the family home, and Ryan was raised by his mother, who was born Lynne Giggs, in Salford, where he developed his footballing touch. Lynne worked two jobs – as a barmaid and auxiliary nurse – though as a single mother never had enough money to be able to afford to buy the best boots for Ryan; but she instilled in him the capacity for hard work. She is a real saint, and Ryan paid perpetual tribute to her when he changed his surname from Wilson.

David Beckham came from a small house in East London and his father worked as a heating engineer. Paul Scholes grew up in a council house in Langley and Nicky Butt hailed from Gorton – both places where you won't see a Bentley parked in the drive. Wayne Rooney comes from a hard neighbourhood in Liverpool and gave serious thought to becoming a professional boxer. Danny Welbeck and Wes Brown both grew up in Longsight, a Manchester neighbourhood known for gang violence. Bryan Robson's dad was a lorry driver. Rio Ferdinand grew up in Peckham, one of the poorest areas of London. The list is endless.

Over the years I became better at judging the influence of background on a British player, because we would know the family backgrounds and the schools that the boys attended. It was more difficult to judge those sorts of nuances, and the character of a player, when we started recruiting from South America or Eastern Europe. Until around the mid-1990s, the youngsters would also understand their place in the pecking order at the club. They would be responsible for removing mud from boots, cleaning the dressing room and doing 'balls and bibs' – collecting the balls and shirt bibs that the players had scattered and dropped on the training ground. The boys would understand that the first-team dressing room was strictly out of bounds. Those sorts of rituals probably just made them yearn for success all the more.

In my last decade as a manager, I often found the traits I had previously found in British players visible in boys who had grown up overseas. Cristiano Ronaldo certainly knew what it was like to struggle. He grew up in a village in Madeira in a family that had very little money and was brought up by his mother. Tim Howard, who made 77 appearances in goal for United, was raised in New Jersey by a single mother who had emigrated to the United States from Hungary, and held down two jobs after Tim's father left the scene. The Da Silva twins were another case. They had grown up in Petrópolis in Brazil, and had an astonishing work ethic. Rafael would show up to our training sessions on the coldest of Manchester days wearing a short-sleeved shirt and shorts, while everyone else, including me, was wrapped in layers. At the end of one season I told the pair of them to make sure they got a good rest over the summer, and discovered that their father built a full-size pitch in their hometown so that they could play every day with their mates.

The majority of the foreign players also made football their ticket to the future. The very best have a deeply ingrained capacity for industry, and intuitively grasp that if you can connect talent and work, you can achieve so much. I came from an era when my father made my Christmas toys, and I suspect some of the foreign players empathise with that. Many of the players we signed came from circumstances every bit as grim, perhaps grimmer, than their British team-mates. Adnan Januzaj, who we signed as a 16 year old in March 2011 was born in Belgium, after his parents fled the brutality of the former Yugoslavia. The Ecudorian Antonio Valencia comes from a very poor background, as did the Brazilian, Anderson. Andrei Kanchelskis, who played for us in the 1990s, grew up in the Soviet Union. Carlos Tévez came from the drug-ridden desolation of the 'Fort Apache' neighbourhood in Buenos Aires. Quinton Fortune was reared in a township in apartheid South Africa.

Sadly, there are examples of players who have similar backgrounds to Giggs or Cristiano Ronaldo, who, despite enormous natural talent, just aren't emotionally or mentally strong enough to overcome the hurts of their childhood and their inner demons. Ravel Morrison might be the saddest case. He possessed as much natural talent as any youngster we ever signed, but kept getting into trouble. It was very painful to sell him to West Ham in 2012 because he could have been a fantastic player. But, over a period of years, the problems off the pitch continued to escalate and we had little option but to cut the cord. There has been little evidence that Ravel has matured and his contract was cancelled by West Ham in 2015.

I have an abiding belief about the virtues of tapping the hunger and drive that can be found in people who have had tough upbringings. Whenever we had a setback at United and everyone needed a bit of a boost, I'd always end team talks before a game by reminding the players that they all came from working-class backgrounds where people didn't have much. I would tell them that it's almost certain that their grandparents or someone in their family used to be working class and worked hard every day just to survive whereas all they had to do was work hard for 90 minutes while getting paid a lot of money. In retrospect the phrase 'working class' might not have meant much to some, especially the foreign players, but I think they all knew people who had been through tough times. We all felt ourselves to be outsiders in some ways, and people who feel like outsiders do one of two things: they either feel rejected, carry a chip on their shoulder and complain that life is unfair, or they use that sense of isolation to push themselves and work like Trojans. I always used to tell the players, 'The minute that we don't work harder than the other team, we'll not be Manchester United.'

## Drive

For years I've tried to fathom out why some people possess greater drive than others. I'm not sure I am any closer to solving that riddle today than I was 30 years ago, but I did learn how to harness that power and as I said, I do know that if I had to pick drive or talent as the most potent fuel, it would be the former. For me drive means a combination of a willingness to work hard, emotional fortitude, enormous powers of concentration and a refusal to admit defeat.

At United, there were many players who epitomised the drive required to become successful. At the forefront were the likes of Bryan Robson, Roy Keane, Steve Bruce, Mark Hughes, Brian McClair and Patrice Evra. One player's drive can have an enormous effect on a team – a winning drive is like a magical potion that can spread from one person to another. Bryan Robson was a foreigner to danger. He came from Chester-le-Street, County Durham, a coal-mining area in the north of England, and would plough right into situations that others would avoid. It resulted in him spending a lot of time on the injury list, but it also made him an invaluable leader. Despite dislocating his shoulder several times during his career, he would regularly engage in a daily regime of one thousand press-ups. I used to show players a photograph of Robson defending a corner. His eyes were almost glazed over; he had shut out the rest of the world, and the only thing he was concentrating on was how to make sure that the corner kick was defended properly.

Roy Keane's relentless drive was inspirational. Steve Bruce played 414 games in the centre of our defence, was fearless and a great organiser, but he didn't quite have enough pace. However, like Tony Adams, he made up for his shortcomings with a deeply rooted will to win that was infectious.

David Beckham had a great thirst for victory, as did Nicky Butt, who made 387 appearances for United and was a local lad. The two Neville brothers who came from Bury (just outside Manchester), and Denis Irwin who, like Roy Keane, came from Cork, all had a distinctive drive. They shared similar characteristics: they were entirely dedicated to the club; all were absolutely reliable players who could be counted on to play in 80 per cent of our games; and all could infect others in the team with their will. None of these players relished the sour taste of defeat. Fortunately, as the years went by, we were able to have more players with this sort of edge in the first team.

By singling out these players I don't mean to detract from the others I managed. The reason I mention them is because they did not possess the innate talents of players like Hughes, Cole, Cantona, Verón, Scholes, Giggs and Ronaldo. I use them as examples of drive because, by the application of sheer will-power, undiluted courage and determination, they more than overcame any shortcomings.

Sometimes the drive got out of control and I had to step in. There was an occasion when we played Middlesbrough that a group of players went after the referee like a pack of dogs and I went off my head with them. But I also wanted to be careful that I didn't inadvertently demotivate them. The minute you start intruding too far, you take the drive out of the man. Believe me, it is far easier to do that than to put the drive into someone to whom it does not come naturally. You usually cannot instil an edge in a player if somehow or other he didn't acquire it before he was a teenager. Every now and again there is an example that gives you hope. Ole Gunnar Solskjaer comes to mind. He grew up in a small, quiet Norwegian fishing village, and when he arrived at Old Trafford in 1996 at the age of 23, he looked like a 14-year-old choirboy; there was a certain soft-ness about him. United offered him his first real taste of what victory could be like. He gradually acquired a taste for this and, as a result, became much more aggressive as a player and developed real conviction.

## Conviction

Most people don't have inner conviction. Their confidence is easily shaken, they blow with the wind and can be plagued with doubts. I cannot imagine how anyone, without firm convictions and deep inner beliefs, can be an effective leader. As a player my confidence was shaken when Rangers dropped me and wanted me to agree to a transfer as a part-exchange for another player. But I was determined that I wouldn't let them beat me, and before training I used to go and play nine holes of golf to clear my head and get ready to attack the day. I just resolved not to give in and, when they sold me to Falkirk in 1969, it was on my own terms.

When I did waver, or at least was not being true to myself, it sometimes took another person to shake me out of my stupor. There was an occasion during my early time at United in 1991 when Jock Wallace, the former manager of Rangers, phoned me and said he was coming to watch us play Southampton. Jock was suffering from Parkinson's but he was as shrewd as ever and, after the game, we went out for dinner and he said, 'That's not an Alex Ferguson team. Once you get an Alex Ferguson team, you'll be all right.' It was a wonderful piece of advice because I hadn't been entirely true to my own beliefs. I knew some of the players weren't good enough but, instead of selling them, I'd been trying to turn them into something they weren't capable of becoming. John Lyall, the West Ham manager, told me something very similar. He said, 'Make sure you see Alex Ferguson in your team.' Both Jock and John were implicitly telling me to be true to my own beliefs and convictions. Today, I use the same line with other managers I am trying to encourage.

I don't remember many periods of self-doubt, particularly after I left Aberdeen. I had worked hard and served a footballing apprenticeship that, from the time I started playing to the time I left Scotland, had lasted more than 29 years, and I had achieved considerable success at Aberdeen. These experiences helped harden my inner beliefs and strengthened my confidence in my own conviction. When I was offered the United job, I was very proud and felt confident in my own judgement and abilities. But after I arrived at Old Trafford, and I saw what I had to contend with regarding the drinking culture, I got a bit rattled. I wondered, 'What have I got myself into?' There was a time in 1989 and the start of 1990 when things just weren't going right with United. Of our opening 24 League games we had only managed to win six, and from the end of November 1989 until early February 1990, it was bleak. We won none of our 11 League games. In fact, after we beat Nottingham Forest on 12 November 1989, we did not win another home game until we played Luton Town on 3 March 1990. The fans were getting restless and the media were sharpening their knives. Compared to the consistent level of success I had experienced at Aberdeen, it was a shock to find myself in that situation. My son Jason, who was in his teens at the time, remembers sitting in the kitchen in tears during this drought, asking whether we could just move back to Aberdeen. He tells me now that I said, 'No. We're going to crack on. It's going to work.'

It's one thing to have confidence in your own abilities. It's a completely different challenge to instil confidence in others. Every player is always competing for their place in the side. If they emerged from the academy, progressed through the reserves and made it into the first-team squad, there was always the prospect of someone else emerging through the youth system, or from the transfer market, who might be better. At the end of every season there were always members of the squad who went on their summer holidays unsure whether their place would be assured when we played our first League game the following August. Young players are usually intimidated by the veterans, in part because they are playing alongside their boyhood idols, while the older players are always battling with the spectre of age and injury. Even if an injury does not bring a rude end to a career or, worse still, the promise of a career, as happened with young Ben Thornley in 1994, it erodes a player's confidence and spirit.

Many players, particularly the younger ones, take their bodies for granted as reliable allies. Yet after an injury, they immediately enter no man's land, where they stop travelling with the team, work through rehab by themselves, and have to deal with the uncertainty of whether they will recover or if the club will buy a replacement. Some are even plagued with guilt about being paid when, in their own mind, they are not contributing anything. Two examples come to mind: when Fernando Redondo joined AC Milan from Real Madrid, he suffered an awful knee injury in one of his first training sessions, and refused to be paid until he was fit to play. It was two and a half years before he made his debut and he didn't take a penny off his new club in that time. When Martin Buchan left Manchester United in 1983 after 11 years of service, he joined Oldham Athletic and received a hefty signing-on fee in the process. Early in his second season he realised that he no longer had what it took to be playing professional football, so knocked on his manager's door, retired, and returned his signing-on fee. Two class acts from men of honour.

Every player can have his confidence rattled during a game.

They may be having an off day, they don't want the ball to come in their direction and, believe it or not, they may even secretly want to get substituted. I always found that strikers and goalkeepers had the most doubts about themselves and, if their confidence was shaken, they completely changed. When goal-scorers don't score, they are convinced they will never score again, and when they score they cannot imagine they will ever miss another opportunity. All my strikers were like that, including Mark Hughes, Eric Cantona and Ruud van Nistelrooy. Mark Hughes, who in recent years has been a manager, played for United between 1983 and 1986, and 1988 and 1995; he was as tough as nails and a man of great determination. Mark was born to be a big game player and could always be counted on in the most important games, but was deeply affected when he didn't score.

Van Nistelrooy's entire identity as a man was bound up with scoring goals. When he didn't score in a game, even if we won, the storm clouds would gather. He had that Calvinist attitude which meant he felt he hadn't earned his keep and didn't deserve to be paid if he failed to score. Without doubt, of all the strikers I managed, he was the most single-minded. His whole existence revolved around scoring goals. After we beat Everton in 2003 to win the League, Ruud ran straight to the dressing room to see whether he or Thierry Henry had won the Golden Boot, the award given to the Premier League player who has scored the most goals in the season. It turned out that he'd won it that year and could enjoy his summer.

As for goalkeepers, Tim Howard has had a wonderful career at Everton since he left United in 2006. However, though he got off to a good start during his first season at Old Trafford, after we brought him over from America, his confidence never seemed to be the same after he made a mistake in 2004 against FC Porto, which eliminated us from that year's Champions League competition. It rattled him to his core, and though he came back into the side, he never seemed impregnable. I feel for goalkeepers because, after they let in a goal, everyone in the entire stadium is looking at them. It's all too easy to forget about the mistimed tackle, the three bad passes or the botched back pass that caused the goal in the first place.

When David de Gea joined us in 2011, he had the unenviable task of filling a role that had been masterfully occupied by the Dutchman, Edwin van der Sar, for six years. David was just 20 and, though he was tall, he had yet to develop the muscular strength to deal with some of the Premier League's bruisers. His first few months were mixed and both the press and the fans were on his back. After one game, I could see that he was down, so rather than talk to him directly, I chose to make my remarks to the whole team. I told them that David was a perfect example of the character of United and that he had come to England not speaking a word of English, didn't even have a driver's licence, and then gets a weekly hammering from strikers who have been ordered to make his life miserable. I could see when I finished that my little talk had lifted his spirits. He is now among the very best keepers in the world, thanks to the work of Eric Steele, the goalkeeping coach, and others.

The other place where the level of individual confidence is revealed is when penalty kicks are taken in a sudden-death finish. Some players, like Patrice Evra, would be spectacular penalty takers during practice but dreaded the idea of being asked to do the same in a game. Paul Ince was the same, and Wes Brown, our long-time stalwart defender, would sooner have played barefoot than take a penalty. I think Wes prayed that the game would be decided before he had to take his turn. Then there were the guys who just brimmed with confidence. On the rare occasion that Eric Cantona would miss from the spot, he had a look on his face that said to the world, 'How did that happen?' I don't think he thought it conceivable that he could miss a penalty. Denis Irwin, Steve Bruce, Brian McClair, Ruud van Nistelrooy, Robin van Persie, Wayne Rooney: all relished hammering in penalties. Rooney seems to excel when he is under pressure. In May 2011 we were trailing Blackburn Rovers 1–0, needed a point to win the League, and 17 minutes from the end of regular time we got a penalty. Rooney absolutely battered it into the top corner. I'm sure it helps that, even before he has taken the field in any given match, Wayne has decided where he will place the ball if he takes a penalty kick.

From time to time, I'd slide players on in the last few minutes of regular time if I sensed we were heading for a sudden-death finish. I did that in the 2008 Champions League final when I sent on Anderson, the Brazilian midfielder, to take a penalty kick. He was only 20 at the time, but he had all the confidence in the world and scored our sixth penalty, helping us beat Chelsea for our third success in the competition.

Sometimes the occasion would overwhelm even the most experienced of players. You can imagine the tension associated with what might have been the biggest single game of a player's career. It is unrealistic to think that all of them can ignore the press build-up, block out the noise and atmosphere inside a stadium and treat a cup final – particularly a Champions League final – as just another game against 11 mortals. Life does not work that way. When we played Barcelona in Rotterdam in the 1991 European Cup Winners' Cup final, Paul Ince, who was 23 years old at the time, was a bag of nerves. It did not help matters that the kick-off was delayed to allow the crowd to finish entering the stadium. Paul had a rocky first half, during which Bryan Robson had been snapping at him. At half-time I said to him, 'Incey, just concentrate on the game. Forget everything that's happened before the game. Nothing bad is going to happen. Just go and relax and enjoy it.' In the second half he was much better and worked brilliantly with Robson to protect our defence.

We also had peculiar situations when a player might voluntarily make life more difficult for himself and increase his own anxiety level. That happened in 1995 when we were knocked out of the UEFA Cup at Old Trafford by Rotor Volgograd. I had picked John O'Kane, who was a gifted player but had only appeared a few times in the first team, to play right-back. Ten minutes before the kick-off, well after the team-sheets had been submitted, he told me he wanted to play left-back. It was clear that he was rattled by the prospect of the game, but there was nothing I could do. It was a death wish because he was up against a Volgograd winger who was a flying machine. I put Phil Neville at right-back, played O'Kane at left-back and pulled him out of the game before half an hour had gone by, after he had been torn apart.

Every now and again, something beyond our control would rattle the confidence and resolve of the entire club. At those sorts of junctures it's vital to boost the collective confidence. When Manchester City started forking out the biggest sums ever seen in Britain, it was natural that everyone at United would be reading the newspapers with a mixture of shock and awe. This was exacerbated when we gave Manchester City the League championship on goal difference in 2012 after we only got ten points out of a possible 18 in the final six games of the season. I know people will misinterpret this, or take it for sour grapes, but City didn't win that championship; we lost it.

I used City's Premier League title to buttress everyone's confidence later that summer. As we reassembled for the following season, I kept reiterating that United expected to win absolutely every game we played. It didn't matter whether our opponent was the reigning Premier League, or Champions League champions, or a fourth division team we'd drawn in the FA Cup. I was just able to keep reinforcing the ideology that no club was bigger than United – no matter whether their owner controlled all the oil in the Persian Gulf, or every coal-mine in Russia.

# 3

## ASSEMBLING THE PIECES

# Organisation

I realise that the system within a football club doesn't have the complexity of what is required to design a nuclear submarine, build 50 million mobile phones or organise clinical trials for a new drug. But like every organisation we needed to be well run and had to be sure that our system was deeply ingrained. Our product just happened to be a football team, rather than a car or washing machine, and our whole reason for being was to make sure all the pieces of our product – all the different players – fitted together.

I've always felt that it's impossible to field a great football team if you don't have a great organisation. Most owners and managers mess around with team selection without any under-lying purpose. They arrange everything back to front and are too impatient for quick results. Before you can field a great team, you have to build a great organisation, and all the elements have to be assembled properly. That takes time, especially in circumstances which business books call 'turnarounds'. At United my responsibility was for the team, while the club's CEOs – principally Martin Edwards from the time I joined the club until 2000, and thereafter my commercial soul-mate David Gill – worried about everything else.

When I joined United there were four or five departments and about 85 people, including the groundsmen, laundry team, kitchen and administrative staff. The club made money from the sale of season tickets and gate receipts. If we were on television, which was rare in the mid-1980s, we'd get a small four-figure sum for a live game. After I assessed the situation, my aim was to build the club again rather than to build the team. I was confident that if we did the first part properly, and people were patient, we'd eventually be able to have the best team. It was also clear that we were not going to be an overnight success.

These days Manchester City and Liverpool are trying desperately to develop their own talent. Manchester City, which doesn't have Liverpool's lineage or history, and has always operated in United's long shadow, is pulling out all the stops. Manchester City spent £32.5 million, on Robinho, the day after Sheikh Mansour's purchase of the club in 2008 and more than £600 million since, but I am not sure that it has bought them much beyond a squad which, at the end of last season, was showing signs of wear and tear. While you might be able to buy your way to short-term success, it does not work over the long term. That requires patience, and the construction of a complete organisation.

## Preparation

The most important aspect of our system was training. Whatever happens on a Saturday afternoon has already occurred on the training ground. If I was starting again as a manager, the thing

I would focus on the most is a player's attitude during training sessions. If they take it seriously and have the necessary talent and determination, good things will happen. If they are inclined to slack off, they will never make it over the long haul. Our training ground was where the real work was done. There was a rhythm to this from which we rarely deviated. The day following a game, all the players would come in for loosening exercises, a massage and Jacuzzi. On Monday we would have a thorough training session and, if we had a midweek fixture, Tuesday would be devoted to pre-match preparation, Thursday would be a recovery day and then the whole cycle would start again. We were very careful to emphasise the need for proper recovery – not just after games but also after big competitions. For example, we gave players who participated in the World Cup a full 28 days to recover from the exertions. I would also sometimes send a few of the older players away for a week's break in December. In the winter of the 1998–99 season, I sent Peter Schmeichel off on holiday to get some sun on his back and rest. From time to time I did the same with younger players. I sent Gary Neville to Malta for a week when, early in the season following the 1998 World Cup, it became apparent that his batteries were low. These breaks helped restore them and ensure they were fit for the rest of the season.

I laid down the ground rules for training and I wanted my ideas to be implemented on the practice field. When Steve McClaren took over training at United in 1999, I was very specific with him. He was going to run the training, but I made sure he understood that I required intensity, concentration and commitment in every training session. I told him that if he was dissatisfied, he either had to start all over again until it was right, or get the players back for an additional session. There had to be no bad sessions.

I just didn't want people tinkering with our training system. When Carlos Queiroz started running training sessions, a couple of the players didn't like the sessions because they were too repetitive. I stopped one training session and told them, 'When I was a player I wished I'd been coached by Carlos. All the repetitive things we are working on will become second nature on Saturday when you have no time to think.' All our planning and preparation was to help guard against a sudden rush of animal instincts in the heat of the moment. When a game starts to go in the wrong direction, it is so easy for players – especially the youngsters – to be controlled by their heart rather than their head. That's the last thing you want. But don't forget that football is an emotional game and there can be bad tackles or refereeing decisions that can affect people. Desire and a ferocious need to win are wonderful attributes, but they have to be tempered by a cool head. Ninety per cent of the time most players are fine, but there can be occasions when raw emotion overtakes the need for discipline. All of our drills on the training grounds, all our tactical talks and assessment of competitors were done as a way to hammer into the heads of the players the need to stick to the plan. It is very hard to persuade extremely competitive spirits to be patient. Yet very often our victories were squeaked out in the last few minutes, after we had drained the life from our opponents. Games – like life – are all about waiting for chances and then pouncing on them.

As the years went by the system became so familiar and so well understood that my assistants didn't need to be reminded. It was helped by the fact that we had players who had been with the club for many years like Vidić, Evra and Ferdinand and, most of all, by the players who had known no other world than United – like Scholes, Giggs and the Neville brothers. The players came to understand my values, and the older players automatically transmitted these values to the younger players or new signings. There was just a consistency of ideas.

It's extraordinary what you can do on the training ground, especially if you have people with receptive minds who are eager to improve. Andy Cole was a standout example. When he joined us as a 23 year old after being at Arsenal, Bristol City and Newcastle United, he just wanted to loiter in the penalty box and score. After about three months of training he had improved immeasurably. He was better on his feet and his overall foot-balling ability had been enhanced. I discovered that this sort of change was not limited to the younger players. One extraordinary example was Henrik Larsson, who was a striker in his mid-thirties when he was loaned to us in 2007 during the Swedish off-season. Everybody kept saying, 'I wish he had been with us when he was a boy.' He just sopped up everything we said to him, but he returned to Sweden because he had made a promise to his family and his club, Helsingborgs. Something similar happened when we signed Michael Owen when he was almost 30. He only made 52 appearances for us but, even though he had played for Liverpool, Real Madrid and Newcastle United, and had been in the England team for a decade, he still had the desire and pride to want to improve while he was at Old Trafford.

When René Meulensteen became our coach after Carlos Queiroz left us for the second time, it was much easier, because he had worked for several years within our system. He'd been on the scene and had helped the players who were then young-sters – Danny Welbeck, Tom Cleverley and Cristiano Ronaldo – develop their technical skills. René inherited all of Carlos's crossing and defending drills, but he also added features of his own. René was also a devotee of Wiel Coerver, the great Dutch coach, who was among the first to emphasise the importance of ankle mobility and its influence on ball control, so he also helped enhance our system. Mick Phelan is another example of the benefits of growing up within a system. He had played for me; I brought him in as a youth coach and he gradually worked his way up the organisation until he became assistant manager in 2008.

I never had a chance to experiment with helping some of United's best players become coaches and – eventually – managers, but I always felt that would have been a great way to ensure the continuity of excellence at Old Trafford. Ryan Giggs, Paul Scholes, Gary Neville and Nicky Butt all had those attributes, but I was never going to suggest to them, 'Quit playing and become a coach.' I had really wanted Neville to be involved with our academy, but he got a contract with Sky and went into the television world. I was disappointed, as Gary's character and attitude would have enhanced the club and Paul is one of the best assessors of a footballer within the game. I feel they were a loss to Manchester United.

I've lost count of the times during my career that I was accused of having a lot of luck, or intimidating referees into providing a lavish amount of extra time, when United were losing at home. There were plenty of times when Lady Luck blew in our direction – it happens all the time in football. Yet preparation had a lot more to do with our success than a few fortunate breaks.

Part of the pursuit of excellence involves eliminating as many surprises as possible because life is full of the unexpected. That's what our scouts, our youth system and the innumerable training sessions were all about. But there were also occasions where we did extra homework because we felt unprepared. For example,

I always wanted to know as much as possible about what we were going to contend with before any game. After I joined United, I had no idea about all the players at the clubs in what was then the First Division. So I asked John Lyall to send me his files and reports on all the teams and players we were up against. He had an experienced eye and reading his material was a great help.

Relentless homework, all of it unglamorous, was a mainstay of United. Here's one example. When we played Bayern Munich in the 1999 Champions League final, we had done our homework. In every game you wanted to have a sense for how the opposing manager might change his tactics during a game. Of course, that is something that is difficult to predict, but thorough preparation can sometimes suggest which players might get substituted. In the 1999 final, the Bayern winger, Mario Basler, who was deadly with free kicks, scored a few minutes into the game. Alexander Zickler, who was a mainstay of the Bayern side for many seasons, played wide left that night. We had predicted that Zickler and Basler would both be substituted. We hadn't rubbed any crystal ball; we had just watched the tapes of Bayern and knew they would take these players off. Zickler came off in the 71st minute and Basler in the 87th. These substitutions deprived Bayern of a lot of their ability to penetrate our defences and, as a result, they were less of a threat and we could throw more bodies forward in search of a goal. Many years later, while we were preparing to meet Barcelona in the 2008 Champions League semi-final, Carlos Queiroz placed mats on the field to show the players exactly where he wanted them – a couple of the mats were almost placed atop one another to emphasise how tightly we wanted Scholes and Carrick to bottle the attacks through our midfield. Barcelona failed to score in either leg.

In the 36 hours before a game there was a rhythm to our preparation. We'd show a short, condensed video of the opponents to the players before we practised and then, at the hotel, on the evening of the game, we'd centre their attention on the things they needed to pay heed to. We kept these videos short because most players, especially the young ones, have limited attention spans. I always liked to dwell on an opponent's weaknesses rather than its strengths. While it was good to look at video of some of the lethal players we would find ourselves up against, ultimately no battles are won by mounting a sterling defence. The way to win battles, wars and games is by attacking and overrunning the opposing side. So I would always dwell on our opponents' weaknesses – partly to exploit them and partly to impart in my players a sense of what was possible. If you overemphasise opponents' strengths, you just plant seeds of doubt in your players.

On the day of the game itself, I'd finalise the team and run through the precise tactics I wanted employed. I paid attention to a couple of other little items. I used to check out which of the players on the opposing team were making their Old Trafford debut. We used to purposefully exert more pressure on these individuals – it was one way we rolled out our red carpet. Another thing I was always mindful about were the talented players we would line up against who were not especially hard workers. These players would always have something left in the last 20 minutes because they had not been busting their guts during the earlier stages. Matthew Le Tissier, who appeared more than 500 times for Southampton, was one of these types. He could be loitering around for a good part of the game and, just when everyone was spent, could ruin our afternoon in the blink of an eye. The others in this category were the so-called 'floaters', the sort of players who would often wear the number 10 shirt in Spain or South America. They drifted around between the midfield and the strikers and you never knew if they would play on the left or right or in the middle of the park. David Silva was one of two or three players who filled this role at Valencia. These type of players are free to roam and would save their energy for when their team had the ball. The fact that they could appear in different parts of the pitch and not operate in restricted areas meant we could not afford a single lapse of concentration.

On our own team, the best players tended to be sticklers for preparation. That's part of the reason why they were good or great. David Beckham, Ryan Giggs, Cristiano Ronaldo and Wayne Rooney would all stay after training to perfect their free kicks. They would not disappear for a long bath, or a massage, or be straight out the door because they had to run down to a car dealership. They would be religious about spending an extra 30 minutes trying to bend balls around a row of mannequins and past the goalkeeper. That's why Beckham became a master of taking free kicks from between 25 and 30 yards from goal; and Giggs from between 18 and 23 yards; while Rooney was better closer to the penalty box. As for Ronaldo, he'd be able to score from free kicks if he took them from behind the moon.

The crowd looked at the goal Beckham scored from the halfway line against Wimbledon in 1996 as if it was some sort of miracle. It was nothing of the sort. He must have practised that same kick hundreds of times so, when opportunity struck in south London, he seized it. The same goes for lots of goals scored by the United players. They had been scored, or certainly practised, for hundreds of hours during training sessions.

I came to admire how some other managers prepared their

teams because the majority of them had the challenge of extracting performance from players who had nowhere near the talent of the Manchester United squad. Sam Allardyce, who played for most of his career at Bolton and Preston before managing Bolton, Newcastle, Blackburn and West Ham in the Premier League, is a prime example. Kevin Davies was a striker who played for Sam at Bolton, but did not move like lightning and was quite cumbersome.

When Sam managed Bolton (between 1999 and 2007) he concentrated on squeezing every drop of advantage from players like Davies, and he did this through preparation and anything extra that technology might have to offer. He would know which sort of ball into the penalty box would be guaranteed to give opponents the most problems and he even went to the extreme of having exercise bikes set up in the dugouts so that the substitutes could be properly warmed up before they took the field. It has rarely been acknowledged, but Sam's belief in the benefits of preparation have paid dividends for him, even if several of the owners he worked for did not have the slightest inkling of how he transformed middling players into decent teams.

There were a couple of times when we suffered setbacks that were so severe, I was forced to re-examine our entire approach. After Chelsea won the 2004–05 Premier League title, I took a fresh look at our pre-season preparation. Chelsea had steam-rollered all the other clubs and wound up with 95 points compared to Arsenal with 83 and United with 77. It was humiliating. We spent an entire season chasing their tail, but there was just no way we could catch Chelsea. I did not want that to happen again.

After Chelsea's first triumph, I paid much more attention to the intensity of our pre-season preparation. Chelsea had just been much fitter than United during the 2004–05 season. We redesigned the pre-season fixtures for 2006–07 – as the schedule for 2005–06 was already in place – so that we played higher calibre and more competitive teams. While it was important for the club to wave the flag in countries where we had a big following, it did not make much sense to play fixtures where Fabien Barthez, who was our goalkeeper for three seasons, could play as a striker. So we made sizeable changes. It was much healthier to play more challenging exhibition games than win a walk in the park 10–0 in Thailand. It was a real lesson to me about the risks of clinging to past practices and not moving with the times.

Despite Chelsea's triumph, I did not want to rush things during the following pre-season period. I wanted to ease the players back into the rhythm of the season in a gradual fashion. High-performance athletes have a tendency to push themselves too much or over-train. For some it is an obsession, while others worry about an erosion of fitness levels that could cause them to lose their place in the team. In pre-season, we would work on mobility, but we would steer clear of serious physical encounters or severe interval training. There would never be any serious, long lectures, detailed post-mortems of the previous season, or dozens of hours of video analysis. We would conduct medical tests on the players. We would set up a series of 15 medical stations in the gym that were manned with nurses and doctors and would run a battery of tests on each of the players. This allowed us to have accurate readings on the players' medical and physical conditions. We ran specific cardiac tests and comprehensive blood assessments; scanned tendons with ultrasound machines and checked to make sure all vaccinations were current. We also scrutinised the players' flexibility, mobility and balance; gave them eye examinations and cognitive assessments so that, throughout the season, we had a benchmark against which to test the severity of concussions. These tests were literally from head to toe, since the players had their teeth examined by dentists and their feet by podiatrists. All this allowed us to figure out how vulnerable each player was to injury and we categorised them in three different buckets: high, medium and low. We then designed gym programmes, customised for each player, for the first block of the season.

The change to our pre-season routine took a little time to bear fruit. In 2005–06 Chelsea won the Premier League title again, albeit by a greatly reduced margin of eight points. And by 2006–07 our fitness improved enough to turn the eight-point deficit into a Premier League title of our own – this time by six points from Chelsea.

In football, just like in other activities, the best-laid plans sometimes don't work and improvisation is required. It actually happens on a fairly regular basis. I would often twiddle things during a game or at half-time. One example that comes to mind is a game against West Ham in the closing weeks of the season in April 2011. A few months earlier, West Ham had whipped us 4–0 in a Carling Cup tie where I had fielded a team of young players. Towards the end of that game, Wally Downes, West Ham's first-team coach, asked Wes Brown, as he waited on the sidelines to replace Jonny Evans, 'Are you going on to make a difference?' That got right under my skin, as did the taunts from West Ham's supporters after the game, who were very aggressive towards me in the car park. I told them, 'We're going to be back here in April and we're going to relegate you.' However, when we were 2–0 down at half-time in a match towards the end of the season, I was a long way from fulfilling my promise. So I tossed our game plan out of the window, pulled Patrice Evra, who had played for France in the middle of the week, out of the game, and moved Ryan Giggs to left-back. Eventually we won 4–2 with Rooney scoring a hat-trick. A few weeks later, at the end of the season, West Ham got relegated to the Championship.

Something similar happened at Old Trafford in 2009 when we trailed Tottenham Hotspur 2–0. At half-time I brought on Carlos Tévez, the Argentinian striker, for Nani, and the effect was dramatic. Tévez was like a clockwork mouse, except you never had to wind him up – he was just tireless. He came on to the field, started hurling himself at every Tottenham player, completely changed the pace of the game and stirred up the fans. We won that game 5–2 and went on to win the League by four points. It's odd to think of the effect of that one change to a plan.

Sometimes we were outwitted by opponents who approached a particular game with more finely tuned tactics and were better prepared. In 1996, Newcastle United thrashed us 5–0 at St James' Park. Kevin Keegan, who was Newcastle's manager, fielded a team full of threatening attackers, including Alan Shearer, Les Ferdinand, Peter Beardsley and David Ginola. The savagery of that defeat was apparent in the last goal, which was scored by the Belgian centre-back, Philippe Albert, who managed to chip a ball over the head of our goalkeeper, Peter Schmeichel, from 20 yards. We were humiliated.

We could be outdone by our own ill-discipline too. You can get into real trouble if players ignore plans or don't stick to them. That happened to United in both our Champions League final games against Barcelona. We lost both because two or three players ignored our plans and played their own game. You cannot do that when you play Barcelona, particularly when the club was managed by Pep Guardiola, because of their ability to keep control of the ball. United were used to having the ball for three-quarters of a game, so as we prepared to play Barcelona we knew, because of their ability to retain possession, that they would throw us off our normal game.

Every now and again we were also undone by the atmosphere we encountered. There were two grounds that always caused us trouble – when we played Liverpool at Anfield, and Leeds at Elland Road (when they used to be regular opponents). We've been to Anfield with some of our very best teams, but the crowd – who are merciless towards visiting teams and refereeing decisions of which they don't approve – whips up such an atmosphere that it erodes the players' confidence and makes them lose their concentration. It only takes a momentary lapse to upset hours of dedicated preparation, and there's very little you can do to help players with that. While there are elements of chess to a game of football, wingers, goalkeepers and centre-backs – unlike rooks, bishops and knights – are made of flesh and blood and emotions.

One other element of preparation worth mentioning is the way I approached the idea of risk. It would not surprise me if some observers feel that much of United's success was due to our willingness to take unnecessary chances. When the crowd at Old Trafford are chanting, 'Attack! Attack! Attack!', it is easy to think that we automatically threw caution to the wind. I never thought about it like this because part of a leader's job is to eliminate as many risks as possible. Some might think that my fondness for horses or cards means that I am a gambler at heart, but that isn't really true. In my private life I have always been very careful about the amount of money I am prepared to spend on a horse or bet at a race-track, and the same caution applied at Old Trafford. We tried to leave nothing to chance. I cannot tell you how many half-time talks centred on the need to be patient and wait for the right opportunity to occur, rather than to be daredevils. I would only want to take a risk during the last 15 minutes of a game if we were trailing by a goal. At that point, it doesn't matter whether you lose by one or two goals, and it was only then that I was prepared to throw the kitchen sink at things.

Frequently when this happened, the opposition played right into our hands by trying to defend their lead. They would substitute a defensive player for an attacker and it could change the entire balance of the game. Suddenly we could surge around their box without worrying as much about their ability to counter-attack. Our opponents probably thought they were eliminating a risk by falling back into a defensive posture, but it gave us an advantage without us having to, in the grand scheme of things, unduly increase the amount of risk we took. And more often than not, the goal would come. The value of last minute goals was the impact on the dressing room, with everyone celebrating, and for the fans, who couldn't wait to get home or to the pub to talk about it.

Our critics would say this was lucky, or down to the pressure to extend the game into 'Fergie Time', but in truth it came down to careful preparation and having a deliberate and thoughtful approach to risk.

## Pipeline

When you run any organisation, you have to look as far down the road as you can. But if your organisation is anything like Manchester United, then your perspective is constantly changing. Sometimes it was possible to look several years ahead, and sometimes it was impossible to see beyond the next challenge; or, in our case, the next game. But prioritising a long-term strategy for the club was crucial, and at United we always had to be thinking about the composition of the team a few seasons ahead. So we had to have a conveyor belt of talent.

Every game requires 11 starting players and seven substitutes, and our whole organisation was designed to produce them. I always wanted to know about what the pipeline of players looked like for the team we would select three years in the future. It is so much easier to produce a consistent level of high performance when you nourish youngsters, help them develop and provide a pathway to success.

This was no easy task, because it meant sifting through all the millions of boys who dream about becoming football players. It means watching tens of thousands of games – many of them in the pouring rain and bleak surrounds. I read recently that Steve Coppell, who played for United between 1975 and 1983 before going on to a career as a manager, said, 'It's like turtles in the South Seas. Thousands are hatched on the beaches, but few of them ever reach the water.' Steve is dead right, except at United we were more interested in the turtles that we thought would be able to survive long journeys in the sea, rather than those who could just reach the water's edge.

When I joined Aberdeen in 1978 we had two scouts; by the time I left we had 17 scouts, who were responsible for identifying promising youngsters who lived in Scotland. The result was fabulous. When Aberdeen played in the European Cup Winners' Cup final in 1983 against Real Madrid, we fielded eight home-grown players who had worked their way through the youth teams and only three players who had been bought (and that number included one, Gordon Strachan, who was at the club when I arrived).

My experience with Gordon only served to strengthen my belief in the benefits of developing youngsters. When I arrived at Aberdeen his head was on the block because my predecessor had decided to sell him. I put the transfer on hold until I had given myself the opportunity to make my own assessment and I liked what I saw. So we kept Gordon, helped him improve his skills – particularly using the entire width of the pitch and getting himself into the right position – and he went on to great things: a sterling career as a player for Manchester United and Scotland and a managerial career which has culminated in him leading his own country.

At United, in the mid-1980s, there were scouts everywhere – all over England and all over Ireland. But there was a gaping hole in the system. There were just four scouts to cope with Greater Manchester and the wider city region, and only two for the whole of Manchester. To combat this weakness we changed the management of the youth system and instilled new energy and leadership under Les Kershaw, who was helped by Nobby Stiles and Brian Kidd, who had both played on the 1968 European Cup-winning team, and who knew the area. Les was a real, and unusual, find. He had taught chemistry at Manchester Metropolitan University, and was scouting part-time for Arsenal when Bobby Charlton mentioned his name. Les brought the detached objectivity of the science laboratory to Old Trafford and had an enormous impact on the way we built the backbone of our youth programme. The scouts were part-timers and we built an incentive compensation scheme. They got a fixed weekly stipend, and bonuses if the boy was signed for the club, made the first team or represented his country. They were also paid extra if the player stayed with the club for multiple years.

In retrospect the greatest evidence of the power of youth was in the United squad that won the Treble in 1999. That squad contained 30 players of whom 15 were under 25 years old. It included David Beckham who was a great advertisement for the youth-team policy. We first heard about David in 1986 when he was 12 years old and he was spotted by our scout Malcolm Fidgeon. The real pull for David came through meeting Bobby Charlton when he attended the Manchester United legend's soccer school. Coincidentally, 1986 was also the year we heard about Ryan Giggs. Ryan and David made their debuts for the first team when they were 17 years old. Nicky Butt and Gary Neville were also 17, Phil Neville was 18 and Paul Scholes was 19 when they first played for the first team.

The full impact of our youth programme became apparent at the start of the 1995–96 season, when six of the 13 players I used during the game against Aston Villa – which we lost – had come through our system. Alan Hansen, the television pundit, surveyed the result and concluded, as he announced to the British public that night, 'You can't win anything with kids.' I have always thought the opposite – you will never win anything without kids.

Youngsters can inject a fantastic spirit in an organisation and a youngster never forgets the person or organisation that gave him his first big chance. He will repay it with a loyalty that lasts a lifetime. For young players, nothing is impossible, and they will try and run through a barbed-wire fence, while older players will try to find the gate. Every generation also raises the level of the game, because they stand atop more shoulders than the previous one. That's truer today than ever before, because of the spread of television and the catchment area of a large club's scouting organisations. Television means that boys all over the world are able to watch Lionel Messi or Cristiano Ronaldo. I am sure there are thousands of them trying to emulate Lionel's feints or Cristiano's moves. Somewhere there are a couple of boys who will be trying to improve upon their heroes' skills, and eventually they too will be inspiring yet another generation to ever more creative heights.

I suspect that the way we approached the young players was a highly magnified, miniature version of the way in which employees are trained to progress through a large organisation. We had distinct layers and a structure, and the road to success was as clear for them as it might be for a graduate from college who joins a company in a trainee scheme and dreams of one day becoming a vice-president, managing director or CEO. At United our layers were the youth academy, the B team, the A team, the reserves and the first-team squad. The FA Youth Cup was important for several reasons. It gave the youngsters a taste for a tough competition, for the sort of preparation that was an echo of life in the first team and a sense of the difference between being a winner and loser.

When we first came across young boys with talent, we were all over them. We gave them endless drills and were not shy about telling them precisely what they needed to do. We wanted to be confident that they had mastered the skills essential for their success, which was why the youth academy was no laughing matter. The boys fell under the gaze of Eric Harrison and they trained with great intensity on Tuesday and Thursday nights, during sessions in which the first-team coaches were also heavily involved. Archie Knox and I made it a point to watch these sessions, and Eric made the boys feel as though these sessions were as important as a cup final. Some of them found their time with Eric far more intimidating than their time with me. As the boys matured, we eased off a bit and, eventually, if they made the first team, we might have demanded that they polish some aspect of their game but, for the most part, the management challenge changed. We knew that they had the skills and trusted in their competence, so our focus started to shift to their emotional and psychological needs. We also shielded them from the press. For example, Ryan Giggs did not give his first interview until he was 20, and then it was with Hugh McIlvanney of the *Sunday Times*, who we knew as trustworthy.

One of the ways we blended youth with experience was out of the sight of the television cameras. Every now and again senior players like Bryan Robson and Darren Fletcher would play with the reserve team. That was a shot in the arm for the players we were counting on for the future. Even if the experienced players just showed up to stand on the side-lines and watch the youth team, the youngsters got a huge boost of confidence. Bryan Robson, Steve Bruce, Brian McClair all did that, and Gary Neville would also help the young players sort out their contracts. They each had their own way of helping the youngsters. Gary would always be rebuking them, but he wanted them to be successful. Oddly, when Gary himself came into the squad, he had been under similar pressure from Peter Schmeichel. When Ryan Giggs made it to the first squad he was really helped by Paul Ince, who took him under his wing. The same thing had happened to me as a youngster at St Johnstone, when three of the older players – Jim Walker, Jimmy Little and Ron McKinven – had looked out for me. At United, Eric Cantona performed one of the most avuncular acts towards younger players when, after the whole squad pooled the pot for FA Cup final media appearances, each individual was given the choice of taking their share or leaving it in for a draw to win the lot. All the young players, like David Beckham and Gary Neville, took their share, but Paul Scholes and Nicky Butt stayed in. When Eric won the draw he gave all his prize money to Paul Scholes and Nicky Butt, who had just entered the first-team squad and for whom, at the time, £7,500 was the equivalent of two months' wages. His reason was typical Eric: 'Because they have balls.'

It is such a tonic for a youngster to feel that he has a mentor whom he can trust and who has his interests at heart. There is more of a natural bond between players than there is between the coaching staff and the players. Some of this is because of the normal organisational gap that exists between an employee and a manager. The other is because of age difference. For example, towards the end of my time at United it would have been much easier for James Wilson to identify with Patrice Evra than with me, since I was old enough to be his grandfather. There is a lot to be said for either picking, or being lucky enough to land, the right mentor. The best ones can change your life.

No matter how hard we worked to blood youngsters, Barcelona is still able to do this better than any club. The way they develop boys into some of the best players in the world is breathtaking. It demonstrates the benefits of long-term investments in people and thorough training in the ways of the organisation. Great teamwork comes from deep familiarity and developing close bonds with others. In a company, people who have worked together for a long time will know how others will react in certain situations, and may even be able to anticipate what their colleagues might say. The same thing holds true on the football pitch. The most magical example was the Messi-Iniesta-Xavi troika at Barcelona. The three of them knew each other so well that the way they passed the ball in a wee circle among themselves made you dizzy. It's like watching a spinning carousel.

At Arsenal, Arsène Wenger has had his own twist on building for the long term. When he arrived in England his policy was based on his knowledge of French football and his method for developing the team was to buy a lot of French players in their mid-teens and early twenties, such as Thierry Henry, Patrick Vieira and Nicolas Anelka. More recently, Arsène has adapted this approach and has spent big sums on Mesut Özil and Alexis Sánchez and also bought young English players like Oxlade-Chamberlain, Walcott and Chambers.

In my last decade at United, we employed a similar tactic. We just cast our net farther afield and bought the Da Silva twins from Brazil when they were 17, Giuseppe Rossi, the Italian centre-forward, whom we later sold to Villarreal, and Gérard Piqué, from Barcelona when he was just 17. In England, players can be offered a professional contract at 16, which can be signed at 17. At the time, Spanish regulations allowed us to offer Piqué a contract at 16, but Spanish clubs could not do this and could not therefore protect their assets. This was also the case when Cesc Fàbregas signed for Arsenal.

Our emphasis on youth strengthened as the years went by, and our system became better tuned. United's global network expanded in relation to identifying the best young players, regardless of which country they were playing in – Macheda (Italy), Possebon (Brazil) and Januzaj (Belgium). During my last few seasons at United we put a whole bevy of youngsters under contract: Tyler Blackett, Paddy McNair, James Wilson, Andreas Pereira and Will Keane. If I had my way I would make sure that any sons of United players with great promise would all be targeted for our youth system. It underlines the importance of investing in the sorts of facilities that will attract youngsters and, in particular, help sway their parents. Every parent wants the best for their children, and the clubs that can demonstrate this sort of support will strengthen their negotiating positions. It makes it far tougher to sell the dream of the future if you cannot point to the staff and facilities that will make it come true.

# 4

---

# ENGAGING OTHERS

# Teamwork

Balance is the key to every team. It is impossible to win a football game with 11 goalkeepers or with a group of people with identical talents. I imagine that's true in other organisations too.

We thought a lot about the age composition of our team, and kept close track of how many players were over the age of 30, between 23 and 30, and aged 20 to 23. I never wanted a team that was either too old, where players had lost a yard or took longer to recover from injuries, but I also didn't want one which was too young, inexperienced and impetuous.

I've read some of the stuff that was written about the condition of the United squad when I retired. You would have thought that I had left 11 corpses on the steps of a funeral home. It's hilarious. At the start of the 2012–13 season I had not imagined that I would be retiring, and I was as intent as I had ever been in ensuring we were well equipped for future campaigns. At the end of that season the average/median age of our squad was just under 26 – or about the same as it had been throughout the previous 25 years.

A lot has also been made of the fact that we had some players who were aged 30 or older. That's true, but it also ignores the fact that these days the player who takes good care of himself can expect to perform at a very high level until he is 35 or 36. That was not the case 25 years ago, before we all started paying attention to the benefits of sports science, nutrition, more modern training regimens and better pitches. Juventus didn't sign a two-year contract with Patrice Evra in 2014 when he was 33 because they were daft. Patrice was part of the Juventus team that beat Real Madrid to reach the Champions League final last year, a starting 11 that included six players aged 30 or over. Chelsea signed 36-year-old Didier Drogba in the summer of 2014, and he went on to make 40 appearances in a season that saw them win the Premier League and the League Cup.

When I arrived at United, the average age of the squad was too high for my liking. I tried to figure out whether I could shape them into something stronger, and went about analysing every detail of our set-up: pre-season preparation, training, the way in which we started the season and the reason we lost specific games. Between 1988 and 1991 I concluded that Father Time was the enemy, and told our chairman, Martin Edwards, to conduct a fire sale and get rid of the lot for whatever he could get for them. Today, I probably would do this more quickly but, in the 1980s, before the dawn of the Premier League and the barrel-loads of television money, we did not have the spending power. I also had hoped that, with time, I could get the players, especially the established internationals, to increase the scale of their ambition and boost their performance. By the late 1980s, though, I was determined to wipe the slate clean and keep as many young people as I could. So we sold Jesper Olsen (27) for £400,000, Gordon Strachan (32) for £300,000, Paul McGrath (29) for £450,000, Chris Turner (30) for £175,000 and Norman Whiteside (24) for £600,000, and gave free transfers to Kevin Moran (32) and Frank Stapleton (31). That cleared the decks and gave me the opportunity to start redressing the balance of our team. In their place we signed Gary Pallister (24), Neil Webb (26), Mick Phelan (26) and Danny Wallace (25). Facing up to the issue, concluding that we had the wrong people and changing the composition of the team, laid the foundation for all our subsequent success. It took me time to confront reality and sell these players and, in retrospect, I was too hesitant. Afterwards, when the deed had been done, I remember feeling like I'd almost gone through a cleansing ritual. It was liberating. I wondered why it had taken me so long.

Getting an organisation into balance doesn't occur once. It requires perpetual work. I felt I was always re-tuning things – although, once in a while, we had to do more than just a simple brake adjustment and oil change. We needed to change with the times, so we did, and this occurred on a regular four-year cycle. Our squad in the early 1990s was British and muscular. By the late 1990s it had become more refined, and a decade later we had a decidedly continental flair. Players like Ronaldo, Nani and Evra would have seemed like oddities in the late 1980s. Whenever we sold popular players who were past their prime or had lost their place in the team, there would always be a lot of flak. It wasn't something I enjoyed doing, but it was just one of those ugly necessities of life. When we sold Paul Ince to Inter Milan in 1995, I got a raft of abusive letters. But what the fans did not appreciate was that I was under considerable pressure to make sure that we could make room in the side for Nicky Butt, Paul Scholes and David Beckham. Ben Thornley, another youngster at the time, also looked as if he would make it, until he was terribly injured in a reserve game. I did not want these players going to other clubs and, at the time, we were getting lots of enquiries about whether Butt was for sale. Something similar happened when I decided to sell Jaap Stam, the Dutch centre-back, in 2001. He was 29 at the time, and Lazio offered us over £15 million for him, which I thought was a very good deal, particularly because I knew that I could sign Laurent Blanc for close to nothing. I felt terrible telling Stam of the decision because I could see he was devastated. I met him at a petrol station to break the news – a venue that probably did not make things easier for either of us. It was the right decision for United, even though Jaap continued to play well for several years after he left Old Trafford and, in retrospect, his sale was premature.

Every member of a team has got to understand that they are part of a jigsaw puzzle. If you remove one piece, the picture doesn't look right. Each player has to understand the qualities and strengths of their team-mates. In football eight players, not 11, win games, because everybody has off-days and it's almost impossible to make 11 people play to perfection simultaneously.

Out of the 2,131 games that I managed over nearly 40 years, I can only point to about 20 games where every player was absolutely magnificent. The one game that sticks in my mind as an example of this was when we played Wimbledon in the FA Cup fifth round in 1994. At the time Wimbledon were in the Premiership, and they had a team composed of big, powerful players who would trample you to death. We never seemed to give the ball away, and there was one goal that we scored after a magnificent passing move. It was one of those rare games where our performance could have been set to music. Whilst the Wimbledon game may be an under-the-radar example, most will remember the 7–1 victory over Roma in the 2007 Champions League quarter-finals. It was the perfect illustration of a team ethic, and co-ordination that was as close to perfection as you can get.

The reality is that there are very few highly consistent players. A guy who might score a couple of goals in one game may just fire blanks in the next. Or a defender who tackles flawlessly in one outing may get a red card in the next. The sheer number of games in a season undermines this drive for consistency. In the top flight of European football, the teams play half a dozen pre-season matches, plus – depending on cup runs and European competitions – between 55 and 65 games during a season that stretches over nine months. That's the equivalent of one game every four or five days. Also, for a team at Manchester United's level, almost every player will be playing for their country as well: that's another eight to ten games each season.

No matter how carefully players are trained, or how much they are cosseted, it is difficult to have all of them at peak performance for every match. I was always sparing in my use of the younger players to make sure we didn't play them too much during their first two or three seasons. They were always raring to go but, at that stage, were still developing both physically and mentally. I also did not want them taking it for granted that they had earned a permanent place in the first team. It was good to keep them hungry. Paul Scholes, partly because of injuries, only started 38 League games in his first three seasons as a first-team player. At the other extreme, it's difficult to rely on players reaching the twilight of their careers, because it takes them longer to recover from injury and they sometimes have recurring conditions that can sideline them for weeks at a time. In all my time at United we had a number of players who you could depend upon to be available for selection and play the majority of the games in a season. These included Steve Bruce, Denis Irwin, Brian McClair, Mark Hughes, Gary Pallister,

Dwight Yorke, Eric Cantona, David Beckham, Phil Neville and Patrice Evra, during the peaks of their careers.

The task of building and maintaining a team is never done. Not only are there injuries, or the fatigue that can set in during a very long season, but you also have to deal with Father Time. There are always youngsters, in the full blush of youth, pressing to get into the first team; conversely, there are players in their mid-thirties who might have been mainstays of the club for many years but are approaching their sell-by date. This means that top-flight teams are in a perpetual state of evolution, and woe betide the manager who gets lulled into feeling that particular players can go on for ever. I was always on the lookout for new players for the first-team squad – either those who were home-grown at United (which was my strong preference) or from elsewhere. Whenever we came across a player of unusual ability, the unspoken question was whether he would serve us better than the current incumbent. This goes for a reserve goalkeeper as much as it does for a potent striker. Another exercise that I used to employ to keep myself honest was to ask myself which member of our first-team squad would be able to command a starting place with Real Madrid or AC Milan or whatever team happened to be Champions of Europe that year. That little mental exercise always illuminated our weaker spots.

When I assembled a squad, I would always try to ensure that I had half a dozen multi-purpose players who could play a variety of positions. It provides a manager with so much more flexibility, either during the course of a season if there is a plague of injuries or, for tactical reasons, during a game. Ryan Giggs, Phil Neville, Paul Scholes and John O'Shea are prime examples of that sort of a player. They could play with great distinction in four or five positions. The other virtue I prized was reliability. I wanted players who were fit to play in every game. Nobody would want to run an organisation whose top performers could only appear for work three days a week. The same goes for football teams, which is why I cherished players like Brian McClair or Denis Irwin, who between them played 1,000 games for United. They were great soldiers, although obviously without the profile of some of our household names. Mick Phelan was similar and would do anything that was asked of him. He would play in any position and would, if needs be, mark a man like a limpet mine.

Durability was another key characteristic. Steve Bruce, Gary Pallister, Denis Irwin, David Beckham, Dwight Yorke, Ryan Giggs and Eric Cantona rarely ever spent extended periods out with an injury. In 1990, when Mark Hughes got injured against Liverpool, I genuinely thought he was going to be out for a month. He was back in the team ten days later. That sort of durability was a godsend to me because it widened my options and also meant that I could field teams where all the players were familiar with each other. In the 1992–93 Premier League campaign, eight players started 40 or more games in a 42-match schedule. It should be no surprise to hear that was the first year United won the League while I was manager.

I'm not exactly sure why Premier League players are more prone to injuries than their predecessors, especially since most of them are fitter and stronger than the players of 20 years ago. My suspicion is that the quality of the pitches has a lot to do with the higher injury rate. The fact that most top-notch venues now have pitches that are as smooth as the surface of a snooker table makes the game far quicker and more attractive to watch. But it also allows the players, who gain confidence from a sure footing and even surface, to hold the ball longer and also to tackle quicker and harder. So the velocity with which players collide is far greater than when I played. This makes it all the more important to have a squad that includes a healthy portion of multi-purpose players.

Some people wonder whether any organisation can survive if it is entirely composed of creative players. I suppose they worry that creativity brings its own negatives in the shape of ego and individualism. People with big egos want to win so that was never a problem for me. It is wonderful to dream of fielding 11 spectacularly creative players every Saturday, but that breaks down in practice because you have to deal with the realities of needing a solid defence to withstand attacks. You need to have balance in your team, but I always found myself drawn to the creative, attacking players. They can see things that others cannot. On a football field, they are the players who are able to penetrate opponents, make a decisive run, are equally comfortable hitting a 50-yard laser pass or carving open a defence with a short pass, like Paul Scholes, or switching the course of play like David Beckham. Creative players can change a game and galvanise a club. When Cristiano Ronaldo was playing for United, I kept telling him that his job was to create opportunities. In the 2004 FA Cup semi-final against Arsenal, my instructions to Ronaldo were simple: 'Don't worry about defending – just attack.' We played three central midfielders and that gave Cristiano the platform, and freedom, to terrorise Arsenal. It is players like Ronaldo, Giggs, Cantona and Scholes who decide matches. Teams filled with players like Steve Bruce, Roy Keane, Jaap Stam, Gary Neville, Patrice Evra, Nemanja Vidić and Bryan Robson would be almost unbeatable, but would not be able to split open a competitor – especially important when your opponents will do anything not to lose. The ones who can slice open competitors are the few truly creative sorts.

The 1999 side exemplified this because we had creativity up

front, and in midfield Scholes was the clever one with the piercing passes, Beckham was a spectacular crosser of balls from the sidelines, and Giggs's bolts of electricity would leave opponents flailing. And behind them sat Keane – the indomitable, tireless driver. There were other combinations that worked well too. Dwight Yorke, whom we signed from Aston Villa in 1998, could skewer the opposition, create something out of nothing, beat a man and was deadly in front of the goal. Ole Solskjaer, Teddy Sheringham and Andy Cole could all have played for any of the top European clubs. Ole and Andy were fabulous finishers and Teddy was a clever passer in the last third of the field. But none of them had that extra gift with which Dwight Yorke was blessed. Dwight's arrival also had the unexpected benefit of bringing out the best in Andy Cole, with whom he developed an extraordinary relationship. In 1998–99 (the season United won the Treble), the pair scored 53 goals between them.

One attribute of the exceptional creative type is that you have to keep them from being bored. Usually it isn't a question of arrogance or complacency, they just don't seem to feel sufficiently challenged. This was sometimes the case with Paul Scholes. Things would come so easily to him that, from time to time, when we were leading in a game, he would just tune out. He'd start to flick balls and do little tricks, as if he was at a Christmas party. I'd tell him, 'Scholesy, stop the carrying on.' He would look at me as if he had no idea what I was talking about. But he knew, and when the going was tough and he had to perform, he rarely ever fell short.

I always had a fondness for the kings of creativity who would play for our opponents, even if I might have wished they were wearing United red. Dennis Bergkamp at Arsenal, Gianfranco Zola at Chelsea, Zinedine Zidane and Dejan Savićević in Europe, Glenn Hoddle at Tottenham and Paul Gascoigne at Newcastle and Tottenham are examples of that sort of extraordinary flair. Gascoigne, at his peak, was the best English player I have seen in my time, with the exception of Bobby Charlton. Xavi, Iniesta and Messi at Barcelona have been the master chefs for the past few years. All of them would get three Michelin stars and you would walk 50 miles barefoot to watch them in the kitchen. Speaking of fondness, I never allowed my personal feelings about a particular player to cloud my judgement about what was best for the team. Obviously I found it easier to get on with some players rather than others, but irrespective of any private feelings, I wanted the very best team on the field. I just think a leader has to keep reminding himself to be clinical about these sorts of judgements. You don't have to love your players or your management team, but you do need to respect their abilities.

As I mentioned, at United we effectively rebuilt the team on four-year cycles – even though it may not have seemed apparent to all but the most ardent fan. For example, little more than three years after our 1999 Champions League final, ten members of the 18-man squad had left the club; five years after the victory, only five of those players were still at Old Trafford. It meant being very clinical about the capabilities of each player, which was not always easy when some of them had played hundreds of games for the club and made huge contributions to our success. But there was no choice. At Aberdeen, if we wound up third in the League, nobody beyond the team and the coaching staff would be too bothered because Rangers and Celtic were always supposed to occupy the top two spots. At United it was another matter entirely. The genetic make-up of the club was formed from victory.

One aspect of team-building that often gets overlooked is the need for old-timers to have the necessary patience with newcomers. Football can be brutal and there is nowhere to hide on a pitch. When new players arrived at United, particularly if they were transfers and immediately thrust into the first team, they were often uncomfortable with our style of play and performing in front of 75,000 people. When Patrice Evra, our great left-back, played his first game for United in 2006, it was in a derby against Manchester City. He spent the game walking around in a trance. It was a disaster and we lost 3–1. I signed Evra in the same season that we bought Nemanja Vidić from Spartak Moscow and the pair of them took about six months to settle in.

I always felt it was important to be careful about the way a newcomer was threaded into the side, especially if he was not a product of our youth system. For the newcomer everything was unfamiliar, and I am not alluding to the Manchester weather or driving cars with steering wheels on the right-hand side. I mean our system of play and, in particular, the habits and quirks of other players. The boys who had grown into men at Manchester United, such as Ryan Giggs, Paul Scholes, Nicky Butt and David Beckham, could almost have played together blindfolded. They knew how their team-mates would react, or where they were likely to be in particular situations, and could communicate without speaking. They trusted each other's judgements and had that sense of fellowship which is the glue for any group of people who want to outperform competitors. The newcomer did not have that advantage, which is why I always tried to make sure that I wasn't integrating a lot of new players into the first team at the same time. It was almost like trying to teach each person a new language, while familiarising them with several local dialects.

Players sometimes also coveted particular shirt numbers. The number 7, which had taken on a mythical status, having previously been worn by George Best, Bryan Robson and Eric

Cantona, was a shirt that David Beckham, who had started his United career wearing number 24, was eager to wear. At that stage, after David had just played a couple of seasons in the first-team squad, I would have preferred if Roy Keane had taken the number. But Roy was not fussed about it and so I gave it to David. I quickly realised that, as a United fan, this number really mattered to him. He wore it with distinction. After my last season, the number 7 shirt became available and was worn by Antonio Valencia, who subsequently felt it added a burden to his game. He switched back to his previous number the following season.

I also found that experienced players are honest enough with themselves to know if they aren't quite as good as another player. That's particularly the case with older players. A 35-year-old player knows he doesn't have the pace of a top-notch 20 year old, and all team members were aware of the difference between themselves and the unnatural talent of a Cristiano Ronaldo or Eric Cantona. The older players aren't competing against the youngsters as much as they are contending with the comparisons with their younger selves.

Another thing I had to look out for were character clashes. If people are so selfish that they are only thinking about themselves, it just doesn't work. When people start butting heads it destroys a team. We had a situation at United where Andy Cole and Teddy Sheringham just didn't like each other and they wouldn't work together on the field. During one game they had an argument in the tunnel at half-time. So I called them into the office and told them that if I saw that again, they'd both be gone. The change was immediate and there was never another problem between them. Whilst they were never going to be the best of friends, they were professional about the whole situation. But Andy did not want to play second fiddle to anyone, and after Ruud van Nistelrooy arrived, it was clear he was unhappy. Some years later there was tension between Ruud van Nistelrooy and Cristiano Ronaldo. Ruud was dissatisfied with the number of passes he was receiving from Cristiano, and his very evident irritation exacted a toll on the younger player.

When I appointed Roy Keane as club captain in 1997, it aroused the ire of Peter Schmeichel. Schmeichel admired Keane as a player and, best as I know, there wasn't any particular animosity between them. It was just that Schmeichel's pride was hurt, and he let me know in no uncertain terms by storming into my office and going completely berserk. I refused to back down and he stormed out, but I just reiterated to Peter his importance to the team while telling him that the decision had been made. This, obviously, wasn't the best way to usher in Keane as the club leader.

Working as a team didn't stop at the touchlines, and it was a sensibility that was required everywhere. When I brought René Meulensteen back to United in 2007 after he had a brief, ill-fated spell as manager of Brøndby in Denmark, my coaching staff were unhappy. René isn't shy about telling others what's wrong with them, so the prospect of his return was not greeted with undiluted joy. I told everybody that the reason René was being rehired was because he was a spectacular development coach and it was good for the club.

I used all sorts of ploys to try to emphasise to the players, particularly the younger ones, the benefits of teamwork. In my office at the Carrington training ground, I used to have a large black and white photograph from the 1930s, of 11 workers in New York, eating their lunch while sitting on a steel girder several hundred feet above street level during the construction of Rockefeller Center. It makes the hairs on the back of my neck stand up. These guys are sitting there, wearing their cloth hats, without any safety harnesses, and one of them is lighting a cigarette. I'd explain to the players if one of the workers got into trouble his mates would try to save him. I'd say: 'That's team spirit – when you give your life to someone. No one at the club ever wins a thing without the other ones.' Of course, some of the boys completely missed the point. Once, when I asked a player, 'What can you say about that photograph?' the reply was, 'They've all got hats on.'

We were very careful about trying to make sure the limelight shone on as many players as possible. Inevitably, the press would focus on the goal-scorers, but there were plenty of ways for us to ensure that credit was shared as widely as possible. We would rotate different players in front of the press for post-game interview sessions. There were also plenty of opportunities in the match programme or on the website or on MUTV to showcase different personalities. Most were willing to do this, although a few, like Paul Scholes, preferred to stay in the shadows, and some of the foreign players who were unsure about their command of English tended to hold back. If we were playing in Spain, or Portugal, we would be sure to line up a player who spoke Spanish or Portuguese. That was just good business, because those sorts of appearances helped broaden United's appeal.

There is one other lesson I learned regarding teamwork, and it is on an odd topic – nepotism. It does not matter whether you are running a family-managed organisation, or one with more widely distributed stakeholders: a leader is always tempted to look at his own kith and kin, or family friends, through a different lens. Some leaders think that if they bring a close relative into the organisation, it will send the wrong message, destroy teamwork and throw everything out of kilter, because people will assume that a surname, or a personal relationship, is more important than ability. These leaders have a firm rule and refuse to hire family members or friends, even if their credentials suggest they are more than worthy. Others will lurch in the opposite direction and turn a blind eye to the shortcomings of their son or niece.

I encountered this issue when one of my twin sons, Darren, wanted to play as a professional. I never really considered signing him for United because I always thought it was going to be too awkward for both of us. So Cathy and I went to see Brian Clough at Nottingham Forest, and Darren was about to sign for him in 1990 when Archie Knox, my assistant manager, argued that I should not let him go to an opponent. Archie's point was that it was only going to be awkward if Darren made the first team. I talked it over with Cathy, who suggested I let Darren decide. I remember going to his bedroom to pose the question and it was Darren who decided he wanted to play for his old man.

As things would have it, Darren made his debut for the first team in 1990 and played 16 games during 1993, the year United won our first League title under my management. He was very unlucky because he got a hamstring injury in a Scotland Under-21 game against Italy and was out for a couple of months. By the time he was ready to return, Paul Ince and Bryan Robson had recovered from injuries, and the following summer I did what I needed to do as manager and signed Roy Keane, who was then 21, to buttress our midfield. That was a tragedy for Darren, because after that he never really got back into the side; he asked for a transfer because he was keen to play regular first-team football. I helped him land at Wolverhampton Wanderers but then, poor devil, he had to endure four managers in as many seasons. While he was in the first team and in the dressing room, it was a bit difficult for both of us. To Darren's credit, he understood that, at

United, I was the manager not his dad, as I found out when I tried to pump him for information about the lifestyle habits of a couple of players. There was no way that Darren was going to squeal on his team-mates. He played his cards very close to his chest. As for moving Darren along to Wolves, Cathy has never forgiven me. From time to time she will remind me with the words: 'You sold your own son.'

## Captains

As hard as I worked on my own leadership skills, and as much as I tried to influence every aspect of United's success on the field, at kick-off on match day things moved beyond my control. On the field, the person responsible for making sure the 11 players acted as a team was the club captain. Even though I imagine some people think this is a ceremonial position, it is far from that. Yes, there are elements of symbolism to the role, because the captain is the man who always gets to lift the trophy – but I only ever wanted a leader, rather than someone who might look good on top of a cake. It is a critical decision. For football managers the club captain is the equivalent of what a business unit leader or a country manager might be in a company. He is the person responsible for making sure the agenda of the organisation is pursued.

I was always a strong personality, and when I selected people to transmit my intentions to others, I looked for the same quality in them. I don't know where it came from, but even when I was playing for my school team and getting into youth-team football, I'd start getting into the players. My dad always used to go to the games and watch and never say a word. But there was one boy whose dad complained to mine and said,

'Could you speak to your son, he's always going on to my boy.'

Every leader has different characteristics and leads in his own manner. I suppose that's true for CEOs of companies as much as it is for football managers or captains. That was certainly the case during my career as a manager when each of our captains had very different personality traits. When I selected the captain I was looking for four principal virtues. The first was a desire to lead on the field. Some of the finest players just did not aspire to do that, even though they commanded immense respect. Paul Scholes is the shining example of this. He was an extraordinary player and an emblem of everything United stood for but, even though he has what it takes to be a winning manager, he never aspired to be our captain. He is a man of few words, doesn't wear his emotions on his sleeve, and has no need for the limelight. However, nobody should be fooled, because deep down he torments himself if he messes up.

The second attribute I wanted was someone I could trust to convey my desires, and the third was a person whom the other players would respect as a leader and whose instructions they would follow. Not every creative person is born to be a leader. They may be incredible members of a team and astonishingly productive individual contributors, but poor leaders. My son Mark tells me this is also true in his line of work, where people who are very gifted as investors often are not the best types to run and lead an investment organisation, simply because the skills required in that role are not their forte. I also wanted captains capable of adapting to changing circumstances. No general is going to win a war unless he has colonels and majors who, in the thick of a fight that is going poorly, can muster the troops, galvanise them into action and help them defy the odds. The same was true for us, even though United's battles were fought on grounds with names such as Anfield, Camp Nou or Stadio delle Alpi rather than Waterloo or El Alamein.

There were a handful of captains of other teams that I came to admire, although I obviously didn't know them as well as the Aberdeen or United skippers. Alan Shearer at Newcastle United, John Terry at Chelsea and Tony Adams at Arsenal are the ones who stick out for me. They were all driven guys who had an edge to their personalities, and their teams were all the better as a result. Johan Cruyff was probably the most influential during my career. The players, whether it was at Ajax or in the Dutch side, probably listened to him more than they did the manager. Cruyff couldn't help himself: he had to direct and control everything.

When I arrived at Aberdeen I didn't have to worry about picking a leader for the team because Willie Miller was the captain – when I got there and when I left – which was a real tribute to his ability and fitness level. At United Bryan Robson was the club skipper when I appeared and there wasn't a player on the field who could match his determination and grit or his ability to read a game. He was a perfect captain and ticked all the boxes. I trusted him to make on-field adjustments to playing positions; he was also someone who would speak his mind, which was something I valued. Robson remained captain until he started getting plagued by injuries, and in 1991 Steve Bruce led the team for most of the season. Bruce was solid, courageous, and stuck his head into all manners of dangerous positions. Not only would he always put his neck on the line, but he also has a natural instinct for taking care of those around him and a great sense of humour. Both Bryan and Steve were invaluable in other ways, particularly when it came to helping young players and their parents understand the possibilities if they elected to cast their lot with United. When Bruce's knees began to give him trouble,

I picked our talisman, Eric Cantona, and subsequently Roy Keane. Eric and Roy were a study in contrasts – one French and the other Irish. Eric was a man of few words, but when he offered praise it had a dramatic effect. It was more meaningful to David Beckham, after he scored his miraculous goal against Wimbledon, on the opening day of the 1996–97 season, that Eric considered it the best goal he had ever witnessed, than the fact that he had pulled off the impossible. Roy, by contrast, was a man whose intensity could intimidate his team-mates, but he was a great leader on the pitch.

Peter Schmeichel became captain when Roy Keane was injured, and was the team leader on the day we beat Bayern Munich to win the Champions League in 1999 when Roy was suspended. Even though there are other examples of goalkeepers who acted as captains, such as Iker Casillas of Real Madrid and Spain and Gianluigi Buffon and Dino Zoff in Italy, there is a natural tendency to select a player who is in the thick of things rather than the one between the posts. So a goalkeeper who becomes a captain has to be a bit larger than life, and Peter certainly was. Not only was he a massive physical presence – taller than many of the defenders who played for United – but he was also able to transmit his confidence, enthusiasm and zest along the entire length of the pitch.

In the downtime between games I would often solicit the opinion of my captains, but they all understood that I was the ultimate decision-maker. I was also keen to hear what they had to say about particular players, but captains tend to toe the line and stay true to their playing comrades rather than tell tales out of school. I remembered this dividing line from my own playing days and respected it. I frequently talked to the captains and other senior players about how we might approach an opponent. In 1996 as we were preparing to meet Liverpool in the FA Cup final, I spent time with Eric Cantona and Peter Schmeichel trying to figure out how we were going to deal with Steve McManaman. Eric suggested that we drop Roy Keane in front of our back four to keep tabs on McManaman, who floated behind their forwards and was a real handful. It was an astute observation, which we followed; as a result, McManaman was silenced and we won what was a tedious, uneventful game when Eric scored the only goal. Eric's advice was crucial. It didn't matter to me that he had come up with the idea rather than a member of the coaching staff or myself. It just made a ton of sense. It wasn't as if I was chasing honours or looking for personal glory or seeking to be the font of all wisdom. I just wanted the team to win.

It was never quite the same in my last decade at United. Some of that was due to the changing nature of the game, the increase in the number of fixtures we played each season and the rise in the number of substitutes used during games which, by the start of the 1995–96 season, had risen to three. A captain simply could not play in each and every game – so the armband tended to move around. These factors led to a spell where Giggs, Ferdinand, Evra and Vidić, whom we all called Vida, wore the armband at different times. Towards the end of my time, when Vida became more prone to injuries, he and Patrice more or less alternated as captain. You could not have found two more different personalities. Vida is dour and uncompromising while Patrice just brimmed with enthusiasm. He came to me once and asked whether he had gone over the top in a tirade in the dressing room. I reassured him and said that he had saved me from having to shout. Patrice's instinctive reaction was great because it showed how deeply he cared and I thought it would goad his team-mates into performing better. It was the mark of a natural leader.

# 5

## SETTING STANDARDS

# Excellence

Everyone has a different definition of 'world class', the two words that seem to have taken the place of 'great' or 'excellent'. If you read the papers, or listen to the television commentators, we seem to be awash with 'world-class' footballers. The same thing seems to be happening in the classroom, because I keep hearing about 'grade inflation' – or the way in which an A* gets given to a lot more students than in yesteryear. In my book there are only two world-class players playing today – Lionel Messi and Cristiano Ronaldo. There are a considerable number of great players, and an even larger collection of good ones, but of the thousands of professional footballers playing today, only Cristiano and Lionel have earned the right to be described as 'world class'. Other players can produce 'world-class' moments – a spectacular goal, an extraordinary pass, or an astonishing save – but there are hundreds of moments in a game and thousands in a career. There are a number of subjective and objective criteria that I use as a way to rank players. The subjective ones include their ability with both feet; their sense of balance; the disciplined fashion in which they take care of their fitness; their attitude towards training; the consistency between games and over multiple seasons; their demonstrated mastery in several different positions; and the way they add flair to any team for which they play. The objective ones that are impossible to dispute are: the number of goals they have scored; the games they have played for several of the best club teams in the world; the number of League championship and cup medals they have won, and their appearances in World Cups. When you employ this sort of measurement approach, it becomes far easier to define the very highest levels of performance. The people who are least confused about this are other players.

There are a decent number of great players in the game today – Thomas Müller at Bayern Munich, Luis Suárez and Neymar at Barcelona and Alexis Sánchez at Arsenal – but I'm sure that all four would admit that they are not at the same level as Messi and Ronaldo. I don't mean to demean or criticise any of the great or very good footballers who played for me during my 26-year career at United, but there were only four who were world class: Cantona, Giggs, Ronaldo and Scholes. And, of the four, Cristiano was like an ornament on top of a Christmas tree. He was the one who added that final touch. Roy Keane, Bryan Robson and Steve Bruce were great players, but they earned that distinction from their attitude, ambition, leadership ability and intensity rather than some of the other attributes.

Looking a little further back, Bobby Charlton, who played 758 games for the club and 106 games for England, including appearances in the final stages of four World Cup tournaments, illustrates what I mean by 'world class'. Bobby seemed to float above the field, was two footed, could play on the left, the right or in the centre, and had an inner confidence and steely resolve. Bobby, despite all his accomplishments, has always been a modest, humble man. He is quiet and shy, but on one occasion when United were trailing at half-time he said, 'Give me the ball. I can win this.' He was not boasting or preening, he just knew what he could do and, more importantly, his team-mates recognised this. United went on to win that game and they did so because of Charlton – a player who was world class.

In football, a manager is fortunate if he has one world-class player in a squad; most clubs do not have that luxury. Yet, even for them, it is still possible to field a very good team. Properly harmonised, 11 good players can form a team that is more than the sum of its parts. Yet I cannot think of a team that achieved great things at the highest level without a world-class player.

Part of the way you develop excellence in an organisation is to be careful about the way you define success. I was always careful about setting specific, long-range targets. I would never say, 'We expect to win the League and two pieces of silverware this season.' First, it conveys the wrong message, because it sounds cocky and arrogant. Second, it applies a lot of additional pressure on everyone without any real benefit. Third, it sets everyone up for disappointment. It was much easier to say, 'At United we expect to win every game,' because that was the case from about 1993 and it also conveyed the spirit of the club. Making sure everyone understood that we expected to triumph in every game set an agenda of excellence and allowed me to regularly administer booster-shots of intensity.

There's a balance that needs to be weighed when conveying a sense of what's possible with the reality of the circumstances. You have to set up each individual for success, which requires considered thought. It's so easy to set unrealistic expectations and I learned this early in my career. At one point in my first season at St Mirren, the team had won eight games in a row and were well placed in the second division. I was feeling buoyant and told the press that we would not lose a game for the rest of the season. Instead, we won only one of our remaining fixtures, and the club finished the season in sixth place.

At United the press would always ask me at the start of the season what I hoped to achieve. My canned response was to tell them that we wanted to win one trophy and we didn't care which one it was. I was careful not to build up false expectations or place too much pressure on everyone. It is counterproductive. However, we never went two consecutive seasons without a major trophy between my first piece of silverware at United and the end of my career, a period of 23 years.

I was also lucky that, with one exception, I never had an owner or director tell me that they expected me to bring home a piece of silverware. The only time it happened was just before I got fired from St Mirren, when a director told me (even though we had been promoted the season before and had a very young team) that he expected us to win the League in the following season. It was the only time anyone ever said to me: 'We need you to win a trophy.' What he failed to acknowledge was that to achieve that we needed two or three new players that the club did not want to buy.

Winning anything requires a series of steps. You cannot win the League with one giant leap. So I would be careful to divide everything up into digestible chunks. Nobody is going to take a climbing team to the foot of Everest, point to the summit and say 'Okay, lads, get up there.' At the start of the season I would avoid communicating any particular objective with the players. My comments to the press about wanting to win a trophy were reasonably generic and the squad were used to these expectations anyway. I would only start to become less vague in November as the shape of the season and the form of our rivalries became clear. At that point, as the afternoons shortened, I would say to the players, 'If we're first, second or third, or within three points of the lead, on New Year's Day, we have a fantastic chance.'

In November 2009 René Meulensteen set a specific target for the points we wanted in the bag at the end of December, but over that period we lost to Chelsea, Aston Villa and Fulham and I felt the target actually became counterproductive. I thought it better to have an element of vagueness about the specific goal. If we came out of Christmas week in fifth place, it was not a complete disaster because, over the years, it became folklore within the club that United always performed better in the second half of the season. We would always say, 'The second half will look after itself.' Of course, it was a bit more complicated than this, but it buoyed spirits to have that outlook. The reality of anything that's fiercely competitive is that very often nothing is decided until the bitter end. In all my time at United, the winner of the League title was only decided two weeks or more from the end of the season on four occasions.

Being willing to reappraise your targets during a game is crucial too. If you are in real trouble, it often seems like an impossible task to set things right. That happened to us in 2001 when we were 3–0 down to Tottenham at half-time. At the break I was realistic with the players and told them we were in a royal mess. There was deathly quiet in the dressing room and all I said was, 'Score the next goal and let's see where that takes us.' I didn't say something like, 'We've got forty-five minutes to score four times.' That would have seemed impossible. When we walked into the tunnel to take to the pitch, Teddy Sheringham, a former Manchester United player now playing for Tottenham, was barking at his team-mates, 'Don't let them score early.' Having experienced life inside Old Trafford he knew how dangerous we could be when coming from behind.

However, we did score the one goal, and that led, inconceivable though it sounds, to a further four. We eventually won the game 5–3.

Once United started winning domestic competitions, I began to have higher aspirations. I shared these with the coaching staff and explained that, while we obviously had to pursue the League title with a vengeance, our new target was to win the European Champions League. By 1993, the year that United won its first League title while I was manager, the club had only won the Champions League – or the European Cup as it was known until 1992 – once compared to six victories for Real Madrid, four for AC Milan and Liverpool, three for Bayern Munich and Ajax and two for Benfica and Nottingham Forest.

I employed the same approach to the pursuit of the European Cup as I did for the domestic trophies. We had to do it step by step. The first obvious goal was to emerge from the group stages with at least ten points. We only failed to do this three times – in 1994–95, 2005–06 and 2011–12.

I operated in a similar manner with players. I never told Cristiano Ronaldo or Dimitar Berbatov that we expected them to score a minimum of 25 goals a season, or instructed Paul Scholes or Roy Keane that they had to maintain a pass completion rate of at least 80 per cent. I never had a particular quota that I expected any player to fulfil, but they all knew I expected nothing but the best from them. Signing a player to a new contract always presented a good opportunity to review performance levels and it gave me room to talk about where they needed to improve. Whenever we bought a player I would make a point of sitting down with him and explaining exactly what was expected of him at a club like Manchester United.

As for myself, I never wrote out a series of personal goals. When I was 17, I did not tell myself that I needed to score 100 goals by the time I was 30 or finish my playing career with half a dozen medals and a score of Scottish caps. It was similar when I was a manager; although I did know, after Aberdeen had established itself as a winning club, that I wanted to work in a larger setting. Once I got to United, beyond a few brief flirtations with a handful of other clubs, I never thought much about working elsewhere. From time to time people suggested that I become manager of England, but that post, irrespective of the decade, has always held little appeal to me. Not only would I have had to deal with the guilt of turning my back on Scotland, but I would also have had to contend with all the frustrations of the position. It's a hopeless job because, before any major competition, the press and the public whip themselves into a frenzy. They tend to forget that a national team manager, even though he might be handsomely compensated, is in a part-time role. He only sees the players intermittently, he doesn't conduct daily training sessions, and it is unrealistic for any group of players, no matter how talented, to instinctively sense, in the way that they can do at their club, what one of their national team-mates might do. I had a taste of the frustrations of managing a national team when I stepped in for a short stint as Scottish manager following the death of Jock Stein in 1985. It was definitely not my cup of tea. In my opinion, international management jobs are for experienced men in the later stages of their career who have the patience to deal with the shortcomings of the post and carry the reputation needed to command a dressing room full of players with whom they spend little time.

After I got to Manchester, I could not imagine a larger stage than Old Trafford. Obviously I'm very aware of Camp Nou and the Bernabéu, which are both great settings, but for me neither has had the allure of Old Trafford. I never gave myself a quota for the number of League titles or FA Cup trophies I had to win before I retired. If I had said to myself, I cannot go until United has won five Champions League titles, I would still be at Old Trafford, even though, privately, I believe we should have achieved that goal under my watch. I never said to myself that my life would not be complete unless United strikers won a certain number of Ballon d'Or awards or Player of the Year awards. I just don't operate like that. All I ever wanted to do was win more trophies. I just could never get enough.

## Inspiring

You don't get the best out of people by hitting them with an iron rod. You do so by gaining their respect, getting them accustomed to triumphs and convincing them that they are capable of improving their performance. I cannot think of any manager who succeeded for any length of time by presiding over a reign of terror. It turns out that the two most powerful words in the English language are, 'Well done'. Much of leadership is about extracting that extra 5 per cent of performance that individuals did not know they possessed.

It was always important that the players erased the memory of the previous season, whether we had won or lost. If we had done well in the previous year, it did not guarantee that we would automatically do so again. And, if we had lost, I had no interest in prolonging any hangover of defeatism. The coaching staff, in particular the sports science crew, would come to me with new ideas before or during the pre-season, but I would never conduct any big post-mortem with the players. I used to gather them around me in a semi-circle at the training ground and re-emphasise my desire to win and use it as an opportunity to set expectations. I used to ask the mature players, who had begun to acquire a taste for United's victory habits, how many medals they had won. I told them that they could not consider themselves to be a United player until they had won ten medals. I remember saying to Rio Ferdinand that he could never think of himself as a United player until he attained the level of Ryan Giggs. Of course, that was mission impossible.

It is much easier to do difficult things if others like you. Though I have never tried to court popularity, I always tried to pay particular attention to people at United – or at the other clubs I was involved with – who worked behind the scenes and were our unsung heroes. It wasn't a false front; it just seemed like the right thing to do. These people weren't getting the multimillion-pound salaries or public acclaim, and didn't wear Patek Philippe watches or drive Bentleys. Some of them – the laundry team, the groundsmen, the hospitality waitresses – took the bus to work. They were the mainstays of the club. At United, some of them have been there even longer than Ryan Giggs. In a way, they are the club's equivalent of the Civil Service – they outlast the governments and, at United, they provided continuity and a connection with our heritage. It was very easy for me to feel affinity towards them, since most had backgrounds much like my own.

Some managers try to be popular with the players and become one of the boys. It never works. As a leader, you don't need to be loved, though it is useful, on occasion, to be feared. But, most of all, you need to be respected. There are just some natural boundaries, and when those get crossed it makes life harder. When I was playing at Rangers, they hired a new manager, David White. He was young and a good man but just out of his depth. He was overawed by the club, while at the same time he was living in the shadow of Jock Stein over at Celtic. The players didn't have much respect for him, and part of the reason was because he was too close to them. The same thing happened at United when Wilf McGuinness succeeded Sir Matt Busby in 1969. Wilf had several things going against him. He was succeeding a legend; he was only 31 years old and had no management experience. But, worst of all, he was managing a group of men with whom he had played. It was an impossible position for him. My immediate predecessor at United, Ron Atkinson, had a similar issue. He had enjoyed much more success as a manager than Wilf, but he too chose to fraternise with the players. It just doesn't work. A leader is not one of the boys.

It is vital to keep some sort of distance. This could be expressed in small but significant ways. For example, I generally rode at the front of the team bus. The players understood the distance, and at the end of the season when they had their parties, I was never invited. They'd invite all the management staff, but they wouldn't invite me. I wasn't offended by this. It was the right thing for them to do. With one exception in Aberdeen, I never attended any of the players' weddings. There was a line that they were not prepared to cross and they respected my position. It also makes things easier because, as a manager, you can't be sentimental about them. Jock Stein told me once, 'Don't fall in love with the players because they'll two-time you.' That may be a bit harsh, but Jock was right that you cannot get too attached to people who work for you. The one time you must have that attachment is when they are in trouble – when they need your advice. I couldn't count the number of times where I helped players with personal matters, and I'm proud of the fact they trusted me and that they knew that discussion would stay private. In these situations I acted as a priest, father or lawyer – whatever it took to make the problem go away. Even to this day, many former players still come to me for advice; this is a reflection of the trust that underpinned our relationship.

When players got too old I couldn't afford to be kind to them at the expense of the club. All the evidence is on the football field. It just doesn't lie. I had to make a lot of horrible decisions and I had to be ruthless. I never expected the players to love me, but neither did I want them to hate me, because that would have made it impossible to extract the most from them. All I wanted was for them to respect me and follow my instructions.

Unless you understand people, it's very hard to motivate them. I learned this years ago in Scotland when I was handed a lesson by a young lad. While I managed Aberdeen, we used to travel down to Glasgow every Thursday night to coach young kids on an AstroTurf field so that we could identify the best young talent. I was down there one night, dressed in my track-suit emblazoned with its 'AF' initials, when I saw this kid, who was about eight, smoking a cigarette. I said, 'Put that cigarette out, son. What would your dad think if he saw you smoking?' The boy looked at me and he said, 'Fuck off!' and walked away. My assistant manager, Archie Knox, who was with me, burst out laughing at the way this kid had chopped my legs off. But when I started thinking about the incident, I realised that I knew nothing about that boy. I had no idea where he came from, what his parents were like, whether he was taunted by his pals and why he harboured such anger. Unless you know those sorts of things and have an understanding of someone's personality, it is impossible to get the best out of them. Before we signed players, especially youngsters, I always tried to understand the circumstances in which they had been raised. The first ten or 12 years of anyone's life have such a profound influence on the way they act as adults.

121

Another crucial ingredient of motivation is consistency. As a leader you can't run from one side of the ship to the other. People need to feel that you have unshakeable confidence in a particular approach. If you can't show this, you'll lose the team very quickly. There is a phrase in football about players 'not playing for the manager', which I have seen happen a thousand times. Once that happens, the manager is as good as dead, because he has failed in his major undertaking – which is to motivate the players to follow him. The time to be inconsistent is when changes need to be made because the world is changing around you. There was always the temptation when things weren't going well to change or to leap to a new lily pad. That doesn't work. Sometimes, if we lost some games, we'd hear that the players thought that our training should be more light-hearted; that our results would improve if, instead of concentrating our training sessions around technical skills, we played mock games. I always refused to bow to those sugges-tions. Any field on a Sunday is full of people playing park games, work games or pub games, but that doesn't make these people better footballers. I just believe that continual devotion to improving technical skills, and the enhancement of tactics, lead to better results, and I wasn't about to change just to temporarily please others.

Leaders are usually unaware, or at least underestimate, the motivating power of their presence. Nobody sees themselves as others see them. I'd never really understood this until Rio Ferdinand buttonholed me one day because I had missed some training sessions while travelling abroad to scout a player. Rio said, 'Where have you been? It's not the same when you are not here.' It didn't matter that Carlos Queiroz was running the training sessions and the routine and drills were exactly the same as if I had been there. Rio had noticed my absence, and perhaps some of the players had eased off a little because I was missing from the sidelines. I don't know whether that actually happened because I wasn't there – and maybe that's the point.

I took Rio's observation to heart. After that, if I had to go and watch a player or check out a team, we chartered a private plane so I could be at the training ground the next day even if I hadn't got to bed until two in the morning. The lesson I absorbed was that even if I said nothing during the practice (and I rarely said much), my physical presence was a more important motivational tool than I had realised. Anyone who is in charge of a group of people has got to have a strong personality. That doesn't mean dominating every conversation or speaking at the top of your voice. Some quiet people have very strong personalities and rooms fall silent when they have something to say. A strong personality is an expression of inner strength and fortitude.

I always got more out of players by praising them than by scorning them with criticism. Footballers, like all human beings, are plagued by a range of emotions that run all the way from profound insecurity to massive over-confidence. Trying to measure where, along this spectrum, each of these players was on any particular day was very important. If you hope to motivate people, you need to know when to prey on their insecurities and when to bolster their self-confidence. People perform best when they know they have earned the trust of their leader.

My father was a man of few words. He didn't dole out praise. His main desire was for me to keep my feet on the ground and retain my humility. After I scored three goals in one game and got home, he just handed out stick. He said, 'You don't shoot enough. You don't pass enough.' I suppose my dad's remarks made me want to work harder so that I could garner praise from him but, after I had played well, it was always deflating to hear him utter those sorts of remarks. By contrast, my mother and my granny used to be full of compliments and praise, and their joy in my successes was evident. In retrospect I sometimes wonder whether my parents inadvertently supplied me with two engines: one that made me want to try even harder and a second that made me feel I was capable of anything.

I wasn't afraid of criticising a player when I felt I could help him improve, but I always tried to couch this in a positive way. For example, I would tell a young player that he would be far more effective if he passed the ball more. That message is more likely to be absorbed than barking, 'You're never going to be any good if you keep hogging the ball.' After a game I would always try to avoid criticising the players. They had enough pressure, without me piling it on in public. I saved my criticism for the private sessions away from prying eyes. I tried to employ heat shields to deflect criticism from a player who had misplaced a pass that gave away a goal, or another who had missed a sitter that could have won us a game. It was always easy to give the press something else to write about – a couple of decisions that had gone against us, a penalty that should have won us the game, a long injury list or a pile-up of fixtures. I tried to take the pressure off the player who did not need me or anyone else to remind him of his mistake. Most players are mortified when they let down their team. My first inclination was always to defend the player and sort it out afterwards.

Every player is different, and I came to learn that they all required different care and feeding. Some would be at one extreme and need little from me. This was particularly true of players who had made a couple of hundred appearances, had inner confidence, and understood me. The youngsters and those who, for whatever reason, were less assured, needed different handling. I'm sure that, from time to time, I underestimated the degree of intimidation experienced by new players. All the youngsters who had been part of the United system for years were intimidated enough by the first-team dressing room. But imagine what it was like for a player signed from overseas who had never played in England and sometimes could not understand what was being said. I know that Tim Howard, whom we signed from the American team MetroStars, in 2003, and quickly started to employ as our first-team goalkeeper, found a massive contrast between his former team, which had been at the bottom of the MLS, and United. He had to quickly adjust to the notion that men whom he had worshipped from afar were now his team-mates, and to our more direct and confrontational style of management. I'm not sure there is anything that can prepare someone for a dose of Glaswegian bluntness, doled out by a shipyard worker's son, particularly when that man is in ultimate control of your destiny.

You might think that team-mates would resent another player who was treated differently. That would probably be true if he was an everyday character. But, once in a while, someone would appear who required something special. Eric Cantona fits into that category. He had been a bit of a wayward character at his other clubs and had gained a reputation for being unruly and difficult. His disciplinary record was longer than your arm. It was almost as if he was considered some sort of demon. That made no sense to me. When you are dealing with individuals with unusual talent, it makes sense to treat them differently. I just made it a point to ignore what had happened in the past and treat Eric as a new man when he joined United. When Eric was with us I would always make a point of talking to him every day – on the training ground, or in the cafeteria or dressing room. He was a sensitive person who was easily bothered by all sorts of things, but he loved talking about football and that was a way to help restore his spirits. I did things for Eric and for the really special players that I did not do for others, but I don't think this was resented, because the players understood the exceptional talents had qualities they did not possess. My relationship with Eric might also have been helped by the fact that neither of us were English and, to some degree, we considered ourselves outsiders. But even the players I thought I understood well could react in unexpected ways. I did not realise until fairly recently that, when he was far younger, Gary Neville was unable to sleep after I handed him a tongue-lashing. It just emphasises how any leader needs to put himself in the shoes of the listener. For example, I was always very careful when I rested a player to emphasise how I was counting on him for a subsequent, crucial fixture. This helped – but probably didn't completely satisfy – their desire to play in every game, and hopefully prevented them interpreting my decision as a lack of confidence in them.

With most players I did not have to urge them to increase their work rate or expend more energy, but there were a few, like Gary Pallister, who played 437 games for United between 1989 and 1998 who needed the extra poke. The irony of this is that Pallister was probably the best defender I ever managed, but he had a laidback attitude towards life. He did not like training, and in games it always seemed to take him 15 minutes to coax his engine into life. There was a first half in a game against Liverpool in 1990 when he just tortured me. At half-time I said to him, 'You are coming off.' Then I thought better of myself, changed my mind and told him, 'No, I'm not taking you off. You can suffer along with me.'

Paul Ince was another. He was a good player but he had a

tendency to run with the ball rather than pass it. Every now and again I'd have to upbraid him and I did so after a game against Norwich in 1992, which we had to win in order to have a shot at the League title, and he went berserk. He started yelling that I always blamed him, and the other players had to hold him back. I told him, 'I'm not blaming you. You made mistakes. You ran with the ball when you should have passed it.'

When I was younger I was more inclined to be severe. I cringe when I think back to a live TV interview moments after Aberdeen had won the 1983 Scottish Cup final against Rangers – three days after winning the European Cup Winners' Cup final against Real Madrid – when I blasted the team for a 'disgrace of a performance'. Later, after I had tucked more experience under my belt, I took a different approach. There is no benefit in engaging in public hangings. It just doesn't buy you anything. It humiliates the victim and does not do much to encourage those around him. So I tried to stick to a few rules. While not always succeeding in the heat of the moment, I would try to reserve my severest comments for a private session with a player. I would always try to meld criticism with support by saying, 'You know you are capable of better. What were you thinking?' It was also important to make everyone understand that any disciplinary action was not arbitrary: it applied to everyone and it was unchangeable. When Ryan Giggs started arguing with me at half-time during a game against Juventus in the 1996–97 season, I stapled him to the bench for the second half. When Paul Scholes, one of the best players ever to wear United red, committed a few daft tackles that resulted in needless red cards, I would always discipline him. His actions had let the side down; however valuable a player he was, he wasn't above the law.

One other aspect of managing high-achievers that is worth emphasising is the need to restrain them from trying to do the impossible. Every now and again someone would pull off an acrobatic goal or some other exquisite form of mastery, but you can never count on these. There is always a temptation when the chips are down to try and resort to stunts that might have worked in the pages of the old comic magazine *Boy's Own Paper*, but were almost always guaranteed to fail in front of 75,000 desperate fans. Whenever we were in a tight game and trailing by a goal, I would always emphasise to the team that we should not panic, and I would implore them not to try and shoot from outside the box. Instead I would want them to keep their heads, retain possession and get crosses into the penalty box. Gary Neville, who was our indomitable right-back for so many years, had this habit of trying to shoot from 35 yards. It drove me bananas. After the game I would always be asking him, 'How many times have I told you it doesn't work?' Disciplined perseverance pays far more dividends than impetuous attempts at individual heroism.

Part of the way to extract the most out of people is to show genuine loyalty when the rest of the world is baying for blood. Football provides plenty of opportunities to do this. After Eric Cantona's famous kung-fu attack on what appeared to me to be – when I reviewed tapes of the incident after the match – an aggressive, foul-mouthed fan at Crystal Palace in 1995, the club, which gave him a four-month suspension (which was doubled, in a punitive manner, by the FA), did everything we could to support him. Eric had been sent into exile and forbidden from training or travelling on our pre-season tour, so it was natural for him to feel isolated and forgotten. I worked very hard to make sure he understood that we cared about him, and eventually, when he was teetering on the edge of departing to play in Italy, our loyalty towards him caused him to stay in Manchester.

Some years later, in the 1998 World Cup in France, after David Beckham got sent off for lashing out at Argentina's Diego Simeone, now the Atlético Madrid manager, we wanted to be sure we were by his side. The entire press corps was convinced that David's dismissal from the game had cost England the fixture, and the headlines reflected this. They were merciless: '10 Heroic Lions, 1 Stupid Boy' was the headline in the *Daily Mirror*, while the *Daily Star* blared: 'Beck Off'. There were effigies of David hanging from lamp-posts, and it wouldn't have surprised me if an immigration officer had refused him permission to re-enter Britain. After I saw what happened, I immediately phoned David, because I knew he would be devastated. He was. I learned afterwards that he had burst into tears when he saw his parents after the game and was almost inconsolable.

The last thing David needed was criticism from me, because he had already found himself guilty. So I phoned him, tried to bolster his confidence, told him that I understood what had occurred, that these things happen to us all, and that Manchester United, and everyone associated with the club, knew he was a wonderful player and were looking forward to his return, and that we would take care of him. United's first away game of the following season was against West Ham, where an effigy of Beckham was displayed hanging from a noose en route to the stadium, and the United team bus was pelted with stones and pint glasses.

Something similar happened when we went to sign Ruud van Nistelrooy from PSV Eindhoven in 2000. We had agreed on terms and I was stunned when Ruud failed his medical test. PSV claimed that Ruud was fit, and to demonstrate this arranged for a filmed training session. He broke down on camera and you can see the film of the session on YouTube, with Ruud howling in pain on the ground. It turned out that he had torn a cruciate ligament. So we suspended the deal but I immediately flew to the Netherlands to see Ruud, who was bed-ridden. I told him that it was not like the old days; that cruciate ligaments could be repaired; that he would regain his fitness and we would then sign him. I think that helped reassure Ruud, and it was also a way of ensuring that he did not go to another club. Just over a year later he was in United red, scoring on his debut.

Occasionally players can face much bigger challenges. Fortunately it is extremely rare for a top-notch player to come down with a life-threatening illness, but when Darren Fletcher fell sick with ulcerative colitis, it presented an opportunity for United to demonstrate unflinching support, because he was out of the side for a very long time. Darren had tried to muscle his way through this debilitating condition for a couple of years, but eventually it made him housebound and he underwent surgery. Coincidentally my sister-in-law had died of complications from the disease, so I was all too aware of the torture Darren had been silently enduring. It would have been easy for the club to consign him to the wilderness, but we made sure that he understood we wanted him to get well and return to the side and gave him a new contract. He had come to United as a teenager and never let us down, so while he was undergoing treatments we made him a reserve team coach so that he would not feel abandoned. I poked my head into one of his half-time team talks and he was spectacular. He was berating the players and I listened to him tell them, 'If you think that performance is going to get you in the Manchester United first team, you have to be joking. You have no chance.' In due course Darren recovered, felt great personal relief when he publicly revealed his private battle and is now the proud captain of West Bromwich Albion.

Though this sounds odd, I would sometimes protect players by leaving them out of the first team. It happened at both ends of the spectrum. For youngsters (as I have mentioned), I thought it best to gradually introduce them to the rigours of life in the first team. And for players in their thirties, I often rested them to make sure they did not overtax their bodies. When Eric Cantona and Gary Neville came to me to say they wanted to retire, I tried to talk both of them out of doing so. I urged Eric to talk to his father, but that didn't work. Gary, being a proud professional, was also adamant. I had urged him to wait until the end of the 2010–11 season to make his decision but he just said, 'No, Boss, I'm finished. I am just kidding myself on.' On more than one occasion I left Wayne Rooney out of battles on Merseyside with Everton, not because of fitness concerns, but because the Everton fans could be merciless on him. Even though Wayne, particularly as he has got older, can shield himself from most abuse, it just did not seem sensible to expose him, or more particularly the entire team, to the abuse that would have been levelled at him. The abuse is so extreme that even Wayne's father, a diehard Everton fan, skips United's games at Goodison Park.

Football provides plenty of opportunities for a manager to show his support. There may be the times, like with Beckham or Van Nistelrooy, where the players were dealing with ugly situations. But, more often than not, it is the little things – helping youngsters improve their technique, making suggestions like one I made to Cristiano Ronaldo that he shorten his running stride when he was preparing to cross the ball, standing by players when they get injured, blooding a teenager when he makes his way into the first team – that instil a sense of loyalty. I was not doing these things because I was trying to emulate Mother Teresa, I was doing them because they would help

United, but they had the side-effect of demonstrating to the player that we had confidence in him. This instils tremendous loyalty; it also helped them to lift their game. Their way of returning these favours was to give that extra 5 per cent during a match. And so, inadvertently, I gradually came to understand this back-door route to inspiring people.

The criticism of others also provides a way to rally the troops. It is one thing for an individual to be singled out for a press savaging, particularly when some of it may be deserved. It is quite another when a whole organisation is pilloried. I almost used to enjoy it when that happened, because it played right into our hands. It would get under the collective skin, it would bring people closer together, and it offered me a convenient rallying cry. In 1996, after we were clobbered in successive League games by Newcastle and Southampton, we lost our third League game in a row against Chelsea and BBC radio broadcast a programme about our supposed demise. It was a perfect tonic for us, and I am sure helped us go on to win the Premier League. In hindsight, I can see why it was such a big story as in my last 20 years at United it only happened on two other occasions.

## Complacency

Complacency is a disease, especially for individuals and organisations that have enjoyed success. I like to think that United's ability to avoid lapsing towards complacency was one of the characteristics that distinguished the club. We were not always successful at doing so, but I was always eager to stamp out the slightest trace of complacency. It's like dry rot or woodworm because, once damp gets into the brickwork or insects into the wood, you don't notice the damage until it is too late. Whenever we played a game I never thought victory was in the bag. People might think of me as a 'winning manager', but just look at the statistics. At United I managed a total of 1,500 games, of which we lost 267, drew 338 and won 895. So overall you could conclude that every time I walked out on to a pitch I only had just under a 60 per cent chance of winning. In the hotel in Moscow in 2008, after we had just won the Champions League and Premier League, I talked to the players about the 2008–09 season and emphasised the need to be prepared for a tough, fresh series of campaigns where nothing was guaranteed.

I received my first high-profile lesson in the curse of complacency in 1968 during my first season as a player for Rangers. We had not lost a game up until the very last match against Aberdeen. We went down 3–2 and lost the League. After the game, thousands of supporters went berserk and were breaking windows and stampeding. It was mayhem. We required a police escort to leave the stadium unscathed. It would not have taken us much to win the League. It was our job to do our job – and we didn't.

Another example of complacency, or over-confidence, sticks in my mind. It comes from tennis. I attended the final of the US Women's Open Championship in 2012, when Victoria Azarenka almost beat Serena Williams. Azarenka was up 5–3 in the final set and gave a little fist-pump to her family and friends in the box. From that point on it was all downhill. She lost the game she was serving to win the championship, and Williams went on to take the trophy. I saw Azarenka's face after she lost. She was devastated. It just shows you should never touch a cup until you have won it.

The same thing happened to the US team in the Ryder Cup tournament at Medinah in 2012, when they were leading the

Europeans by 10 points to 6 and only had to win 4½ points from the remaining 12 in order to win the trophy. I'm sure a degree of complacency had set in – it is just human nature. The moment that happens, things start to go wrong, and it almost always leads down the road to perdition. At Medinah you could see uncertainty start to creep into Team USA after they gave up one point. Then, after the next one went out of the window, confusion started to set in. It wasn't long before they were panicking, and by then the jig was up. Players forget what they are supposed to do, are incapable of calming themselves down and commit mistakes they don't usually make. Eventually they capitulate.

I've seen this happen a million times. It begins with uncertainty which leads to confusion. Then panic starts to set in and, before you know it, the team has capitulated and defeat becomes inevitable. Meantime, the behaviour of their opponents starts to change: their confidence begins to build, their concentration sharpens and they block out all distractions. They can smell the scent of blood and, before you know it, complacency has scored another ugly victory.

We weren't immune to it ourselves at United, and there are a few specific games that I am embarrassed to recall. In November 1998 we played Blackburn Rovers and were coasting towards what looked like a straightforward 3–0 win, made easier by the fact that they were only playing with ten men. Then Blackburn scored two goals in the last 25 minutes and we disintegrated. It was absolute mayhem. We were clearing balls off the line and booting them into the stand and I was saying to myself, 'If we lose, I'm going to kill every single one of them.' We scratched out a narrow victory on that occasion, but it was complacency, perhaps compounded by some substitutions I made, that nearly caused us profound embarrassment.

Without doubt our worst dose of complacency occurred in 2012 when we played Everton at Old Trafford. It was April, we had played 34 games in the Premier League season and were first in the table, five points in front of Manchester City. Goodness knows what happened in that game. Maybe everybody thought it would be a humdrum affair and a routine win. Maybe we all thought we were about to add yet another trophy to our collection, particularly since it had been the best performance of the season. We were 4–2 up with seven minutes to play; one or two of the players got a little lazy running back to their defensive positions and stopped doing their jobs.

I think about that game a lot, and even now I cannot account for what happened. We were 1–0 down after 33 minutes. We got the equaliser just before half-time and the next three goals were unbelievable. We sliced Everton to bits and were leading 4–2. The irony was that we were haunted by Darron Gibson, a strong midfielder we had only just sold to Everton. I kept telling the team to not let Gibson get in a position with the ball in the middle of the pitch. But, for some reason, we didn't, and wound up with Darron Gibson actually running the show. And in the 85th minute Everton dragged the score back to 4–4. One week later we played Manchester City at the Etihad Stadium and lost 1–0 – a result that was partly caused by a couple of mistakes I made with team selection, and by Roberto Mancini's emphasis on defence. Manchester City wound up winning the League.

In my last season as a manager, in March 2013, we were 2–0 up against Chelsea in the FA Cup at Old Trafford and it looked as if we were coasting to victory. That was the trouble – we were coasting. Chelsea made a couple of substitutions that changed the momentum and got a goal back before equalising soon after. By the end of the game we were under extreme pressure and just managed to hang on for a draw. The match went to a replay at Stamford Bridge which we lost; our complacency had turned a comfortable victory into defeat.

I was always careful not to exude any sign of over-confidence. That was not a pantomime show or a false front, it is how I feel about pursuing anything that others also want. You just cannot take anything for granted. If United happened to be at the top of the table and there were five games left to play, I would never say, 'If we get three points here nobody stands a chance of catching up.' Instead I would say, 'Let's get this game out of the way. Just get the job done.' You win by taking one step at a time.

One final exhibition of complacency lodges in my memory and it was the last home game of the 2006–07 season against West Ham. We had already wrapped up the title the previous week, but I had lectured the team before the game that they owed it to everyone to make sure we won. West Ham, for their part, needed to beat us in order to stay in the Premier League. I had left Ronaldo, Giggs and Scholes on the bench because we had the FA Cup final the following week but, right before half-time, Carlos Tévez scored for West Ham. I put our three best players on after half-time but we still lost. The complacency of the United team on that occasion made me furious. I let the players have it full throttle at the end of the game. It was an appalling way to end the season, it was an awful display to our fans of what Manchester United stood for, and it left a terrible taste in my mouth. The players might have thought it was a meaningless game – but I didn't.

Complacency can often start seeping into an organisation that has had a string of triumphs. More money starts flowing around; travel policies are loosened so that people start booking expensive airline seats or five-star hotels. Then plaques and mementos of victories, or important milestones, begin popping up on desks and office shelves. Some organisations, and United certainly is one of those, even have a museum where their old products – or, in our case, trophies – are on display. At United, as the years passed by, the essentials of life certainly got easier. We started chartering planes to ferry the team around, the comfort of our buses increased immeasurably, and it was all too easy for us to take these luxuries for granted.

Nonetheless it is important for all the people associated with an organisation to feel part of a big success. A few days after we secured any of our trophies, I'd gather all the staff at Carrington together and we would toast our success with a glass of champagne before getting to work. I always felt that the trick was to celebrate our triumphs without for a moment losing the edge and depth of desire that had taken us there. I just wanted to be on my guard that victories weren't seen as auto-matic guarantees of future success, and that celebrations did not sow the seeds of complacency.

People who have given everything to achieve the impossible deserve recognition and praise. However, I have never been a big fan of celebrations. While I was at United and participated in many, the commercial side of the club organised all those sort of events. Whenever one of my players won the Ballon d'Or, or the Professional Footballers' Association Player of the Year award, I would be sure to attend the banquets. But I cannot pretend I enjoyed all the drinking that accompanied them.

I loved celebrating goals, particularly ones like the bicycle kick Wayne Rooney pulled off against Manchester City in 2011. For me the final whistle of a game was always salvation. The final whistle is the greatest moment. It is definitive, and marks the time when you finally achieve something. I only felt in a celebratory mood for a couple of hours after a big victory. It didn't matter if it was a League Championship or Champions League. Celebrations after victories are exhausting. As a manager, after a game, you need to give the press interviews, return to a hotel, freshen up and attend a reception. By the time the day was done it was one o'clock in the morning and I would be dying to get to bed. I'd usually lie in bed for a bit and feel a sense of satisfaction, but by the time I woke up that was gone.

I recognised that a victory or major event had a different meaning if you are a player, or supporter, or director – you can celebrate as long as you want. It was always very rewarding to see the amount of happiness a team can provide – especially to a community that either does not have much of a share of the limelight or has been down on its luck. The victory in the European Cup Winners' Cup in 1983 was a great tonic for Aberdeen – a city which, despite the business brought by North Sea oil, is easily forgotten. Aberdeen is closer to Oslo than London, and in winter there can be fewer than six and a half hours of daylight. Even in May, when we had our homecoming parade, there was a freezing wind howling off the North Sea. The city council declared an official holiday, and all the schools closed except one – the Albyn School which, at the time, was an all-girls' school. However, when we passed the school, all the girls were outside or looking through the windows, cheering the bus.

Even though Manchester is much bigger and better known, the United victories meant a lot to the locals. The whole area had known its share of misery – and I'm not talking about Liverpool's run in the 1970s and 1980s. I'm referring to the local economy, the decimation of almost every manufacturing busi-ness, and the enormous hardships this caused for numerous families. For many of these people, United's victories were the best thing that happened in their lives. I'm sure that, for some, our open-topped bus processions through Manchester were better than Christmas.

In 1999, after our Treble, it was extraordinary. In Deansgate, the main road through the centre of Manchester, there was a building that was under construction which had 'DO NOT ENTER' signs plastered all over it. That didn't stop anyone. There were people standing on the open concrete floors and steel beams. Everyone was singing the favourite United songs and throwing scarves and hats at the bus. The same thing happened in 2013, after we won our 20th League title, and the team was taken out on to the balcony of the town hall. For several seasons, when we had won the League, I'd have the staff over to the house for a spread and some drinks.

While I took great pleasure and satisfaction in seeing what we had done for others, I cannot say that I felt as happy. I always felt I had to be in the vanguard of tomorrow. I'd immediately start to think about ways in which we could improve, and players who were coming to the end of their best days. For me, the questions going through the back of my mind during any celebration were, 'How do we top this? How do we get another triumph?' I never wanted us to be torpedoed by complacency.

# 6

---

# MEASURING PEOPLE

# Job Hunting

Unlike a lot of my fellow managers and, more importantly, unlike a lot of the people I grew up with in Scotland, I've never had to contend with the soul-deadening experience of months or years out of work. I can only imagine the devastating effects of being tossed on the ash-heap. Fortunately, I always had a job when I was looking for a fresh challenge, but that did not prepare me for interviews – particularly at the start of my career.

I have done thousands of interviews, but those have been with the press. I've only really done a few job interviews in my life – at Queen's Park in Scotland in 1974, Wolverhampton Wanderers in 1982 and Barcelona in 1983. My interview for the position as manager of Queen's Park was a disaster. I was completely unprepared. I wasn't sure who I was going to meet and I certainly hadn't thought about the questions I would be asked, let alone have a list of topics that I wanted to discuss. So when I arrived, thinking I was just going to see the chairman of the club, I was surprised to find a large interview committee, including men I had played with. There must have been 12 of them in the room. I was nervous. I didn't know how to handle myself. I was shockingly bad. I spent the whole interview trying to justify myself and my record, rather than just being myself. When I came out of the room I knew I had failed and I felt really disappointed. They gave the job to Dave McParland, who later became an assistant to Jock Stein at Celtic.

Over time I discovered that interviews, or meetings, with the principals of other clubs were very revealing. They gave me glimpses of the tone and tenor of each organisation. My encounter at Wolves was astonishing. I had been led to believe that they had already decided to offer me the job, and then I found myself in a hotel, with the whole board, being asked what I would do if I found a player had taken £5,000 from the club's bank account. I thought to myself, 'They don't need a manager, they need an accountant.' I could not get back to Aberdeen quickly enough.

At about the same time, I met Irving Scholar, then the chairman of Tottenham, who offered me the manager's job at White Hart Lane. At the time the club had an incumbent manager, Keith Burkinshaw, and there was no way I was ever going to take anybody's job away from him.

Later in my career, I met with a representative of Massimo Moratti, the long-time owner of Inter Milan. That went out the window the moment he showed me a list of players they were going to buy and sell, which is just as well because I would never have persuaded Cathy to move to Italy.

It's strange to think, looking back, that the job that came to define me – the manager's post at United – was offered to me without a formal interview. Few businesses would think of offering a job to someone they haven't interviewed, or didn't already know pretty well. But that is not always the way it works in football. When I received a telephone call from United, the club was hovering in the first division relegation zone and flirting with disaster. Previously I only had fleeting contact with the Manchester United board when, in 1984, I had helped them buy Gordon Strachan, the midfielder, from Aberdeen, at a time when the player had already agreed to a transfer to a German club. Apart from that, and the briefest of sideline conversations with Bobby Charlton during the 1986 World Cup in Mexico, I had never spoken to any of them about the job. When I finally met them at my sister-in-law's house in Bishopbriggs, just outside Glasgow, it was to discuss the financial realities of the position. They had already decided they wanted me in Manchester, and I was so eager for the job that I moved to Old Trafford for less than I was being paid in Aberdeen.

Over the years I have picked up far more experience of being on the other side of the table – of being the interviewer rather than the interviewee. When I interview someone, I want to know how ambitious they are or whether they are just thinking about a job as a stepping-stone to something else. Apart from their qualities and qualifications, I want to measure the level of their commitment. I always look for enthusiasm, for a positive attitude, for eye contact and for personal courage. As United became more successful, I could see that some job candidates were quite nervous when they came to see me. So I tried to put them at their ease by offering them a cup of tea. I just wanted them to relax enough so that I could get the measure of who they really were.

You can pick up the signs of someone's character in many different ways during an interview – and it's often the little things that make a difference. For example, someone who sits up properly and is leaning forward a little is showing that they are eager to start. That is way better than appearing cocky or over-confident or not seriously interested in the position. Some people are often afraid to ask questions during interviews. That's daft. Interviews should not be a one-way street. You need to know what your employer can offer you. I often get a measure of someone by listening to the questions they pose. It shows how they think; offers a sense of their level of experience and degree of maturity.

In my 26 years at United, the most important interviews I ever did were for the role of my assistant. At United I had seven assistant managers – Archie Knox, Brian Kidd, Steve McClaren, Jim Ryan, Carlos Queiroz, Walter Smith and Mick Phelan. After Brian Kidd left in 1998 I got more serious about interviewing, and the process became more meticulous. We looked at several people but narrowed it down to David Moyes and Steve McClaren.

David was about 35 at the time and was managing Preston North End. He was very tense when I interviewed him and that showed in the seriousness of his face. Steve McClaren was the opposite of David. He was bright, breezy and enthusiastic. He had worked at Oxford United and Derby County, where the players liked him, and he was a voracious consumer of books and videos about football and training techniques. At that point Steve had a lot more experience in the top flight of football than David, and that swung my decision.

The most impressive interview I ever did was with Carlos Queiroz. I'd been looking for a foreign coach who could speak several languages, to help us with the foreign-born players. Andy Roxburgh, the former manager of Scotland, referred me to Carlos, who was coaching South Africa at the time. Quinton Fortune, who is South African and played for United, was also complimentary about Carlos. When Carlos came to the interview he just did everything right. I'd never met him before. He was dressed as if he was going to get married and I could see by the way he sat that he wanted the job. He looked at me intensely – I always watch to see whether people can maintain eye contact because it is a good measure of their confidence. Carlos had good ideas and asked good questions. He was experienced and he was eager and I didn't hesitate in hiring him.

René Meulensteen had a different way of demonstrating his appetite to join United. He had been coaching in Qatar and had been referred to us by Dave Mackay, the great Tottenham Hotspur and Derby County player. In 2001, when he came to seek a job at United, René told us the best way he could advertise his skills was to demonstrate them in action. So we went out on to the training field and he ran a technical session with some younger players and that clinched it for him.

Figuring out whether a coach could do his job was different from taking the measure of a player. The proof of that came when we watched him play. Interviewing a 16-year-old centre-back is not going to tell you very much about his footballing ability, although it will give you some insight into his determination. The only real way to tell whether a player has the toughness and perseverance to flourish for a long time is by the performances he turns in. When you meet new people and try to assess the most vital component – their character – you are only making an educated guess. Sometimes you are right and sometimes you are wrong. The only real test of character comes with the passing of the years and watching them perform – particularly when they are going through a bad spell or recovering from a setback. The ultimate judge of performance is Father Time.

# Networking

My 11 grandchildren are the greatest networkers I've ever seen. They're always using Facebook, Instagram, Snapchat or Twitter. I've never been a great networker, in either the new-fangled or old-school manner, but I really believe in what – these days – are called networks.

Decisions are simpler when you are dealing with people you know well. It is far easier to gauge their opinions and weigh their judgements than the observations of strangers. Many of my best appointments – both as coaches and players – stemmed from the referrals and assessments of this informal network, which developed over the years. It wasn't something I consciously sought to assemble. I didn't consciously try to cultivate or ingratiate myself with people because I thought they would do me a favour or be useful to me during my career. A network takes time to develop. Part comes through the passage of time, part from the way you treat others and part from reciprocity. But it all begins at home.

If the people within your organisation feel they are part of a community that has their interests at heart, they will develop great loyalty. And it often starts with what seem like small issues. When we were planning our Carrington training ground in the late 1990s, the architects and the chairman wanted to have two separate dining rooms – one for the players and one for the staff. It was a hangover from our old training ground, The Cliff, where the only people allowed in the dining room were the players and the medical staff. But I disagreed. I wanted everybody together. I wanted the younger players to be able to mingle and eat lunch with the older players and the staff too, including people like the laundry team and groundsmen.

It's great for a young lad to be able to talk to Ryan Giggs, and it was good for all the young players to see and mingle with the first team. It gave them role models and something to aspire to.

Sometimes if I saw a young player, a lad in the academy, eating by himself, I would go and sit beside him. You have to make everyone feel at home. That doesn't mean you're going to be soft on them – but you want them to feel that they belong. I'd been influenced by what I had learned from Marks & Spencer, which, decades ago in harder times, had given their staff free lunches because so many of them were skipping lunch so they could save every penny to help their families. It probably seems a strange thing for a manager to be getting involved in – the layout of a canteen at a new training ground – but when I think about the tone it set within the club and the way it encouraged the staff and players to interact, I can't overstate the importance of this tiny change.

There were, of course, much more high-profile examples of networks in action. The most glittering example must have been the way we uncovered Cristiano Ronaldo. Carlos Queiroz, who had been born in Mozambique, then a Portuguese colony, was my assistant manager for a total of five years. He had encouraged me to strike up a relationship with Sporting Lisbon, because of their ability to develop young players. We liked Carlos, and it seemed like a smart idea, so we started to exchange coaches so they could experience different settings. In 2001 we sent Jim Ryan, who spent 21 years on the coaching staff at United, to Lisbon, and he spotted a 16-year-old striker playing for Sporting's youth team by the name of Cristiano Ronaldo.

Part of the deal with Sporting Lisbon was that we would help open their new stadium with an exhibition match in August 2003, and so we flew directly to Portugal at the end of a summer tour of the United States. The day before the stadium opened, Jorge Mendes, Ronaldo's agent, had told me that both Real Madrid and Arsenal were also in pursuit of his client. It was a brilliantly timed little aside, because the next day Ronaldo played against us and was unbelievable. At half-time I sent Albert Morgan, our kit man, to fetch Peter Kenyon, who was then the club CEO, and told him we were going nowhere until we had that boy signed. We huddled with Cristiano, Jorge Mendes, and the president of Sporting Lisbon, and agreed on a price: £12.24 million. We arranged for a charter plane the following day to fly Ronaldo and his mother and sister, Jorge and Ronaldo's lawyer, to Manchester. So, thanks to the network created by Carlos Queiroz, we got six years of Ronaldo before he fulfilled his lifelong dream to play for Real Madrid, who paid United £80 million for the best player in the world.

Some of our most experienced players formed parts of our intelligence network. I could always count on Ryan Giggs, Paul Scholes, Gary Neville and Rio Ferdinand for sound opinions on players from other top-tier clubs we were scouting or contemplating signing. They all knew what was required of people we would bring to United. They would tend to have very sharp opinions about other English players, and I'd always ask them whether they knew anything I should worry about. I always used to ask the players in the England squad whether they considered any players from other clubs were good enough for United. In 2006 that led us to sign Michael Carrick from Tottenham.

The players would also work hard to try and help me sign prospects with whom they had some tie. Ryan Giggs was relentless in his quest to try and land his fellow Welshman, Aaron Ramsey, from Cardiff City. We flew Aaron up to Manchester but it was too late. I had got word from Dave Jones, the Cardiff manager, that Aaron had originally wanted to play for us, but Arsène Wenger had somehow managed to turn his head and convince him that his future lay at the Emirates. A couple of years later I got my revenge when Roy Hodgson, then the manager of Fulham, was instrumental in helping us snatch his defender, Chris Smalling, away from Arsenal.

Great networks often extended well beyond the current crop of first-team players. It's easy to forget about someone who has left an organisation and assume that because they've retired, or because their most fruitful years are behind them, they are no longer of any use. Quite the contrary. If the organisation has done right by them they will usually have fond memories of it, harbour considerable affection for it and be very happy to help. We tried to do this at United – inspired, in part, by what I saw at Bayern Munich.

In the mid-1990s I approached Martin Edwards and suggested that United take a leaf from Bayern's book and cultivate the talents of some of our best former players. They were familiar with the club, knew what we stood for, appreciated our pursuit of excellence and had the standing and reputation to act as role models. Bayern did this very well, and their greatest players were effectively running the club.

I could never persuade Martin of the benefit of doing this and I think he might have been a bit suspicious that I was trying to rearrange the board of directors. So he just paid lip service to the idea and all we ever did was use former players such as Norman Whiteside, Paddy Crerand and Wilf McGuinness to help entertain supporters during the lunches and dinners that bracketed home games.

When David Gill became the CEO, he embraced the thought because I wanted former players to help with the increased burden of the commercial side. These days we have a number of former players who do a lot of very useful work for the club. Obviously, Sir Bobby Charlton stands in a class by himself, having been a club director since 1984 and who, for 35 years before Ryan Giggs eclipsed his record, had played the most games for the club. But there are others, too, who act as club ambassadors and go on tours or spend time making sure that our commercial sponsors are happy and we retain them. Some of United's all-time greats, like Peter Schmeichel, Andy Cole, Dwight Yorke, Bryan Robson, Denis Law, and, more recently, Ji-sung Park, all do this; it removed a lot of the burden from my shoulders and those of other members of management.

Maybe the most important benefit of our network is the way we threaded former players into the coaching organisation. It's a marvellous way to ensure continuity and excellence, because they know what enormous success tastes like and what is required to achieve it. Over the years we had plenty of other former players sprinkled through the coaching organisation, such as Brian McClair, Tony Whelan, Jim Ryan, Mick Phelan and Paul McGuinness. Ryan Giggs is today's standout, in his role as Louis van Gaal's assistant manager, but Nicky Butt is also assisting in coaching the reserve team and Paul Scholes returned to the club, albeit briefly, to assist Giggs when he was made caretaker manager. We also tried to stand by former players. For example, after Bryan Robson was sacked as the manager of Middlesbrough, I invited him to keep his hand in the game by helping with training sessions at United.

If, as the years go by, some of United's great players have earned their managerial stripes and come back to help run the club, I will have succeeded in bringing a touch of Bayern Munich to Manchester.

I also tried to ensure that our club network extended to the supporters. Just as I was eager to know what was going on in the dressing room, I also liked to know the sentiment of long-time supporters. There were three guys I counted on for this: Norman Williams, Jim Kenway and Bill McGurr. I invited them to watch our training every Monday and Friday because I knew they would be discreet, keep their own counsel and refrain from blabbing to the press. I always used to chat with them while the players were warming up because they struck me as representing the heart and soul of the club and I knew they wouldn't mince words. Every big club has factions among its supporters who are upset about one thing or another, and I just liked keeping my finger on the pulse. In 2011, after we overtook Liverpool's Championship record, Norman Williams turned up to congratulate and thank every player. He was in his eighties and Manchester United was his life – I felt, in hindsight, that this title win completed his life. He certainly said as much to the players when he told them all the same thing: 'You've made my life.' He died the same night.

Oddly enough there was another vital part of our network, and that was my fellow managers. Whenever I called another manager for an assessment about a player I was contemplating signing, I always got a candid assessment. In 1989 I went down to spend a day with John Lyall to get his opinion about Paul Ince, whom he had managed at West Ham. John was glowing in his praise, and Paul made 281 appearances for United and played 53 games for England. In 2010 I briefly flirted with the idea of signing Mario Balotelli, the talented but controversial Italian striker. I did my homework on him, speaking to a few Italian contacts, but the feedback I got confirmed it was too big a risk. I don't know whether this sort of candid, professional courtesy exists in other fields, but for me it was a godsend. And in return I was always careful not to beat about the bush with other managers when they wanted my opinion on a particular player.

Fellow managers steered me away from players but, on occasion, they also stiffened my backbone when I was trying to make a decision. In 1991, I was looking around for additional defensive help, as Steve Bruce – who was then 30 years old – was becoming more prone to injury. We had heard that Everton had made a bid for Paul Parker, who was playing for Queens Park Rangers, and so I phoned their former manager, Jim Smith, to get an opinion. He was unequivocal and said, 'Sign him. He's quick, he can defend, he recovers well. He's like a Rottweiler.' Parker had actually travelled to Everton, but we managed to lure him to Old Trafford the same summer afternoon. I took him out on to the pitch to look around and he was amazed that there were dozens of United supporters in the stands just watching the grass grow. He signed for us that afternoon and went on to make 146 appearances for United – which could have been a lot more had it not been for niggling injuries.

I tried to return these kinds of favours whenever a fellow manager called with a similar question, or to ask my opinion about whether they should take a job at a particular club. In football there's an odd camaraderie between managers. On Saturday afternoons or Wednesday evenings we may be going at each other hammer and tongs and, during negotiations, we're inevitably trying to get the better of one another. Yet, maybe because we have this odd bond, there is always an inclination to extend a helping hand if someone is going through a rough time. I learned about this in Scotland, and when, eventually, I was in the position to continue the tradition, I tried to do so.

When I used to phone Jock Stein to ask for a favour or to see if he could help me get tickets for some game, he always used to say, 'If I can.' That was a great retort. It's easy to forget about the troubles of others but, if you take the time to remember, it goes a very long way. In 1978, when I was coaching St Mirren, we had lost a cup tie to Kilmarnock; the following morning I was feeling pretty despondent when the phone rang. It was Jock Wallace, the manager of Rangers, phoning to cheer me up. So, decades later, when a journalist phoned me to let me know that Chris Wilder, then the manager of Oxford United, was having a lot of problems with the club chairman, it was just second nature to try and help. I gave Chris my phone number and we talked on a number of occasions. I speak to Steve Bruce fairly often, and in the past couple of years have chatted with Alan Pardew, Sean Dyche and Neil Lennon. It is an informal network – full of wisdom and good humour and sympathy – but one I have always valued. Every manager feels lonely when he has to make an important decision. He can consult with his staff but ultimately he needs to make that decision himself. I know what it feels like for these men because as Premier League managers, they are under constant pressure and others keep their distance – either because they see them as damaged goods or because they don't want to intrude. Either way, if I can help some of them when they are in a tough spot, I am more than happy to do so.

## Firing

Nobody should look at football for lessons about the way to fire people. It's terrible. I got my first taste of that at Rangers when they fired their manager Scot Symon in 1967. He'd been there 13 years, won 15 trophies and had been incredibly loyal. John Lawrence, the chairman of the club, sent an 80-year-old accountant to tell Symon he was sacked. It was unbelievable. The same thing happened to another pal of mine, John Lyall, who, as both player and manager, devoted 34 years of his life to West Ham United. His reward? When he was fired in 1989, the owner did not even have the grace to thank him for his loyalty. I also never forgot the shabby way in which the board of Celtic treated Jock Stein after his 13 years at the club – in an era where the best teams in Scotland could more than hold their own with their English counterparts – during which he won the European Cup, ten Scottish League championships, eight Scottish Cups and six Scottish League Cups.

Carlo Ancelotti was brutally fired by Roman Abramovich in 2011 after Chelsea lost to Everton, having already lost to United and drawn with Newcastle in the previous two weeks. Carlo had won the 'Double' of the Premier League and the FA Cup for Chelsea the year before and was only the fifth manager ever to do so. Carlo kept his composure, didn't blast Abramovich and behaved perfectly. I don't think I would have been able to do the same if I had been in his shoes.

Most football managers are treated without a shred of dignity. Some owners don't even pay them the courtesy of talking to them in person. They will fire them over the phone or even by text message, or they will use a surrogate, like an accountant, to deliver the message. The reasons for the dismissals are often ludicrous. One manager I know got fired because he banned the chairman's wife from the players' dressing room. Mark Hughes's dismissal from Manchester City in 2009, while he was in the midst of re-fashioning the side, was just a high-profile example of the madness that occurs at clubs every week.

I've always found it hard to get rid of people I liked. Harry McShane was aged about 85 and had been associated with United since the 1950s, first as a player and then as a scout (as well as spending time as the club's stadium announcer). Les Kershaw, our chief scout, wanted me to do the dirty work, so I invited Harry to lunch and tried to talk to him about quitting. He knew exactly what I was doing and didn't make my life easy. He kept saying, 'Aye. Get on with it. What is it you want to say?' And I just couldn't bring myself to fire him and instead copped out. I told him that we'd continue to pay him but wanted to change his roles and he could come to watch the first team and offer me advice about them.

While we sold lots of players and gave others free transfers, I actually did not fire many people. We had one doctor who I agreed could spend time on another job for a limited period. When he decided to extend that period I felt I had to act. I felt let down. He had betrayed my trust, so I got rid of him. But for the most part there were very few dramas among the staff at Old Trafford who fell under my authority. When players leave, especially those who have been pillars of the side, their departure, even if expected, is often tinged with mixed emotions. Sometimes, but not often, the partings were abrupt and took people by surprise. That was the case in 2005 when Roy Keane left after over 12 years with the club. When I broke the news to the players, I was careful to praise all his enormous contributions to United and said that these should be recognised in any comments they might make to others.

By far the hardest conversations were with youngsters who, from the time they had sat on their father's lap watching football on television, had dreamed of playing in the Premier League but were just not good enough to step on to the pitch at Old Trafford. From the moment I started managing, I dreaded these sessions. At St Mirren I decided to make my life a bit easier by delivering the same message to five boys simultaneously. One of them broke down crying and I concluded that, while I was making it easier for myself, I was making it a lot tougher on them. Whether it was at St Mirren, Aberdeen or United, the only message they heard was that I was not hiring them. Conveying that message to teenagers was far harder than selling most first-team players, who had been given an opportunity to demonstrate their value. These boys, and their families, had frequently given up everything to pursue their dreams. Goodness knows how many times the parents had accompanied their boy to practices and games. Lord knows how often they had endured rain and cold to cheer on their son at a game everyone else had forgotten. I felt as bad for the parents as I did for the boy and, quite frequently, all three would break into tears. I would try and console them by explaining that the boy had enough talent to make a life in football and that, just because he wasn't being signed by United, about the hardest club to join, that did not mean his future in the game was closed off.

There were plenty of examples of players who had thrived after being released by Manchester United, and I sometimes used the example of David Platt. He was given a free transfer by United shortly before I arrived, but went on to captain England. Platt had plenty of company. Robbie Savage never played for the first team, but he went to Crewe Alexandra and three years later was playing in the Premier League for Leicester City. There are dozens of Premiership players who have been through the United academy, such as Ryan Shawcross, Phil Bardsley, and Kieran Richardson. It says much about the quality of an organisation if you can help ensure comfortable landings for people who just don't quite have what is required to make it within your own.

If players in the prime of their careers have not been seeking a new club, the news that they are being transferred from Manchester United is akin to hearing that they have been fired.

Sometimes, the arrival of a new player, whether a youngster or a purchase, who begins to command a spot in the first XI can also spell extinction for the lad who once owned the position. Though there were a handful of players whose departures were a relief, for the most part I tried to make sure we engineered a good landing for those we transferred. We tried to do everything we could for all the players we released to help them have a career in the game. My coaches and I were on the phone trying to create opportunities for these boys. We were also regularly contacted by other clubs to see what our plans were for our young players. As a result, many of them already had options on the table by the time they were released by United. I was only too aware of what life was going to be like for these players. They would be going from playing in front of 75,000 people and enjoying some of the best training facilities available anywhere, to a far smaller stage. It's a cruel adjustment to play in front of 15,000 people, disappear from the back pages of the newspapers, have a much smaller pay-cheque and, most of all, know that your dreams of playing at the pinnacle of the game are finished. It can destroy the soul.

Firing people, irrespective of their age, is never easy. I gradually learned that there was no point beating about the bush by taking somebody out for dinner or sending his wife a box of chocolates or flowers to try and soften the news. The gimmicks don't change the message. If you have decided you are going to get rid of someone, nothing beats honesty.

# 7

**FOCUS**

# Time

My father always said, 'Don't lie, don't steal and always be early.' I cannot stand being late. I've always been early for meetings. I was always the first into work. It just came naturally. I've always been an early riser so it was no great hardship for me to get to work early. I remember talking to Jean-Claude Biver, the CEO of the watchmaker, Hublot, who told me that when he had applied to work at Omega, the person who interviewed him asked him to show up at five o'clock in the morning. During the interview, Jean-Claude enquired about why he'd been asked to appear while it was still dark. The interviewer said, 'I start at five o'clock in the morning so I'm three hours ahead of everyone. I'm working while you are still asleep.' I was a bit like that.

Youngsters think they have all the time in the world. If you are a boy who has just had his tenth birthday, your next one seems an eternity away. That's because the single year that stretches ahead amounts to 10 per cent of the time you have been on earth. It's a different sensation when you turn 50, because the distance to your 51st birthday amounts to just 2 per cent of the time you have been alive. As you get older and more experienced, you start to think about how you allocate time. You gradually come to appreciate that an hour – or weekend – squandered is time you will never recapture.

As a teenager, part of my desire to squeeze the most out of every day was born of necessity because I had to hold down two jobs. I was working as an apprentice tool-maker, which meant leaving home at 6.45 a.m. and putting my card in the punch-clock at 7.40 a.m. After work or at the weekend, instead of going to the pub or snooker halls with the other apprentices, I was playing football. When I was training with St Johnstone I used to have two and a half hours to practise and usually didn't get home until 1 a.m. I did this three times a week and each trip involved multiple bus, train and tram rides.

After players retire and go into management, they often have a series of nasty shocks. One thing that always surprises them is the length of the workday. As a modern player, unless it is on the eve of a game, the day is always done soon after lunch. These days most of them go home, relax, and park themselves in front of some digital device. When you become a manager you discover three things. There is an endless set of tasks to complete and people demanding attention; the day does not stop and there is never enough time.

When I began managing, I had no idea how to budget my time. I was pathetic. I tried to do everything. This was exacerbated by the fact that – when I became manager of St Mirren in 1974 – I was also running two pubs that were three miles apart. Fergie's was in Kinning Park, near Govan, and Shaws was in Bridgeton. I only got into the pub business because playing and managing East Stirlingshire on a part-time contract did not put enough bread on the table for a young family. Although St Mirren paid me, I sometimes wonder whether I would have fared better at the club if I had not been managing the pubs simultaneously.

The combination of managing St Mirren and running my pubs meant that the only time I saw my boys was on the occasional school run, and the only time we would be together as a family would be for a few hours on a Sunday. When I started managing Aberdeen I sold the pubs, because I wanted to concentrate entirely on football. At Aberdeen my workdays were always 12 or 14 hours long, and I didn't stop work when I got home. Then I was on the phone to scouts, coaches or players. I might have put in more hours every week than my father, but I'm not complaining. His work was far tougher than anything I ever did.

In Manchester I continued with a similar daily and weekly rhythm, although the demands were much greater. I'd be at the ground about seven in the morning and would have a stroll around with my cup of tea. I'd always keep eight to nine in the morning wide open so that if anyone wanted to see me – a coach, a doctor, or a player – I was available. At about nine o'clock we'd go to the video analysis room and watch edited footage of previous games or opponents we were about to face. I'd remain at the training ground throughout the day to watch the youth academy work in the gymnasium. I'd get home around nine o'clock in the evening on Monday and Tuesday and sometimes also on Thursday. On Wednesday, if we were playing, I would either be with the team or I would be watching the reserve team, a future opponent or a player we were interested in. When United were based at their old training ground, The Cliff, I used to go to Old Trafford in the afternoon to do some paperwork or make telephone calls. The Carrington training ground included an office for me so, after we moved there, that's where I'd do my paperwork in the morning. Fridays, whether at The Cliff or Carrington, were always a bit different. Every Friday morning David Gill, United's CEO, would come to see me, and after that I would have a pre-game press conference at nine o'clock.

Nights and holidays were not sacred. If I woke up in the middle of the night, I'd usually sneak upstairs to my study and watch a game. I didn't see the point of wasting perfectly good time trying to go back to sleep. I also husbanded my time by never taking the holidays to which I was contractually entitled. From 1995, I was allowed five weeks' holiday a year, but that seemed like an excessive amount of time not to be working. So I always just took two weeks a year and would usually go with the family to mainland Spain or Majorca. It wasn't until I was in my fifties that I started taking three weeks a year. By then our boys were older and starting to live their own lives and Cathy and I made some trips to America. When the two of us started going to the south of France about 15 years ago, I often had meetings with players we wanted to sign in the restaurant of our hotel. It has a fabulous view over the Mediterranean and Cap Ferrat, and I never encountered a player whose contract couldn't be closed at that corner table.

As I got older, two things happened. First I discovered my body slowed down a bit and I found it harder to maintain the energy levels I had when I was much younger. When I was a young manager I could get by on four hours of sleep, but I needed more as I grew older. So I'd often go home and take a nap for an hour before going back to the ground. Then Cathy kept warning me that I was going to kill myself if I kept working so hard. I was painfully aware of how stress had contributed to the heart attack that led to Jock Stein's death during the Scotland–Wales game in Cardiff in 1985, when I was at his side as his assistant manager. So I took Cathy's advice seriously and developed interests outside football – horses, wine, reading. None of these hobbies took up a huge amount of time, but I enjoyed the distraction and the distance they gave me from football. I used to nip down to Newmarket the morning after Champions League games at Old Trafford to watch the horses train. Those early mornings were quiet and peaceful, and I also received an education in some of the nuances of the sport. Not only did I enjoy drinking the wine I bought, but I got interested in monitoring the price fluctuations. It was absorbing and would take my mind off the daily worries. I found that helpful ideas would sometimes pop into my mind from out of nowhere while I was playing cards or reading a book or going through a wine catalogue. I'm sure the same sensation occurs to other leaders when they are riding their bikes, pruning their roses or climbing a mountain. But I didn't find that these pastimes were a miracle cure. I still often found myself unable to sleep or awake in the middle of the night thinking about something concerning United.

## Distractions

I have yet to encounter anyone who has achieved massive success without closing themselves off from the demands of others or forgoing pastimes. I'm not suggesting that being completely obsessed with a pursuit leads to a healthy lifestyle or eternal happiness, but I just cannot imagine how, if you aspire to be better than everyone else, you can have balance in your life. If you have two people of equal talent it will be the way in which they marshal their ability that will determine their eventual success. Some people are just better at shutting out the rest of the world than others, and that means they have more time to foster their talent or improve their organisation. One of the most vivid examples of an obsession, mixed with devotion, is the tale of my fellow Glaswegian, Jimmy Sirrel, who managed Notts County. He and his wife were extremely close and, after 40 years of marriage, she suddenly died – early on a Saturday morning – at the age of 60. Jimmy was devastated, phoned his two children to break the news but then, without informing the players of what had happened, managed his Notts County team against West Bromwich Albion to a 1–1 draw that same afternoon.

When you are in your teens or your early twenties, it is fairly easy to concentrate on your obsession – especially if, as a footballer, you steer clear of alcohol and the party scene. A 16-year-old player brimming with talent might have a casual girlfriend and a few mates but, apart from those, the only thing in his life will be football. It will occupy his every waking moment and also enter his dreams and nightmares. All he will dream about is playing for the first team, representing his country, scoring a winning goal or lifting the World Cup. The urge to improve himself dominates everything. Ten years later, everything can be different. He might be mentioned in the newspapers every other day. He might have a wife and young children. He may be a millionaire many times over. He will be unable to walk down a street or enter a restaurant without being asked for a picture or autograph. He may not have a moment's peace unless he is behind the gates of his large house. The same goes for managers of high-profile clubs.

I was fortunate that I had a wife and sons who did not make me feel guilty about spending so little time with them and allowed me to be selfish. I always tried to make sure nothing intruded into the heart of my work life and, unless there was a dire emergency in our family, football always came first. Cathy took care of raising our three sons and I was absent for a lot of the time. For example, I did not watch the boys play in their school games because at weekends my job was to be with Aberdeen or United. For me the Christmas break never really existed, because it falls in the middle of one of the heaviest periods in the top flight of English football. I didn't really appreciate it at the time, but now, with the help of perspective, it's clear that my family gave me the greatest gift that I have ever received: time to concentrate on my obsession with the round ball. I never had to deal with the tension that exists between so many husbands and wives, or parents and children, when the spouse or the young ones feel they are not getting enough attention and that a family member, even when physically present, is emotionally absent.

When I got to United I still hadn't mastered the art of eliminating distractions. I'd automatically accept most invitations to charity dinners or supporters' club events. For my first 12 years at Old Trafford I used to read every letter I received and, during some weeks, I'd get a couple of hundred. I just felt an obligation to take care of these because many of them were from people for whom Manchester United was the most important thing in their lives. We'd get letters from people notifying us of a death in their family and asking us to send a note to the bereaved. We'd hear from parents who had a sick child in the hospital asking for an autograph, or there would be people requesting a message to be read out at a birthday or wedding. I used to dictate answers to all these letters.

I gradually became better about controlling my time. Lyn Laffin, who became my assistant shortly after I joined United, started shielding me from many of the incessant telephone calls, and dealt with some of the fans who used to call with suggestions about players who should be sold or new tactics I should employ.

I never did get used to e-mail, so I didn't have to worry about this perpetual, intrusive distraction that can play havoc with even the most concentrated train of thought. During my last ten years at United Lyn took care of almost all the correspondence, because she knew my prose style, so all I had to do was approve it and add my signature.

There were some other rules that also helped me make the most out of every day. I would never accept a lunch invitation, except for sponsors' lunches at Old Trafford and the annual Football Writers' lunches in Manchester, because before you know it, especially if a drive is involved, those midday breaks can gobble up three hours. I also started to eliminate many of the charity functions. As manager of United you are expected to make some appearances to help the cause. Part of this was just a case of getting older, because the midweek dinners aren't as easy when you are 65 years old as when you are a 35 year old. Some were just rituals like meeting with sponsors, charity events and award ceremonies. I would always attend the annual League Managers Association dinner, United's annual dinner on behalf of UNICEF, and the events for the charity I formed, The Elizabeth Hardie Ferguson Charitable Trust. Whenever one of our players won the Professional Footballers' Association Player of the Year, or the Ballon d'Or, I'd be sure to attend those festivities.

I stopped attending supporters' club dinners about a decade before I retired. They usually made for very long nights, with never-ending queues for autographs and photographs. I don't mean to sound ungrateful or aloof – the supporters at Manchester United are the best in the world – but my job was to win trophies, not sign autographs, and I always felt that I was better off focusing on that. I also became more disciplined about which teams I'd go to watch. In my last decade at United I tried to limit it to teams we'd be pitted against in European fixtures. Mick Phelan, my assistant manager, and I would fly out in a chartered plane, have dinner, watch the game (leaving ten minutes before the end) and be back in Manchester by 1 a.m. That might seem like a long day, but it was an abbreviated version of what I did when I was younger.

Learning to concentrate on the essentials was a skill I gradually acquired, and it was something I was keen to hammer into the skulls of all the players. Young players, being teenagers or 20-somethings, usually have two things on their minds. One is football, the second is the other half of the human race. All the nightclubs in Manchester have always been eager to attract United players because they know that word would soon spread among the young ladies. They used to dole out special passes to the players; these allowed them to jump the queues and gain free admission. I have yet to meet a 15-year-old aspiring footballer who wants to live like a monk. It is impossible to completely remove the boy from the man, particularly the young man.

It's no accident that the best players, and the ones who play at their peak for the longest, tend to be those who can shield themselves from the demands of others. Cristiano Ronaldo was among the very best. He didn't drink and he didn't smoke. When he came to Manchester his mother and his sister lived with him. Every now and again he might appear in a TV advertisement or on a magazine cover or, during the summer break, in a Los Angeles nightclub. But don't be deceived, Cristiano knew how to manage himself and his time.

Apart from his skill and his fame, Cristiano – and players of his generation – have far more distractions than I did as a player. They need far more internal discipline to shut off the outside world than people of 50 years ago. When I was a boy, the biggest distractions were the radio, the newspaper, a book – and church on Sunday. I listened to the great boxing matches on the radio with my dad – Randolph Turpin, Sugar Ray Robinson and the last fights of Joe Louis and Jersey Joe Walcott – and we would also tune in to hear the music hall singer, Ronnie Ronalde, on a Sunday, or the quiz show, *Top of the Form*. The local cinema, The Plaza, was about a hundred yards from our door – so that was always good for *Tarzan* and the *Flash Gordon* films, featuring Buster Crabbe. But beyond that there were only street fights, snooker, games of dice and football. There was no telephone or television, let alone 60-inch colour screens with 300 channels, or mobile phones with millions of apps, e-mail, Facebook and the internet.

I was always alive to pressures on my players and kept an ear cocked for word of distractions they might be facing. The constant worry with the English players is drinking and the bookies. Weakness for the bottle has destroyed many careers, while gambling is a cancer in a dressing room. I usually had a pretty good sense of which players had been out and about because I would get calls from club owners or fans alerting me to the fact. At least for me, these pursuits were less of a concern with the foreign players. We also tried, best as we could, to ensure that they didn't squander their money, although one look at our car park would suggest we weren't that successful. From time to time there were distressing stories in the papers about some players who would blow a king's ransom in the betting shops. We would bring in financial consultants and lawyers to offer advice. We even had one person suggest that players contemplating marriage should exchange vows in Scotland where, according to him, the law is more favourable to husbands than in England. That prompted Cristiano Ronaldo to say that when the time came he would only get married in Scotland.

It is true that few footballers spend a lot of time studying or trying to excel in school examinations. That's one of the reasons why they are successful on the field. When the academy system started, the structure was 12 hours' education and 12 hours' coaching (including matches) per week, which, to me, was an imbalance. My job was to produce footballers. But if any player wanted to pursue qualifications – or if his parents wanted him to do so – we agreed that the club would pay for it. This was a rare occurrence; these boys wanted to be footballers. I understand the benefits of a fine education and how it equips people for their journey in life. I recognise too that many footballers who get injured at the age of 25, or whose careers end in their early thirties (particularly those playing in the lower leagues), don't possess the education, skills or financial cushion required to have a decent life in today's world. Yet the job of a football manager is not to make sure that a boy can become a biologist or geophysicist, or that he is equipped for the 40 or 50 years that will follow his playing career – it is to make sure he will be a great right-back or winger. Eleven Nobel laureates are not going to win the FA Cup.

We faced this issue with my eldest son, Mark, who could probably have carved out a life as a professional footballer. He played for Aberdeen's reserves as a boy, but he had other interests too, and Cathy and I could tell he was ambivalent about a life in football. We were careful not to exert any pressure on him to follow in my footsteps. It's just as well, because he studied at Sheffield Hallam University and at the European University in Paris, became enchanted by the world of investments and, after five years at Goldman Sachs Asset Management, helped form Generation Investment Management, a much-respected fund manager in London.

I'm sure it would be wonderful if one of my young players

had had the grades to gain admission to Cambridge University or Imperial College London, but I can more or less guarantee that, if that were the case, they would not have been able to devote the time required to progress to the first team. There would have been a significant impact on their momentum as footballers. More experienced players are able to deal with this and the example of Vincent Kompany, who combined his studies at Manchester Business School with his role as Manchester City's captain illustrates this. In all my time at United I cannot think of one player who had a degree. Colin Murdock, who did not make the first team but played on our youth team in the early 1990s, got a law degree from Manchester Metropolitan University in the mid-1990s while playing for Preston North End. But Murdock is the exception that proves the rule.

Distractions exact a heavy toll on individuals and organisations and it demands incredible discipline to keep them at bay. At United the players always had demands from the commercial, business side of the club. It was understandable, because the commercial department was responsible for bringing in television and sponsorship revenue, selling executive boxes, staging profitable events and running the hospitality organisation. Without all this revenue we couldn't have done some of the things we did, such as sign some big contracts, pay hefty salaries, improve our training facilities or use private jets for travelling to games.

The sponsors all wanted contact with the players and the demand was insatiable. As the television revenue kept increasing and as United got ever better known around the world, the number of sponsors started to climb. Shielding players from the requests of the commercial team was a big part of my job. Mick Phelan was a dab hand at juggling all this. The commercial guys who, quite naturally, wanted to be able to provide sponsors with behind-the-scenes glimpses of United would produce all these ideas and the stream of requests was endless. Mick would be our intermediary and he'd dole out favours as if he was passing around manhole covers. He made sure that a lot of these were fulfilled during the pre-season, so that we could say with a straight face that our obligations had been satisfied and this allowed us to rebuff demands during the playing season. Some sponsors would want to come and watch the training, which made me queasy because I didn't want others to see who was training and who was injured. So I limited access to a handful of minutes at the start of a session and, otherwise, would make a few appearances at lunchtime and attend one or two dinners during the season.

At United we always wanted to try and support local charities. Every Friday the players would sign around 100 shirts that could be given away to charities or auctioned for a good cause. The one global organisation we supported was UNICEF, and when we were on foreign tours we would take the players to witness some of their work. In Thailand we went by river, in skiffs, to visit a school to see kids who had been rescued from child prostitution, and in South Africa we visited orphanages. These were eye-opening experiences for all of us. But most of our charitable work was done close to home because we wanted to be good citizens and demonstrate that we cared about people all around Manchester. In 2006 we formed a special group, The Manchester United Foundation, to take care of the club's charitable activities – particularly the local schools and hospitals. The players would go and visit schools and the bedsides of seriously ill children. All of these were great things to do, but I kept an eagle eye on them because the most important thing was winning a game on Saturday. The fans aren't going to thank you if you're doing charity work and it costs you three points.

Big games have the most distractions. When I had my first taste of this at Aberdeen after we reached the European Cup Winners' Cup final in 1983, one of the first things I did was make sure that the players' wives and girlfriends understood their role. So, in jest, I wrote a memo to all of them explaining it was their responsibility to pack toothpaste, blankets and other essentials for the trip to Sweden and summoned them to a meeting at Pittodrie where they would hear more of what was required from them. Through the grapevine I very quickly heard that my joke had misfired and gone down like a lead balloon. I walked into the room in Pittodrie where I was greeted by a collection of wives and resounding silence. I apologised for the joke that had backfired and told them that the real purpose of my memo had been to bring them together so that we could prepare for what would be the most important game in their husbands' careers, and perhaps the biggest occasion in which they would ever participate. I made sure the wives understood that their one task was to make sure that their husband was as well prepared as possible for the game and that, under no circumstances, should they do anything that could distract him. After I finished speaking I asked whether they had any questions. There were none. They all understood what I wanted: no distractions.

There are fans that mob you at the airport; the hotel lobby where the team stays can also be teeming with autograph hunters. When United played in the Champions League final against Barcelona in Rome in 2009, I actually asked the hotel management to close off the hotel to fans, because I wanted to eliminate the hubbub. As the years ticked by, I found that I was able to close myself off from the frenzy and tittle-tattle that surrounded United. From time to time I'd notice that the coaching staff were chatting about something and I didn't have a clue what they were discussing because I had been lost in my own thoughts. When we were approaching big games I'd isolate myself in a mental cocoon. Unless somebody brought up an issue relating to the team, I would barely hear anything that was said. I just tried to concentrate on the one big thing – my job. When I was lost in my own thoughts, Cathy would always say, 'You're not listening to me.' She was right.

From time to time there were distractions that could have been avoided. An example was the legal scrap I got into in the late 1970s when I sued St Mirren for wrongful dismissal. I acted emotionally and impulsively and, in retrospect, it would have been better for me to have spent every second thinking about how to turn Aberdeen into a title contender.

Whenever we got caught up in a big match, I always told the players, 'Don't play the occasion, play the game.' There's all the other frippery that doesn't matter: the bands, the pre-game theatrics, the new suits and all the travelling supporters buzzing with anticipation. The first time I took United to a Wembley final in 1990, I was as excited as a teenager on a Saturday night and distracted by the surroundings. I did what I had seen everybody else do and took the team out to inspect the pitch. It was a boiling hot day and we were roasting in our suits and I suddenly realised we were being daft and the players were getting dehydrated. An inspection of the pitch wasn't going to influence the result so I ordered everyone to get to the dressing room. There's only one way to enjoy a final and that's to win it. Nobody ever remembers the losers.

# Failing

When you look at a successful person, you cannot imagine that they've ever failed or had a brush with failure. You watch sports stars like Roger Federer, Serena Williams or, in the old days, Muhammad Ali and Stirling Moss, and it's impossible to conceive of them as losers. The same extends to other walks of life, where someone of great accomplishment puts his wares on display. If I look at paintings by L. S. Lowry, the Mancunian best known for his bleak renditions of urban, industrial life, I have a tough time believing that he ever made a bad picture, or if you read one of Robert Caro's books about President Lyndon B. Johnson, you cannot imagine him worrying about writing a paragraph that didn't contain a carefully buffed phrase. But we are all haunted by failure. It paralyses some and motivates others. It was my own inner determination to avoid failure that always provided me with an extra personal incentive to succeed.

After I left Rangers in 1969, it would have been easy for me to feel like a bit of a loser. I had tasted life in the top ranks of football, but I knew I was never a key part of the manager's plans and, when I was transferred after two years at the club, all I had in my silverware drawer was a runners-up medal from a Scottish Cup final. We had got pipped at the post in the final game of the 1967–68 season for the Scottish League when we lost against, of all clubs, Aberdeen. So I could have been overwhelmed by self-pity when I was off-loaded to Falkirk, but I was determined not to be cowed.

I would like to think that, somehow, the people I went on to work with at both Aberdeen and United came to share that same positive attitude towards failure. For me, that whole approach to life could be boiled down to the 101 seconds of injury time that it took United to turn what had looked like a 1–0 defeat by Bayern Munich in the 1999 Champions League final into a 2–1 victory. Bayern Munich's ribbons had already been attached to the Cup in anticipation of the victory ceremony, and the president of UEFA was preparing to present the trophy to them, when our refusal to give up meant those ribbons were changed to red.

As we prepared for the Champions League final nine years later in 2008, I played the DVD of the last three minutes of the 1999 game to emphasise to the players the importance of never, ever capitulating. For me, the only time to give up is when you are dead.

When I started my life as a coach, I never dreamed that I would wind up as the manager of Manchester United. All I thought about was survival. Each time I joined a club – East Stirlingshire, St Mirren and Aberdeen – I just thought to myself, 'I'm not going to fail here.' It was one of the things that drove me. I always had that fear of getting humiliated, and failure was always that wee thing at the back of my mind. I kept silently saying to myself, 'Failure. Don't fail.' When I joined East Stirlingshire as a manager, the only qualifications I had for the job was that I had been a player, had earned my coaching badges and could make a decision. I didn't know anything else. Four weeks earlier I had been a 32-year-old player. Suddenly I was a manager, albeit a part-time manager, who was just hoping to survive long enough to figure things out. After I had been at St Mirren, and got my first wee taste of managerial success, I had a hunch that I would do well when I got to Aberdeen. It was the first time I was a full-time manager and the club had the nucleus of what it took to win – it was a one-town team which had a good owner, decent facilities and a healthy stock of players.

It was only really in my last year at Aberdeen that I started mapping out a path for my future. Prior to that I was just concentrating on surviving and not failing. The complete perfection that Celtic achieved in their 1966–67 season, when they won five competitions, seemed like the stuff of miracles and myth. Even in our strongest seasons at United the fear of failure and the striving for perfection drove me on. Although I helped fill the trophy cabinet at Old Trafford, the club, under my leadership, never managed to go through the entire League season – like Arsenal did in 2003–04 – undefeated. The experience of defeat, or more particularly the manner in which a leader reacts to it, is an essential part of what makes a winner.

Before games I always had a churning in my stomach. It never left me. It was always there. I could never find a way to get rid of it. I remember feeling acutely nervous when I played at Rangers because I never felt that the manager had confidence in me and I always felt I had to justify my place in the team. But in some ways it may actually have got worse as the years went by, no matter how many cups lined the trophy cabinet, because the expectations, and the pressure, increased. Whenever we went to Anfield to play Liverpool I always had butterflies in my stomach.

The worst time was always during the pre-match warm-up. I hated it. If we had a 3 p.m. kick-off, I would give the team talk between 1.15 p.m. and 1.45 p.m. Once I had delivered my piece I would leave the players alone. We had prepared as best we could and last-minute instructions always leave players wondering whether they command the manager's confidence. At 2 p.m. my assistant manager would take our team-sheet to the referee and we would discover what team our opponent had decided to play. Then, after everyone was in their warm-up gear, the dressing room would empty about 2.15 p.m. I detested the next 30 minutes, which always seemed to drag on and on. I was often by myself in our dressing room and the pair of clocks on the wall never seemed to move.

During the pre-match warm-up, when we played at Old Trafford, I used to sit in my office and read the match programme or flip on the television and watch the horse racing. I'd sometimes wander about and try to find someone to talk to. Occasionally a visiting manager would come and have a cup of tea. The loneliness was much worse when we played away games because I had no office to use as a refuge. Then, I would often find myself sitting alone in the dressing room. I don't think this feeling, certainly in my later years as a manager, was caused by worrying about failing. Rather it was prompted by the apprehension, anxiety and uncertainty that always surrounds a big occasion, which might be exacerbated when you depend on others to implement your wishes. I'm sure other leaders experience similar feelings, no matter how worldly and important they may seem to others.

Even now, when I'm watching United from the directors' box or at home on the television, I feel twinges in the pit of my stomach. I never tried to get rid of this feeling. Maybe some people, before a big performance or important encounter, try to calm their nerves with breathing exercises or a dram of whisky, but I never did so. I just accepted that nagging anxiety as part of my job. It accompanied me through life and it would have been a big warning sign that I was no longer up for the task had that anxiety – which really was a sign of how badly I wanted to win – ever disappeared.

The old adage that you learn more from defeats than you do from victories has certainly been true for me. While I am sometimes inclined to say that I never look back, it isn't really true. I wouldn't harp on at the players about defeats, and I would certainly try to mask whatever I was thinking, but privately I always spent more time contemplating games that we lost than the ones we won. It's also true that if, during any season, we failed to win a major competition that we should have won, I found myself stewing on the reasons during the summer so that I could correct whatever was wrong before the start of the next season.

My record is full of defeats. Between 10 August 1974, the day I first managed East Stirlingshire, to 19 May 2013, the day I left the field for the last time as manager of Manchester United, my teams lost about two out of every ten games that they played. There were also plenty of draws that I considered as bad as losses. So I had plenty of opportunities to learn from defeats and setbacks. Though I never got fixated by statistics, my overall win rate as a manager was just under 60 per cent. In United's best season we won nearly 72 per cent of the time.

On occasion we got badly punished and I did not like it one bit – such as the two consecutive League games we lost in the 1996–97 season: 5–0 to Newcastle and 6–3 to Southampton. I don't recall any other times we conceded 11 goals in two consecutive games. In 1995 we lost the League and FA Cup in the space of seven days – one to Blackburn Rovers and the other to Everton. However, I don't ever think I had to contemplate a series of setbacks as severe as those that Bayer Leverkusen suffered in 2002 when they played in a League decider, the German Cup final and the Champions League final – and they lost all three. You would need more than a couple of aspirin to get over that.

At Aberdeen and United, once the squads were properly organised, I always felt our defeats, or disappointing results, were caused by what we failed to do rather than what our opponents did. I found it healthy to approach disappointments in that manner because it meant we were in control and could improve. I was always a better manager after a loss. For whatever reason, it made me sharper. I suppose sometimes I wanted to prove I was not a loser, and at other times I wanted to avenge a defeat. After the 1993–94 season, every year when we did not win the League title seemed like a failure to me. At some point in my life the desire and need to win outstripped my fear of failure. Winning was a matter of pride. It did not matter whether it was the first team or reserves. Losing is a powerful management tool so long as it does not become a habit. I felt that way to the end of my career. After we got pipped at the post for the Premier League by Manchester City in 2012, we were subjected to ugly taunting by some diehard Sunderland fans at the Stadium of Light (which, at that moment, seemed poorly named). Afterwards, in the dressing room, I told all the players – and emphasised it to the younger ones – that they should remember the treatment they had just received every time they returned to play Sunderland. And they did. The following season we returned and beat them 1–0.

Defeats rarely got the better of me, though I am aware that, especially in retirement, it is easy to put a gloss over the past. There is no changing the fact that, beginning in 2008, we reached the Champions League final three times within four years yet only won once. So while I was elated on one occasion, I was disappointed on three. There were some moments of profound despair. In October 1989, as a favour, United had travelled to St Johnstone for a mid-season friendly to help them open their new stadium, McDiarmid Park. We won 1–0 but our performance was worse than pathetic. After the game I went back to my hotel room, eager to escape. Archie Knox, my assistant manager, knocked on the door and told me I had to attend the reception being held for the teams. I was in my bed and told him, 'I'm not going. I can't face those players. They're not good enough.' Archie was right. It took me some time, but eventually I did drag myself downstairs, although I can't say I was good company. A few other defeats stand out because I could not get to sleep after Aberdeen's loss to Dundee United in the 1979–80 Scottish League Cup final, and went home to bed after United's 5–1 defeat to Manchester City in 1989. The two worst defeats were probably both Champions League fixtures – against Borussia Dortmund in 1997 and Real Madrid in 2013. Those defeats were more painful than the humiliations of a 5–0 trouncing by Newcastle in 1996, the 5–0 thumping by Chelsea in 1999 and our League Cup final defeat to Sheffield Wednesday in 1991.

When I knew we were going to be beaten, I always tried to make sure we didn't get smashed to smithereens because of the effect on morale. We played Manchester City at Old Trafford in October 2011 and got beaten 6–1. It was our worst thumping by our crosstown rivals in 22 years, and our biggest home League defeat since 1955 when United were hammered 5–0, also by Manchester City. The irony of it was that for most of the game we outplayed them. City scored two goals either side of half-time, and though we scratched our way back to 3–1, we conceded three goals in the last 13 minutes. In retrospect we should have just bolted the door, prevented City's last three goals, and avoided the embarrassment of the terrible newspaper headlines and the jubilation on the other side of Manchester. More importantly, we lost the League to City that year on goal difference, which made this result even more painful.

Handling the press in the moments after a defeat was really difficult. I might make some general comments about the team but I tried never to single out a player for criticism; though I do recall, to my chagrin, saying something negative about Nani after we lost 5–4 to Chelsea in a League Cup game in 2012. If a striker fluffed a chance, or there was a fatal back-pass or the goalkeeper had a lapse of concentration, the player himself would be more than aware of what he had done. Many of the best players are their own sternest critics and they did not need to read a disparaging comment from me in the Sunday papers. That wasn't going to help. Usually, I tried to deflect the reporters' attention away from both the team and the players, by pointing an accusatory finger at the opponent's tactics, or a refereeing decision. I could always find plenty of reasons for us losing a game that had nothing to do with us, even though I knew in my heart that we had nobody else to blame. I always thought my role was to act as a player's heat deflector in a moment of crisis.

A major loss or pounding can exact a heavy toll on a group of people. It can shake their confidence and, if you aren't careful, the consequences can linger. Whenever we lost an important game in which I knew we had played well, I tried to say very little. Nobody can absorb a message in times like that. You can whisper sweet nothings but the words aren't heard. So I would just go around and pat each of the players on the head. They understood that message – maybe because they felt it too. In football, a whiff of vulnerability is tantamount to giving your competitors an adrenalin shot that would turn a mule into a Derby winner. When you lose, particularly if you get thumped, you carry that loss around. In football it doesn't matter if the team has a lot of changes for the following game, everyone knows the club lost the prior outing. The players know it, the fans know it, and the press are baying like jackals. It adds unwanted pressure that can build on itself. It's like getting a wee tear in your jacket. If you don't get that tear sewn up immediately, it will only get worse. The reverse is also true. Taking to the field when your competitors are concentrating on survival is like having one or two goals in the bag before a boot has touched the ball.

Back at the training ground on the morning after a defeat, I'd gather everyone around me and ask, 'Are we enjoying the headlines this morning?' or, 'Anybody enjoy what happened to our football club last night?' I'd have a scowl on my face and I wouldn't make it easy, but I was also intent on rebuilding the players' confidence. After any defeat I would tend to withdraw and become sullen. The players would be looking to me and muttering between themselves, 'Bloody hell, he's in some mood today.' I am sure most of them did not want to come anywhere close to me in the canteen. I'd say something like, 'If you don't meet people's expectations, you only have yourselves to blame. There's no one else you can blame. We all know we're better than this and we let ourselves down. At our club losing a game is big news, so let's try and avoid the big news. Let's talk about all the good things that we've got – all the good and great performances. I want to come out for the post-game press conference and say, "Fantastic. It was a fantastic performance." I want to be able to say, "Well done Rooney, well done Welbeck, well done Chicharito."' Players who knew me well understood how much I valued winning. They would gradually absorb this sensibility into their own pores and eventually would be transmitting it to newcomers. We had a virus that infected everyone at United. It was called winning.

Manchester City's Premier League victory in 2012 was painful at the time – particularly because it was based on goal difference. It was also something of a tonic because it gave us something to work towards, and the following year we won the League. City finished second, 11 points behind. After my first League win in 1993, every time we finished second, which happened five times during this period, we won it the following season. There's some merit in getting defeated – even though I'd never want it to be a habit. Team members who are hungry for victory and take great pride in their performance will be eager to avenge defeat.

Football is full of setbacks beyond the simple pain of defeat, but it's useless drowning in self-pity. I do not remember a time when every single member of the squad was at peak fitness and ready to play. Somebody was always injured. It was normal for a tenth of the squad to be injured. I also don't remember a time when one of our long-time competitors was not fielding a player we had missed signing. Take December 2009 – it was a horror show. We had 14 of the first-team squad laid up by injury – including two goalkeepers, seven defenders, three midfielders and two strikers. A fit 11 picked from the injured 14 could have beaten any club in Europe. Yet, while they were on the bench, or with the doctors, we lost at home to Aston Villa and away to Fulham. We also occasionally got hammered by viruses that swept through the squad; at the end of 1994 and start of 1995, things were so bad that I even considered closing the training ground. Nine of our players were felled by the flu and, while they were in bed, we dropped points to Nottingham Forest, Leicester City, Southampton, Newcastle United and Crystal Palace. There is nothing I could have done about either the injuries or the flu; we just had to make the best of bad situations.

We made plenty of decisions that we came to regret in the transfer market, but you cannot change history. United probably could have won a couple of League titles with a team composed of players we scouted but did not sign. In 2003 I went to see Petr Čech in goal for Rennes in a game against Auxerre. We thought Petr was a bit young for the bruisers in the Premier

League, but Petr went to Chelsea and in the subsequent decade kept 220 clean sheets for the club. We got our wires crossed on another goalkeeper too, in 1999, after Peter Schmeichel had announced his intention to retire. There had been some preliminary interest in Mark Bosnich, who was playing at Aston Villa, and I was also very interested in Edwin van der Sar who was at Ajax. By the time I informed Martin Edwards, the club chairman, that we had received bad reports on Bosnich, it was too late. Martin had already shaken hands on a deal and Van der Sar went to Juventus.

Didier Drogba was another. He was playing at Olympique de Marseilles and we went to check him out, but the club wanted £25 million for him and Chelsea moved in for the kill before we had made up our minds. Thomas Müller, who scored five goals for Germany in the 2010 and 2014 World Cups, was a ten year old playing for an amateur team several miles from Munich when we first heard about him. We had him watched and the following day he committed himself to Bayern Munich. We wanted to sign Ronaldo, the Brazilian striker, from Cruzeiro in 1994 but we could not get a work permit, and he went to PSV Eindhoven in the Netherlands. We looked at Robin van Persie when he was about 16 and playing for Feyenoord's reserve team, and even then the price on his head was about £6 million. Jim Ryan, who was on our coaching staff for 11 years before becoming United's director of youth football for another decade, watched Van Persie get sent off and subsequently exchange insults with the supporters. Jim wasn't the only person unimpressed by Van Persie's temperament on that occasion, because his club immediately suspended him. There were plenty of other players I would have liked to sign – such as Alan Shearer, the striker who became a thorn in our side while he played for Newcastle, or the Argentinian, Gabriel Batistuta, who spent most of his career playing in Italy, or Samir Nasri who went to Manchester City in 2011. Then, in 2011, I hurtled down on the train from Euston to Lille to sign the young French defender Raphaël Varane. David Gill was getting into the finer points of the contract with Lens, Varane's club, when Zinedine Zidane got wind of this and somehow scooped him up for Real Madrid from under our noses. I don't think José Mourinho, who was then managing Real Madrid, had ever seen Varane play.

I could have let these decisions eat away at me, but I tried to avoid this. We made these choices, nobody else did. You also cannot field a team with players that you don't own, so what's the point of flogging yourself?

As time went by, these missed opportunities and the setbacks and defeats we suffered along the way eventually helped me become a better, or at least more gracious, loser. When I was a young man I was a very bad loser. After any defeat I would go home and sulk. In Aberdeen, after one particularly bad defeat, I ran the players through the town centre so the punters could all give them stick. When we got back to the dressing room I told them, 'Let that be a lesson to you.' Every winner hates to lose. In football all the best players are bad losers, although they display it in different ways.

The most gracious lesson I received about the manner in which to handle defeat was given by Ottmar Hitzfeld, the manager of Bayern Munich between 1998 and 2004, and 2007 and 2008. After we beat Bayern in the Champions League final in 1999 by scoring two goals in the last three minutes (after a campaign that for United had consisted of 63 games and 96 hours of play), I could tell that he was devastated. Within 180 seconds he had gone from thinking the trophy was his to seeing his players either prostrate or holding their heads in their hands. It must have been soul-destroying, but he was most gracious and that was amplified a year later when I went to Munich to watch Rangers, who had a player that interested me, play Bayern. After the game he invited me to have dinner at his table with his two brothers, and they were all so gracious and warm. Then some of the Bayern players came and shook my hand and offered congratulations, even though they must have hated losing. It was a great display of the quality of the club.

Perhaps the most important lesson in how to handle failure was handed down to me by my own dear mother. When I was 21 I'd been playing part-time for St Johnstone and had been in and out of the team, and only played about 50 first-team games in four years. I was really disillusioned. I had broken my nose, cheekbone and eyebrow in a reserve game, and then, after I recovered, the reserve team got destroyed several games in a row. So I went to Canada House on Waterloo Street in Glasgow, and took out papers to emigrate to Canada, because all my dad's family had already moved there. I just didn't want to play another game for the club.

So one day I got my brother's girlfriend to pretend that she was my mother and call Bobby Brown to tell him that I had the flu and couldn't play. He wasn't fooled and sent a telegram to my mother, because we didn't have a phone, telling me to ring him. I went up the road to the phone booth, dialled Stanley 267 (which is a number I suppose I remember because of the embarrassment), and Brown ripped into me. He said, 'You're a disgrace. You think you're kidding me. You got someone to pretend to be your mother. I've got a whole team down with the real flu and you're playing tomorrow and you report to the Buchanan Hotel at twelve o'clock.'

In that game I scored a hat-trick at Ibrox – the first player from a visiting team to do so – and that wee bit of luck changed my life. I had come within a whisker of quitting. My mother had read me the riot act after she'd discovered what had happened. She taught me never to give in and, ever after, one way or another, I have tried to convey the same lesson to others.

## Criticism

Football is one of those subjects in which everyone is an expert even if their knowledge of the game couldn't fill a thimble. It's like other forms of entertainment or creative endeavour, where it's easier to be a critic than a practitioner. Everyone has opinions about restaurants, airlines, films, cars and paintings, even if they couldn't cook a boiled egg, fly a kite or draw a square. It's different when you get into more exotic fields and the man on the street is intimidated from passing comment because of ignorance. Only real experts can offer a valuable opinion about the mechanics of a suspension bridge or the best way to set up a laboratory experiment. That's just not the case in football, where managers of top-flight teams have millions of critics – from those closest to them, to fans on the other side of the world.

Some leaders have to contend with criticism from within their own organisation. They might have ambitious underlings vying for their job, or a board of directors muttering between themselves. Whenever someone new assumes a role, there will always be doubts about his capabilities until he has proved himself. If a leader has had a long stint at the helm and encounters a bad patch, he will often have to endure times when people ask whether he is past his sell-by date.

There were only a few times when I had to contend with carping inside the place I worked. At St Mirren, where I was the manager between the ages of 32 and 36, I was politically naïve and got on the wrong side of the owner so, to some extent, I helped stoke his criticism.

There were a few periods when I found the criticism demoralising. Although I don't remember ever being booed by United fans, I do remember a particularly tough time in 1989 when, during the whole of December, we failed to win a game. We had lost or drawn ten out of 15 games. Somebody held a banner high up in the Stretford End that said: '3 YEARS OF EXCUSES AND IT'S STILL CRAP . . . TA RA FERGIE'.

I suppose my confidence was shaken a bit because the day after the game I phoned my brother Martin; I knew he would be objective, give me a fair assessment and tell me where I stood. He said, 'You're just going to have to dig in,' which was a sentiment I found reassuring. Years later, the person who had held up that banner wrote a book titled *Ta Ra Fergie*, and a copy showed up at the house. I mailed it back to the publisher. But on the whole I think I weathered the criticism fairly well. Certainly in 2004 and 2005 when we were not playing well and some fans were on my back, it didn't really bother me.

It is sometimes tricky to put criticism in its proper place when you are under a lot of pressure, haven't had enough sleep and everything is going wrong. It might have been a bit easier for me because growing up in Govan was not for the weak. It was a tough neighbourhood – physically and emotionally. There was no option but to be able to protect yourself from bullies and bruisers, and as boys we would get into fights about everything. My brother, a cousin and I would have fights with the five brothers of the Granger family who lived nearby, and from a fairly young age I had become accustomed to physical pain, the taste of blood in my mouth or bad bruising.

I always found it helpful to put criticism in perspective and these memories of my childhood helped. It's easy for me, decades later, to romanticise aspects of my childhood or my playing career, but both had more than their share of raw moments. Yet physical pain is one thing, mental anguish and emotional pressure are entirely different.

I've seen lots of people crack from the emotional pressure of playing or managing. Obviously I might not have been privy to their personal problems, but there are tremendous pressures. The worst example is Robert Enke, the German international goalkeeper who committed suicide in 2009. He had had a difficult few years playing in Spain before joining the Bundesliga team, Hannover 96, and his personal life had been savaged by the death of an infant daughter. After Enke died, his wife revealed that he had been struggling with depression for many years. Fortunately, we never had to deal with anything as distressing during my time at United.

Everybody has their fears; all footballers want to be in the first team, and many will torture themselves when they are injured or have been dropped, fearful that their playing days are ending. There are plenty of them who have turned to drink or gambling and got sucked into a rat-hole of despair.

Managers, most of whom are on short-term contracts, are not immune to the unrelenting pressure and know that the guillotine blade can descend at any moment. Ralf Rangnick, who managed, among others, Hannover 96 and Schalke 04; Gérard Houllier, who worked at Liverpool and Lyon; and Johan Cruyff, after his stint at Barcelona, stepped away from management because of stress. Pep Guardiola took a sabbatical from football after leaving Barcelona to recharge. You have to wonder whether Kenny Dalglish, the great Celtic and Liverpool player, who later managed Liverpool, was ever the same after the horrors he endured in the aftermath of the Heysel stadium disaster in 1985, where 39 fans died, and the Hillsborough disaster in 1989 that claimed 96 lives. And of course I have always lived with the memory of Jock Stein's collapse and tragic death.

If you're in the public eye, the press coverage creates other issues – especially if you are in the sports business. The press helps inflame irate fans. After we moved to Manchester we used to get so many abusive phone calls that we had to change our home phone number several times.

When things were at their darkest for me at United, I remember my wife Cathy asking me what I'd do if I was sacked, and I told her that we would just have to go back to Scotland. I'm sure I would have been crushed if I had been fired, but I always knew I'd be able to support my family and it wouldn't have been the end of the world.

The press can certainly play their part too. Matt Busby told me, 'I never read the papers when we lost a game. They're not going to write nice things about you. So just don't read those stories.' While Matt Busby's advice made sense, it's impossible to be completely oblivious to what appears in the press. In Scotland I was in the habit of reading the match reports, but after I got to United I would very seldom read the papers. Even if I didn't read the papers or watch the football programmes on television, friends would ask whether I'd heard about what somebody had said or written about me, and United's press officer would brief me on inflammatory stories or rumours that had made it into print. But I learned to deal with it and, during my last ten years or so as a manager, I found the press criticism far less troublesome than when I was younger.

The best protection against attacks from others comes from a few people whose opinions you really care about. The yells of a horde of abusive banshees always fade away when you have the support of a few people that you respect. If we lost a game in Aberdeen I usually had to face the chairman in the boardroom after the game. He would be drinking his Coca-Cola – because he never touched alcohol – and would let off steam by giving me stick about the line-up or a particular player. All his criticism stayed in that room and it usually blew over after ten minutes. Either way, outside the room he was unstintingly loyal. The fact that he never voiced a word of criticism behind my back was probably more helpful to me than pounds of praise or a big hug.

At United, especially in the early years, I found it very re-assuring to know that Bobby Charlton was on my side. I never went out of my way to curry favour with him, but he had originally helped advise the board to sign me as a manager and I always felt he was in my corner. During bleak times he often said, 'You'll be all right. You're doing the right thing.' In the months following our 5–1 loss to Manchester City in September 1989, I was feeling a mite vulnerable, and Bobby's backing – particularly during this period – counted for a lot. Not only did his opinion carry a lot of weight through the club, but a few well-chosen words lifted my spirits too. Every leader needs an ally like that.

# 8

---

## OWNING THE MESSAGE

# Speaking

As a manager I communicated with a number of different constituencies and each required special handling: the owner, the coaches and other club staff, the players and the supporters.

Having a healthy, open line of communication with the boss is vital. Few of us don't have a boss. Perhaps the founders of successful companies have designed things in such a way that they don't feel they have anyone they need to please – beyond their inner demons – but the rest of us do. I might have been seen as 'The Boss' by the players, but in football the real boss is the owner, who can hire and fire the manager at will.

I learned this the painful way at St Mirren when I was always arguing with the chairman, Willie Todd, the owner of a painting and decorating company, who had bought the club shortly after I joined. He didn't know much about football and I helped educate him. Before long he began to think he knew a lot about the game and we were soon at loggerheads. It was a very nasty experience, and got to the point where we were not talking to each other. In retrospect, there was only one way it was going to end – and that was badly for me. It did. I was sacked. Managers have to find a way to talk to their bosses, regardless of their differences in character; otherwise it will only end miserably.

At Aberdeen, I wasn't about to repeat the mistake. The personality of Dick Donald, Aberdeen's chairman between 1970 and 1993, was very different from Willie Todd's, and I found him easier to get along with. Though we became close, our conversations were always tinged with formality. I addressed him as 'Mr Chairman', and he always called me 'Mr Ferguson', which helped show I understood the difference between our roles. It was important to establish these boundaries because he was a constant presence around the club, and we would talk almost every day. My other key relationship at Aberdeen was with Archie Knox, my assistant manager. We went everywhere together – working during the day and socialising, when we had time, with our wives in the evening. When I moved to United in 1986 I insisted that he came with me. His last name could have been Ferguson and, while I understood his decision to leave United in 1991 to help Walter Smith at Rangers, it ended a wonderful working relationship.

By the time I got to United I was 44, had experienced success at Aberdeen (where we had won ten trophies and a number of players had earned Scottish caps) and learned that maintaining a healthy relationship with the owner and club chairman was vital. I used to go and see Martin Edwards, United's owner and chairman, in his book- and trophy-filled office at Old Trafford a couple of times a week. No subject was off limits, and I kept him fully informed of everything I was working on and concerned about. We saw eye to eye about most things, with the exception of my own compensation.

This was a time of great change at Old Trafford and in football in general. During the 1990s, the combination of the huge rise in television revenues and the 1995 European Court of Justice's 'Bosman ruling', which lifted many transfer restrictions, gave greater impetus to the business side of the club. After Martin's decision to float United on the Stock Exchange in 1991, the nature of its ownership was altered. The club's stock was no longer concentrated in an individual, but rather distributed among dozens of investment fund managers and hundreds of individuals. For me this meant that, apart from making an appearance at the club's Annual General Meeting, I was no longer in direct contact with all the financial owners of the club, but it was vital that I kept communicating closely with Martin and the board.

The other thing that changed was the gradual increase in authority of the chief executive officer of the club, stemming from the blossoming of United's commercial activities. In 2000 this resulted in the appointment of David Gill. David was responsible for building and running the business activities of United. Over the years David and I became like blood brothers.

After the Glazers took control of United in 2005, the nature of the organisation changed again. Unlike Dick Donald in Aberdeen and Martin Edwards in Manchester, the Glazers did not live near the club they owned. Instead they lived in America and their principal conduit was David Gill. I had talked to Malcolm Glazer after his family bought the club, but I never met him in person. The two family members I saw the most were Joel and Avram who, best as I could tell, were its most enthusiastic football fans. However, it was David who kept the Glazers updated on the health of the club and relayed my requests about purchases of players or upgrades to our training facilities.

After the owner, the next most important constituency I had to talk to was the coaching staff. They were the pipeline for conveying my ideas to players – whether members of the first team or boys coming through the youth system. I am hard pressed to think of a day when I didn't talk to any of the coaches. Even during those very rare times when I was ill in bed, I'd still talk to the staff on the phone. I understood intuitively that if there was a breakdown in communication with my staff, or if instructions were misunderstood or garbled in the re-telling, it would only lead to confusion on the pitch. So, first thing every morning, I would talk to the coaching staff at the training ground and set out my key priorities for the day.

I would talk to the players in one of three settings – during training, on match days, and also by themselves in a one-on-one setting. In some circumstances, especially when I was talking to people I didn't know well, I found it tricky to assess whether I was drilling my message home, so I got into the habit of imagining that I was in the shoes of the listener. I knew from my own experience as a player what it was like to listen to a manager drone on, especially if it was the day before a game, and you were just raring to get on to the training field and blow off some steam. As a result I always tried to keep my team talks short and punchy. I remember once saying this to the players, 'This must be my thousandth team talk,' and Brian McClair, who played 471 games for United between 1987 and 1998, chirped up, 'Yeah, I slept through half of them.' Managers often make things more complicated than they are. The best way to make sure people understand what you expect from them is to be clear and concise, and that was especially true as the number of foreign players increased, since some of them needed subtitles to deal with my Scottish accent. I'm sure there were a few that probably couldn't tell whether I was speaking in English or Welsh.

I took pains to convey to the players that because I was not intimidated by the opposition, neither should they be. I was also careful to remind them of the necessity for us to win all the individual battles that take place during a game. And, more often than not, I would urge the team to be decisive in the final third of the game. At half-time I would relay to the players what I had seen in the first half, make observations about some of the opposing team, and try to tighten everything up. I made a habit of never going around issuing reminders to individual players. It just plants the seeds of doubt in their minds and they are left wondering whether the manager trusts them. Similarly, I never felt it made any sense to be perpetually barking instructions at players during games. If you have to resort to that, it means that you have not prepared or communicated your plan correctly, or you do not trust the players to do what they are supposed to do. Either shortcoming reflects more poorly on the manager than the players.

Bill Shankly, the long-time manager of Liverpool who, like me, came from Scotland, had a reputation for keeping things to the point. I often tried to emulate the effectiveness of one of Bill's favourite lines which was, 'If we get the ball, why don't we pass it to each other? It's a wee bit harder when the other team have got it.' The instructions that I gave most frequently were very short. They were nothing more complicated than 'Keep the ball' or, 'Do not let them score'.

One message that seemed to strike home (at least judging by the number of players who appear to have remembered it) were the words I used at half-time during the 1999 Champions League final when we were trailing Bayern Munich 1–0. I said, 'When that Cup is going to be presented, just remember that you can't even touch it if you're the losers – you'll be walking past it with your losers' medals, knowing someone walking behind you is going to lift the Cup.'

With players, the manner of the delivery of the message could have quite an effect. While I had a reputation for sometimes steam-blasting players, I found that I rarely lost my temper (especially in my later years) in crucial games where we were trailing badly. Then it was vital to stay calm and be very precise with my feedback. Sometimes, Mick Phelan might tell me it was time to give everyone a bit of a roasting, particularly the new players, but tantrums quickly lost their effect. At half-time when we were ahead by a couple of goals, I would frequently put a bit of a bark into my instructions, to ensure that the players did not let their concentration lapse and allow complacency to seep in. I also wanted to notch up as many goals as possible in case an entire season might be decided on goal difference. By contrast, silence can be as effective a way of communicating as anything else. Sometimes, after we had a bad result, I would finish what I had to say to the players and then sit down on the bench and say nothing. The subsequent quietness was probably more effective than anything I said.

Whether the audience is one person or 75,000, you need to assemble your thoughts, know what you want to emphasise and just say it. In team meetings it's important to maintain eye contact and look directly at the players because it adds intensity to the delivery of the message, although I tried to avoid staring at those who I felt might wither under my gaze. There are some managers who will enter a dressing room at half-time with a pack of notes. When they talk to the players they will use their notes as prompts. I cannot imagine how that is an effective way to communicate. If you have command and control of your subject, you don't need notes. No player is going to believe that someone is in control of his material, or is an authority on a subject, if he has to keep resorting to notes. I relied on my memory and my own assessment and, that way, when I was talking to the players, I was able to maintain eye contact. I'm sure I got some stuff wrong. I'd miss a deflection or a foul but, in the grand scheme of things, those tiny details don't count. It's the message, the command of that message and its delivery that pack the punch. Everyone has their own style, but using notes when trying to motivate people is not mine.

If I wanted to convey a particular message, I might summon a player to my office at the Carrington training ground. There was a phone in the dressing room that I used to relay the invitation to come upstairs. I'm sure, when the phone rang, some of the players thought they were being hauled into the headmaster's study for a caning. Some of them were right.

While I was always fixated on both physical and mental freshness, I was careful never to say to a player, 'You look tired', even if I thought that he did. I knew that if I uttered the phrase he would immediately feel tired. Instead I'd say to him, 'You're so strong, nobody is ever going to be able to keep up with you.' Before a game, especially at Old Trafford, I'd emphasise the size of our pitch, which was daunting for most of our opponents, and the need to maintain a high tempo, rhythm and speed. I wanted to plant in their minds that we would have the opponents knackered out by the last 15 minutes of a game.

I used to lie in bed thinking about new themes to talk to the players about, because I never wanted them to feel that I was about to deliver a sermon they had heard the previous week. Once, after I had been to see my very first performance of a classical concert with Carlos Queiroz in Manchester, I talked to the players about the experience. They must have thought I'd gone off my rocker, but I was trying to explain to them how the conductor of the concert, which featured Andrea Bocelli, was trying to obtain the same things from his orchestra as I was doing at United: control, harmony, tempo, timing, rhythm. I knew that the players had never heard this story before because it was brand new, but I'm sure my message was lost on some. There were some stories about teamwork that I'm sure Ryan Giggs or Paul Scholes feel they heard dozens of times, like my tale about large flocks of Canada geese, which can migrate thousands of miles because of the way they work as a team. The birds take turns breaking the air at the front of the flock and, at the back, if one gets injured, a couple drop away from the flock to look after it. I was not asking them to fly for thousands of miles, I was only asking them to play 38 games of football.

Making sure players grasped where they stood was very important. Like all of us they are fragile human beings and it's easy to send unintended messages. If I was not planning to pick a player in a particular game, I'd always try to find a way to explain the reason. They would be worrying that they had fallen out of favour or I had my eye on someone else to fill their boots. Instead I'd try to let them down gently and provide reassurance. Sometimes it was because I was resting them for a more important game. I'd take pains to explain the bigger picture – that the campaign was more important than the game and that we needed to plot out a way of winning every game. In the bigger European games, where we would travel with a squad of 24 players, I would need to explain things to the 13 who were not included in the starting line-up. I tried to make them feel they were part of a squad and that it was the squad – rather than the starting team in any particular game – that would eventually win the League or a cup.

It was all well and good to be chatting with the coaches or the players in quite small groups, but it was another matter to be speaking in front of crowds of people. As you encounter success, more people tend to get interested in what you have to say. I never thought when I first became a manager that I would ever address a crowd of 75,000 people, not to mention the millions more watching on TV – which is what happened after my last ever game at Old Trafford.

Tons of people have told me they are scared witless about speaking in front of others. For some reason it's never bothered me. Even as a boy I was always busy organising other people, and I've long been accustomed to some form of public speaking, even though I am not pretending for a moment that I could deliver a Churchillian speech or the Gettysburg Address. As a teenager I had my stint as a shop steward and, later, when I ran my two pubs, I often had to say something to all the customers. Neither of these settings required great oratorical skill, but I suppose they are one reason why I've never been plagued by the nervous butterflies that afflict many people when they have to stand up and address a group.

I've always marvelled at the way in which some highly skilled public speakers' command of language allows them to convey their thoughts in a powerful fashion. In Scotland in the 1960s and 1970s, everyone paid attention to Jimmy Reid, the trade-union leader and one of the guiding forces of the Communist Party of Great Britain. Love him or loathe him, he knew how to command the attention of a crowd. He was one of the last great political platform speakers – whether it was in the shipyards of Clydebank or in less raucous settings. I spoke at his funeral in 2010 at the Govan Old Parish Church and remember saying that while my education had consisted of football, Jimmy's took place at the Govan library. Words just seemed to flow from him. The speech he made when he was installed as Rector of Glasgow University in 1971, during which he implored the students to reject the rat race, was reprinted in full by the *New*

*York Times*, which described it as the greatest speech since Abraham Lincoln's Gettysburg Address.

When Nelson Mandela spoke at the Laureus Sports Award dinner in Monaco in 2000, you could have heard a pin drop. He didn't speak for long, but his remarks made the hairs on my neck stand up. Such force; such presence. My pal, Hugh McIlvanney, is no politician, but he is probably the greatest sports writer I have encountered and his control of language is fantastic. I could listen to him all day because he speaks in complete paragraphs.

I don't pretend to command language like a Reid, a Mandela or a McIlvanney, but as a football manager I frequently found myself speaking in public, and sometimes in front of a stadium packed to the gills. Talking to smaller groups is a useful way to practise speaking to bigger audiences. The principles are the same. You need to know what you want to say; you have to contemplate how you are going to deliver the message; and you have to maintain control of the audience. If someone has belief, they can find the words to express it. I've never been one for reading verbatim from a speech written out in longhand, nor have I ever used a Teleprompter. For me it's been more important to plan what I want to say, have a mental road map for the points I want to emphasise, and then try to maintain my train of thought. I'm quite comfortable improvising, particularly when the subject has something to do with football. Usually this works but, on occasion, it's an approach that has failed me.

In 1974, after four months as manager of East Stirlingshire, I became manager of St Mirren, where I was also just relying on instincts. Nobody had given me public-speaking lessons or public-relations tips, so I did what I thought was appropriate. St Mirren was a club located in Paisley, a town that had been hard hit by the closure of the cotton mills and a slump in the automobile industry. Glasgow, which is only ten miles away, cast a long shadow over Paisley, and each weekend bus-loads of men would disappear to watch Celtic or Rangers. The whole town had a major inferiority complex, and I was determined to lift spirits and convince the people there that their football club had a bright future. I decided that some public speaking would do the trick.

St Mirren's crowds were barely larger than a church choir, so one weekend I resorted to communicating with brute force. The club electrician taped a loudspeaker to the roof of a van and, like a politician casting about for votes, I toured Paisley, microphone in hand, imploring people to turn out to support their team. We stopped in the city centre, where I extolled the virtues of the team. It worked, and the crowds began to increase.

I had to do some public speaking when I was managing in Scotland, but the level of activity – and scrutiny – increased when I moved south. Manchester United had charity dinners on the first Monday of every month and I sometimes used to speak at these events. The first one was a fiasco. I tried to make a joke about England and Scotland but it just sailed over the heads of the audience. I had expected a few laughs but all I got was silence. Jokes are tricky things to deliver with any degree of assurance, and I understand why comedians go to small clubs to test out their routines before appearing in big venues or going on television.

As much as it's essential to maintain eye contact when talking to a small group of people, I always found it disconcerting to catch someone's eye when speaking in front of a big room. I tended to look towards the audience because I knew that staring at notes on a lectern is one sure way to lose a crowd's attention.

However, I never looked at any particular individual. Instead, I'd pick a spot at the back of the room slightly above the heads of the audience.

It's easy to get thrown off your horse if you look directly at someone in a crowd of people. Eric Harrison, United's youth coach between 1981 and 1998, discovered the perils of this in 1992. He had asked my advice about public speaking and I'd told him to look at the wall at the back of the room and also to move his head as he spoke so that the entire audience felt included. Instead, he made the fatal mistake of locking eyes with one member of the audience, which was not a smart move, particularly as Eric was speaking in Liverpool, and the crowd consisted of Liverpool and Everton fans. He came scuttling back to Manchester with his tail between his legs because the person he had picked out of the crowd did two things. First, he had slowly crossed his throat with his index finger, and then, when that didn't throw Eric off his stride, he started to wave a white handkerchief. That did the trick and Eric, thoroughly rattled, had to sit down.

When Sir Matt Busby died in 1994, I was asked to speak at his funeral mass at the church of Our Lady and St John in Charlton-cum-Hardy near Manchester. It was a big event, and thousands of United fans had lined the route of the cortege. The church was packed to the rafters. I was speaking from notes, which I don't usually do, and I got a roasting from my harshest critic, Cathy, my wife. She said, 'You were hopeless. I told you not to use notes. You're useless when you try to speak from notes.'

Speaking without notes is not for the faint of heart, and sometimes it's been my comeuppance. I gave a talk at Goldman Sachs in London some years ago, and I thought it went well enough, but Mark, my son, lambasted me for hopping from point to point and for an overall lack of structure. I discovered that, with or without notes, there's always someone ready to skewer you – one of the perils, I suppose, of opening your mouth in public.

## Writing

There were only two ways for me to communicate with the broad base of fans – either via the press or through the notes in the match-day programmes. Every now and again there would be an opportunity at a dinner, or special event, to transmit a message to season-ticket holders or supporters' clubs, but those formats don't offer a way to communicate with 75,000 people, let alone millions of fans scattered all over the world. Communicating through newspapers or on television programmes is fraught with peril. Publishers and broadcasters have their own agendas, so it is very easy for a message to get garbled or taken out of context. However, I knew that I could count on the match-day programme as a vehicle with which to convey messages to the people who came to watch us at Old Trafford.

At St Mirren, Stan Park, a local journalist for the *Paisley Daily Express*, would come in once a week, and I would tell him what I wanted to convey. He ghost-wrote my programme notes, but I would always proof-read them before they went to press to make sure Stan had captured the nuances. That routine seemed to work, so I followed this format at Aberdeen, where I sometimes used the programme notes to exhort the supporters to be more vocal. The running joke, which was a bit harsh, was that the crowd at Pittodrie sometimes made more noise unwrapping their sweetie papers than they did supporting the team.

At United I worked with David Meek, a reporter for the *Manchester Evening News*. Early in my tenure I tried to convey a sense of the possible at United, because when I arrived there was tremendous disaffection, not just with the performance that had the club second from bottom of the old Division One, but also at its ownership.

I used the programme notes to show that, at least on some issues, I sympathised with the supporters. For example, I felt that the ticket prices were too high and had conveyed precisely the same sentiment to Martin Edwards and the rest of the board. I also tried to inject a sense of intimacy, so that the notes weren't just about a recent performance or a new signing, but about the softer side of our club. Every now and again I'd pay tribute to a former player who had died, or to friends, like Douglas Smith, who founded and ran one of my first clubs, Drumchapel Amateurs, or Sean Fallon, Celtic's assistant manager. People don't want mundane recitals of the obvious. They want to read something different and learn about the unexpected.

While I was at Aberdeen I published my first book, *A Light in the North*. I wrote it as a way to supplement my income, but it was more a blow-by-blow description of my time at the club and was written in the wake of our 1985 League victory. The first book I paid real attention to was *Managing My Life*, which came out in 1999 after United won the Treble. I collaborated with Hugh McIlvanney on this work and I found it a cathartic experience. It was a busy period in my life and I found myself scribbling down thoughts and memories during spare moments. Eventually I handed Hugh over 200,000 words of notes, assembled on all sorts of different sheets of paper. He sorted them all out and wove them into prose, but I took great relish in – and derived a lot of consolation from – recounting my childhood years and relaying the tone of the setting and the era in which I was raised.

My most meaningful pieces of writing were probably the shortest – notes or letters written in reply to the correspondence that used to come pouring into the office. Remember, the majority of my managerial time was spent before the era of e-mail and texting, so a personal response came in the form of cards or letters. As the leader of United I felt that it was expected of me, depending on the occasion, to send condolence or congratulatory messages or just to thank people for suggestions they had sent to the office. And every year I send out about 2,000 Christmas cards. Some people might say: why not send that money to charity instead? It's a fair point, but my reason for sending these cards is to let people know that I am thinking of them. I like receiving Christmas cards for precisely the same reason.

## Answering

There aren't many areas where I would claim that I've been under more pressure than other leaders, but dealing with the press might be the one. These days it is probably only the leaders of the world's biggest countries who find themselves in front of more microphones and cameras than the football manager of one of Europe's best football teams. It's funny how politicians, particularly when they are campaigning for office, are desperate for press coverage. There were many times when I pined for the opposite and wished that reporters would just leave me alone to concentrate on my job. If United won, we were on the back page of the newspapers. If we lost we wound up on the front pages.

It was one thing to deal with the press in Scotland. At East Stirlingshire in 1974, all I had to do was talk to a young reporter from the *Falkirk Herald*, whose circulation was only about 40,000. The stadium at Aberdeen didn't even have a dedicated press room. I used to have to give my post-game interviews in the foyer of the Pittodrie stadium.

Manchester United was another matter, because it attracted the local and national newspaper, television and radio reporters, and – in the past decade – the growing crowd of internet bloggers who would appear for the regular briefings at United, or the hundreds of international journalists who would come out of the woodwork before major games, and whose reports would almost instantly be transmitted to tens of millions of people all around the world. At Old Trafford they even have cameras, microphones and tape recorders in the players' tunnel, some of which feed the club's own demand for content for its website, TV channel, radio station, magazine and match-day programmes. After a regular game, I'd give three or four television interviews.

During my last few years at United, a comment at a press conference – or even a video taken surreptitiously on a mobile-phone camera at a private function – would quickly be relayed in newspapers and magazines, on Sky Sports News, in innumerable blogs and via an ever increasing number of apps. Here's just one example of how the world cannot get enough of football. Eric Cantona's infamous 'kung-fu' kick at Crystal Palace in 1995 has now garnered over two million views on YouTube. All this for an event that took place 20 years ago – before many of today's football fans were even born! – and ten years before YouTube was even founded.

I've long understood that the press gravitates to what's popular and what will sell newspapers or boost television ratings, even if what is published sometimes isn't closely related to reality. It's easier to get more readers and viewers when writing or talking about popular topics. The press isn't going to spend much time writing about a steelworker who lost his job or a wee guy in a call centre who was fired because of a recession. Those things don't mean a thing to the general public. Football does.

When I joined Rangers, the manager, Scot Symon, had no time for the press. He would not give them the time of day. On one occasion Rangers were playing Sparta Rotterdam in a European Cup tie, when thick fog obscured visibility. A journalist phoned to ask Scot whether the game would be played and he answered, 'No comment'. Imagine if you gave that answer today.

Ron Atkinson, my immediate predecessor at United, had a different approach. I think he spoke to the press every single day of the week, and probably on every single day of the year, because I bet he took telephone calls on Sundays. Ron also allowed the press near the players at the training ground. Ron is a big, outgoing character and he enjoyed the interaction with the press, but his approach was not my cup of tea. First, I would not have known what to talk about if I had met the press every day. I might have been able to say something about the weather or the wine that I had drunk the previous evening, but I would quickly have exhausted my supply of fresh material – at least as it related to United. There was also the bigger issue, which was that I didn't want to have the press in my hair every day, asking me to respond to all sorts of inane questions so that I would blurt out something colourful that they could use to create a story where none existed. I immediately eliminated all the daily briefings and, instead, limited my meetings with the press to the day before a game and immediately after the match. Eventually these sessions just became a waste of time after the more prominent journalists began to skip them as they went in search of the players instead. After a game at Tottenham in the early 2000s, I walked into the press conference and all the main journalists were in the tunnel trying to get hold of the players. There was a smattering of young wire reporters. It was a waste of time.

Encounters with the press, which come in many guises, are all about control. Complete control is easy when you're issuing a press release or a pre-recorded video, when you can edit every word and clip. It's more difficult to retain control during a press conference, or if you get ambushed at an airport when everyone is looking for a chink in your armour. The press are looking for the slightest of slips. The journalists are waiting for a verbal slip while the cameramen are like hunters, ready to snap the shutter as soon as you purse your lips or grimace.

The rulers of North Korea or Cuba may be able to control their press, but it is sheer fantasy to think that anyone in England is going to be able to do the same.

Jock Stein, the manager of Celtic and Scotland, had his own technique. He seemed to know everything about the journalists covering Celtic. He used to know the ones who had drink problems or were gambling too much. He knew all their failings and all their weaknesses. He understood who they were and they knew it. I'm sure that many of them thought twice before writing anything that might embarrass Jock.

While I developed friendships with some of the reporters who covered United – Glenn Gibbons, Bob Cass and Hugh McIlvanney – and came to trust a handful, I never had the easy rapport with the press that Jock developed. They frequently got under my skin, and every now and again I would lash out at one of them in response to something they had written. The reporters would usually blame it on their editors but, if you are the victim of a distorted account, that doesn't matter. I was always determined to communicate with the press on my own terms and, to the best of my ability, control the messages we wanted to disseminate. This revolved around answering questions or, more precisely, not answering questions. If reporters peppered me with questions about injuries or my Saturday line-up, I'd either change the subject or, depending on my mood, tell them it was none of their business. The journalists didn't own the press conferences. I did.

It is important to remember that the reporters are not always asking questions of their own. Frequently, they are planting topics suggested by others. Football reporters have close ties with many of the more important agents. They rely on them for morsels of information that the agents themselves have heard from the players they represent. So when an agent is eager to provoke a bidding war for one of his clients, it's easy for him to plant a question at a press conference by getting a friendly reporter to ask whether we were interested in a particular player.

When journalists or news organisations abused their power, I cut them off. There were always plenty of others eager to take their place. After a series of run-ins with the BBC, I refused to talk to any of their journalists or appear on any of their radio or television programmes for seven years. There were a few reporters who got my goat. Over the years I must have banned over 20 journalists who manufactured stories. I wasn't going to accept it – I would give them the chance to correct it; if they refused to do that, I refused them access. Even though he became a friend and I eventually trusted him, I banned Glenn Gibbons, a Scottish journalist who had grown up in the same area of Glasgow as my father, multiple times. Glenn would always try to appeal to my better instincts by saying, 'What would your dad think of you – banning a boy from the Cowcaddens?' Sometimes I found MUTV, United's own football channel, irritating, and there were some occasions when I just needed a breather and stopped giving interviews to MUTV for a week or two.

It's hard to control your emotions, especially if you've been going through a tough spell, or a player has done something daft that's embarrassed the team. I always tried to be aware of the fact that journalists and photographers would be paying as much attention to my body language as to my words. Paul Doherty, head of sports for Granada Television, told me to always rub my face before I gave a press conference so that I appeared bright and cheery and did not display a hint of tension. He had told me that I was showing too much concern at press conferences and instructed me to, 'Go in there emotionless, with no expression on your face. If you are straight as a die, it will kill them. They are all looking for a weakness.' I took that to heart and, before walking into a press conference, I always used to rub my face. However, to remain emotionless is a lot easier to say than to do, and I remember marvelling at the way President George W. Bush was able to maintain a completely impassive face after he was informed of the 9/11 attacks while sitting in front of a classroom of children and the Washington press corps. I don't think I could have pulled that off. No matter how hard I tried, my emotions and body language changed depending on the circumstances. If things had gone poorly, it was hard not to grimace or have pursed lips and, by contrast, when we had just thumped an opponent it was important not to appear too confident or smug. Either way, I was always aware that a confident air went a long way with the constituency that mattered the most – the players. I also always remembered another piece of advice that Paul Doherty gave me. He said, 'You have to walk out of every press conference unhurt.'

Once in a while I was so upset that I chose not to face the press for fear that I would say something about the referee or assistant referees that would get me into hot water with the authorities. When United lost the second leg of the Round of 16 Champions League tie against Real Madrid in March 2013 because of the bizarre decision of the referee, Cüneyt Çakir, to give Nani a red card for committing a foul on a player he didn't even see, I was beside myself. I knew that the journalists waiting for me in our press room would be like a hundred matadors waving red capes, and I was not about to risk charging at every single one of them. Instead, I sent Mick Phelan to deal with the ridiculous judgement of the referee. I knew on that particular night I would break my own rule and commit the cardinal mistake of actually answering the questions.

It is probably fortunate for me that I did not have to contend with social media for most of my career. The legions of fans following United on Twitter, Facebook or Instagram massively outnumber the fans tracking the club through the *Sun* or *Daily Mirror*. I would wager that younger managers might even start gradually bypassing the major newspapers, skipping the big, formal press conferences and just communicate directly with fans. They say you need a thick skin to deal with some of the abuse on Twitter, but – though it may come from many more quarters – beyond the foul language it isn't any worse than what a manager experiences from newspapers and the television pundits. At least the social networks provide a platform for precise control of the message that you want to communicate, and a way to answer questions, even if they sometimes provoke an unexpected backlash. No matter how savage the treatment in the press, no matter how many questions I didn't answer, I probably was harder on myself after we lost a game than any journalist. If I lost a game it affected me more than anyone else. The journalists could file their column and go to the pub. I had to figure out why we lost and set about fixing the problem.

In retirement, I have found myself watching the way other managers deal with press conferences. I love it, because I want to see where I can help. Every now and again I will phone one of them with some advice. Last season, when Leicester City was lodged at the bottom of the Premier League, I phoned the manager, Nigel Pearson, and told him that he looked too relaxed and over-confident. I told him that he had to show some concern without looking vulnerable. By contrast, when I talked to Sean Dyche, manager of Burnley, who also had a tough season, I tried to reassure him. Sean, who always had a bit of a wee joke with the interviewer, reiterated how hard his team was working, and – while not oblivious to where Burnley stood in the table – he managed to convey a feeling of confidence. Last season, I also took it upon myself to offer Alan Pardew some unsolicited advice before he left Newcastle United to take the helm at Crystal Palace. I asked him, 'What's happened to you? You don't argue with anybody any more. You've given in. You've chucked it. If you want to keep your job, start being Alan Pardew.' He phoned me up a couple of weeks later and said, 'Thanks.' He didn't need to. I know how difficult the job is. I am always happy to help a fellow manager.

# 9

## LEADING NOT MANAGING

# Owners

Authority, and the exercise of control, rests on possessing the confidence of those who provide it. No leader stands a chance if the people he is supposedly managing sense that his hold on his job is tenuous. In football the providers of this authority are the club owners. If they are unequivocal about their confidence in – and support of – the manager, they make his job a lot easier. When I applied for my first managerial job, the part-time role at East Stirlingshire, I was so eager to get my foot on the ladder that I didn't pay any attention to the condition of the club or the personalities who controlled the purse-strings. As the years went by, I quickly gained an appreciation of how important it is to understand the person, or people, to whom you have to report and are accountable.

Most of us don't think about the nature of our employer, or boss, or the tone and atmosphere they cultivate inside their organisation. That's really important in football, which is littered with bad owners. I cannot say enough about the benefits of a long-term, stable ownership that's prepared to make the necessary investments to create a vibrant organisation. It's a priceless foundation for management in any walk of life. I've read quite a lot about Warren Buffett and Berkshire Hathaway, and I imagine that the people heading his various companies all think much more about long-term prosperity than the CEO of a publicly listed company who is worried that the investment fund managers will be at his throat if he produces disappointing earnings in the next quarter. If you have owners, or shareholders, who only think about short-term results, it brings about a never-ending cycle of misery for everyone. That's especially true in football.

Football managers should look for their own modified version of Warren Buffett – people who care about the long term; who provide them with the money they need to build their team; who don't meddle in daily management; who are available when needed; and who understand that their job is only to make two decisions. The first is to replace the manager or CEO; the second is to sell the club. Unfortunately, these people are almost impossible to find in football, and the problem only seems to have been exacerbated by the way in which ownership, over the last 50 years, has gradually shifted from local businessmen to foreign oligarchs, sheikhs and hedge-fund managers, chasing their share of the television money that now floods the Premier League.

For their part, owners need to understand that football is different from the businesses they themselves run and where they have enjoyed success. The clubs aren't supermarket chains, banks or electronics wholesalers.

Football is live entertainment, conducted on a scale that has no parallel. You just cannot manufacture wins with the reliability with which you can produce phones or razor blades, because everything hinges on the performance of individuals and the random influences of emotion, chance and injury. Any owner also needs to be realistic. A devoted fan may come to the stadium for every game expecting a victory, but an owner has to be much more grounded.

Between the time I took over at Manchester United and my retirement in 2013, the 48 clubs that have occupied the remaining slots in the Premier League went through 267 permanent managers (not including caretaker roles). It makes you wonder why some clubs even bother to pay managers. At the start of the 2014–15 season, Arsène Wenger had managed almost as many Premier League games as all his fellow managers combined. The real title of the top football man in most Premier League clubs should be 'temporary manager'.

Chelsea ran through 13 full-time managers (not including caretakers) while I was at United, and Manchester City went through 14 (not including caretakers). It would not surprise me if Chelsea has paid as much as £40 million in settlement payments to fired managers. Chelsea and Manchester City have plenty of companions. The Premier League is littered with examples of poor hiring practices. Take Liverpool in 2010 after they sacked Rafael Benítez. The owners looked around and fastened on Roy Hodgson, who had just taken Fulham to the UEFA Cup final. Liverpool hired Roy and within six months they had fired him. I'm not sure it is any better in Europe. Bayern Munich made 14 changes of manager (not including caretakers) while I was at United, although several of the same men held the post on different occasions. It is all so silly, since there is no evidence that frequent sacking of a manager leads to better results.

Years ago there used to be much greater longevity among football managers – perhaps because the owners came from the surrounding communities and were more vested in the long-term success and stability of their club, rather than many of the people who own clubs today. United obviously had Matt Busby for 25 years between 1945 and 1969 (he returned to the club for 1970–71); Joe Harvey was manager of Newcastle for 13 years between 1962 and 1975; Arsenal had Herbert Chapman for 9 years between 1925 and 1934, and his successor, George Allison, was there for 13 years between 1934 and 1947. Scot Symon was at Rangers for 13 years (between 1954 and 1967) while, before him, Bill Struth held the job for an extraordinary 34 years (1920–54).

There's nothing more reassuring for a manager than to feel that he has the support of his boss. It's as true for young people taking their first job, who are at the bottom rung of an organisation, as it is for a leader wanting to know that he is backed by his board of directors. Your boss can make or break you. I learned that while I was at Aberdeen managing under Dick Donald. The greatest gift he gave me was unerring confidence in my capabilities.

This was particularly true in my first year at the club, when we had a bumpy time. I also had to deal with the legacy of the previous manager, Billy McNeill, who had left to manage Celtic and had been popular with the players. In March 1979 I was feeling pretty despondent after Rangers beat Aberdeen 2–1 in the Scottish League Cup final. A couple of the players had made no secret of the fact that they preferred my predecessor, and the local newspaper, *The Press and Journal*, had been questioning my credentials; I said as much to Dick. He just said, 'I hired you because you can do the job. I'm not interested in what the press say. You just get on with your job. Don't moan. Be a man.' It really lifted my spirits.

I received the same sort of support at United, particularly during my early years at the club before the trophies started to appear. In 1990 we travelled to Nottingham Forest in the FA

Cup and the match was billed as do-or-die for my career. The day before the game, Martin Edwards called me with a simple but much appreciated message, 'Whatever happens tomorrow, your job is safe.'

I was fortunate, at both Aberdeen and Manchester United, to have principal owners who had an abiding pride in their ownership of the clubs. At Aberdeen Dick Donald had been involved with the club from 1949, and became its chairman in 1970. He was not about to tolerate any other shareholders meddling in its affairs. His Annual General Meetings were almost always dispatched within three minutes; the longest extended to about seven minutes when a local businessman engaged in a bit of agitation. Even though Dick had played stints of professional football as a young man, he understood the dividing lines that separate owners from managers. I never felt that he wanted to show he knew more about football than me. That was an enormous blessing. The greatest bosses also take great pride in making sure that if employees who have served them well choose to leave, they go on to greater and better things. That was certainly the case with Dick Donald, because when, in 1986, I began to mention to him that I was thinking about leaving Aberdeen for the challenge of a larger club, he was emphatic that I should only contemplate one: Manchester United. This was well before I had any inkling that Manchester United were interested in me, but Dick's allusion to the club was not just characteristic of the man, but also bolstered my confidence. When I finally left Aberdeen, I knew that he didn't want me to go, but I also left with his blessing in my pocket – a priceless benediction.

Today, I tell managers who are casting about for a club to be sure they find a chairman who understands the complexities of their job. The greatest luxury any manager can obtain is sufficient time to either develop a club or turn things around. It takes years to implement your ideas and put your structure in place. If they are fortunate to find an owner who understands the job and is willing to give them time (and those people are rare human beings), they stand a chance. Otherwise, if they don't get results they will be sacked. Every football manager has been sacked. I was sacked – albeit not for football reasons – and José Mourinho, Arsène Wenger and Carlo Ancelotti have all been sacked. The only football manager who has not been sacked is the one who is two minutes into his first job.

There have been some really good owners of clubs but, unfortunately, they are in a distinct minority. The Cobbold family, who controlled Ipswich Town for many years, were gems. They were deeply rooted in the surrounding community and were brewers and pub owners. Both Alf Ramsey and Bobby Robson worked for them as Ipswich managers, for whom they must have been a godsend. Today there is a VIP club at Ipswich Town called the 'Cobbold Club', even though the family hasn't been involved for quite a long time. That speaks volumes. Most clubs would probably like to forget their former owners. Arsenal has also been blessed by owners with a long-term view. For many decades it was owned by a pair of families – the Bracewell-Smiths and Hill-Woods – and then David Dein (a shareholder and vice-chairman), who was responsible for attracting Arsène Wenger to Arsenal and was the club's driving force for a long time.

When I arrived at United, Martin Edwards was the chairman and largest shareholder. He had inherited the position and stake from his father, Louis Edwards, who himself had first bought control in the early 1970s.

As I noted earlier, Martin shared some of Dick Donald's traits. He did not feel impelled to demonstrate his knowledge of football. He was not confused about the difference between an owner and a manager and, on the whole, we got on well.

The Glazer family have taken a lot of flak during the time they have owned United. People have criticised them for paying vast sums in interest payments to the banks that loaned them the money to buy the club, and for the various fees that have been charged. Others have said that the reason United is once more a publicly traded company is so the Glazers can cash in on their investment. I used to get calls from the people running the various supporters' clubs asking for my backing in various campaigns to get rid of the Glazers. Whenever one of these efforts cranked into high gear, somebody would argue that if I announced my resignation as manager, the Glazers would be forced to sell the club. That never made any sense to me. I told the agitators, 'If I quit, do you think United is going to take the field on Saturday without a manager?'

While I was manager, the Glazers caused me no bother. It might surprise people but, from my perspective as a manager, they have been very good owners. A manager wants four things from the owner: no meddling; money when it is needed to buy a player; support; and fair compensation. When they bought the club, the Glazers said it was a long-term investment, and I took some consolation from the fact that, at the time, they had owned the Tampa Bay Buccaneers, the American football team, for a decade. After they took control, they did not come barrelling in with all guns blazing. It was quite the opposite. After they bought the club, nobody got fired. They valued continuity. There was not one change to any of the commercial or coaching staff and they never exerted any pressure on me regarding the squad or our results. That says a lot about their approach.

They never said 'no' or refused to do something that I cared about. I was also probably manna from heaven for them because I never asked for ridiculous amounts of money. When we signed Robin van Persie in 2012 for £24 million which, at the time, was the largest amount we had ever paid for a 29-year-old player, the only question the Glazers asked was about his age. It was a fair question because in 2008 we had bought Dimitar Berbatov from Tottenham for £30.75 million when he was 27 years old. Berbatov's stylish but languid approach did not work out at United, even though he scored 21 goals in 2010–11 and was joint top scorer in the League. In 2012 we sold him to Fulham for £3 million. So I could see why the Glazers had questions about Van Persie. It was entirely reasonable. But when a player of his calibre becomes available, you have to act.

If I was an aspiring football manager, or dreamed about running a big company, I'd take a very careful look at the composition of the ownership before accepting any job. The former chairman of Birmingham City, Carson Yeung, is – as I write – in jail. Former Manchester City owner Thaksin Shinawatra is in self-imposed exile and cannot return to Thailand. There are plenty of inept British owners too. It does not matter where they come from, these people breeze into football. If they buy a club at the bottom of the Premier League, they are all anxious to get a slice of the revenue from European football that accrues to the top sides; if they go fishing for a club in the lower divisions, they all dream of promotion to the Premier League.

Even the dimmest owner knows that if there is a dispute between an individual player and a manager, it is crazy for them to back the player. As soon as they do that, they have let anarchists into the club. Every now and again there will be an example of a manager who antagonises his entire squad, but that's very different. It has been reported that Paolo Di Canio got sacked by Sunderland in 2013 after a group of players marched into the chief executives' office, but there are not many examples like that. I always knew that, even if a player was stirred into a frenzy of self-pity by his agent, the owners would never side with him.

Most former players who decide they want to become managers are like I was when I joined East Stirlingshire. They are too desperate and willing to jump at any offer. They cannot stand waiting at home hoping that the phone will ring, and a period of unemployment can cause anyone to doubt themselves. But managers are invariably too anxious, getting themselves into a position where, on the day they sign their new contract, they are simultaneously signing their own death certificate. The turnover is preposterous. A housefly has a longer life expectancy than the manager of a Premier League team.

Despite this overwhelming evidence, eagerness and ambition often seem to triumph over cold facts. A couple of years ago Ole Gunnar Solskjaer, who was a great striker for United, and scored the winning goal in the 1999 Champions League final against Bayern Munich, was negotiating to become the manager of Cardiff City. After he had retired as a player, Ole had managed United's reserves and then returned to his native Norway to manage Molde, which he did most successfully. After a few seasons in Norway, Ole was pining to manage a Premier League club, and I read in the papers that he was in the finishing stages of discussions with Vincent Tan, the owner of Cardiff City, who had just fired Malky Mackay. I thought to myself, 'Surely he's not thinking about taking that job – it's bound to be a nightmare.' So I texted Ole and gave him some very firm advice. I told him, 'Tomorrow is the strongest you will ever be with the owner. So get everything, down to the smallest detail that could interfere with your management style, written into your contract.' Nine months later, the inevitable occurred and Tan decided that he would pick a new manager. The good news for Ole was that he had a watertight contract and his talent is bound to be recognised by a more appreciative owner.

Then there are victims of misfortune who suddenly find themselves reporting to new owners. That happened to Sam Allardyce at Blackburn Rovers after it was bought by the Rao family, owners of the V. H. Group, a company that operates chicken-processing farms in India. A few weeks after they bought the club, the new owners fired Allardyce, who had managed the club for two years. Even though he was forced to manage on a shoestring, Sam had always ensured Blackburn placed respectably in the Premier League. The Raos had brought in an agent, Jerome Anderson, as a consultant, fired Allardyce, and replaced him with his deputy, Steve Kean. Then, just to demonstrate their complete lack of understanding of football management, the Raos insisted that Kean, towards the end of his time at the club, had to fly out to board meetings in India. They fired Kean two years later and replaced him with a former United player, Henning Berg, who had called me after he had been offered the job. I warned him about the owners, but he was eager to get into the game after being fired by the Norwegian club, Lillestrøm. Fifty-seven days later, they fired him too, and were forced by the courts to pay him £2.2 million to buy out his contract.

There are also too many cases of managers who have contributed sterling service receiving terrible treatment from the owners they have served. Jock Stein served Celtic for 13 years and won 25 trophies for the club before retiring in 1978. It's hard to imagine a better leader than Jock. He didn't drink or smoke, never took any credit for himself and diverted all praise towards his players. After all this, the directors refused to offer him a board seat. Instead, they told him he could work in the Celtic shop. They did the same to his assistant, Sean Fallon, who had spent 28 years with the club. It was a shocking way to treat people who had given their all.

Every now and again I had assistant coaches who wanted to leave United because they knew I wasn't going anywhere – and I always told them to be very careful about where they chose to go. Steve McClaren had replaced Brian Kidd as my assistant at United but, after three years, was chomping at the bit and wanted to leave to manage a club. He had offers from West Ham and Southampton, but elected to go to Middlesbrough because of the reputation of the owner, Steve Gibson. He was young and prepared to invest in the club. Middlesbrough had a fantastic training ground and it all worked out well for McClaren. He picked the employer that was right for him. Steve's decision showed the value of taking time to assess the situation. He did his homework, he spent time assessing the club and, most importantly, he made a judgement about whether he would get the support he desired from the owner. It shows the value of taking sufficient time to make an important decision, rather than quickly hopping on to whatever lily pad happens to float by.

## Control

The popular caricature of me is an authoritative tyrant with a lust for power. Not surprisingly, I beg to differ. I'll plead guilty to having a thirst for winning and being fixated on maintaining complete control but – in my book – those are requisites for effective leadership. The skipper of any ship incapable of controlling its course, or altering its speed, is not going to arrive safely in port. The same goes for a football club. A leader who seeks control is very different from one who craves power.

There's a big difference between control and power. The leader of any group usually has considerable power, but it's something that can be easily abused. One of the side-effects of the abuse of power is when someone leads by fear of intimidation. As time went by I learned to control my temper. Some of this was just the passage of the years but, more importantly, I realised that a display of temper is more effective if used sparingly. I just don't believe that you can get the most out of people if they are perpetually afraid of you.

There's nothing wrong with losing your temper for the right reasons but, if you explode at the slightest provocation, it can paralyse an organisation. When I lost my temper, the thunder-clouds would tend to blow over in a day or so. There were some players who wouldn't buckle when I delivered my so-called 'hairdryer treatments', but I'm sure there were plenty of others, particularly the younger ones, who quaked in their boots. Sometimes I didn't realise the effect that a few words from me might have on a player. People used to say that some players would be terrified if I so much as raised an eyebrow or just happened to look at them. I'm sure most leaders are not aware that they scare other people, especially if they rarely raise their voice or have never smashed a teacup on the floor. They probably think of themselves as reasonable and compassionate. Yet anyone who can raise a salary, or fire someone, is almost bound to be seen as intimidating or terrifying – or both. I'll also say, in my defence, that the press sometimes made it appear as if I was in a perpetual bad temper. If you look at all my teams it was evident that they enjoyed playing and they tended to express themselves in an uninhibited fashion. People do not do that if they are quaking in their boots or if their boss has made them afraid of their own shadows. If that had been the case at United, people would have seen a team that concentrated on avoiding defeat rather than winning.

I always thought of myself as tough but fair and found it hard to understand how anyone could view me as a monster but, as the years went by and United became ever more successful, I did gradually come to understood that a wink, a nod or a frown could play havoc with the confidence of a few of the players. In team talks I'd be careful not to single out any of the young players who were new to the squad, and would concentrate on the ones who could look me in the eye. When I knew for certain that a word from me, no matter how carefully phrased, would cause a player to have a sleepless night, I usually got somebody else like Mick Phelan, who eventually became United's assistant manager, to convey the message. Harsh outbursts and temper tantrums can, when used sparingly, have an effect, but it's a negative and corrosive way to run anything. It's far better to give people a belief in themselves, and faith in the direction of their organisation, than to rule like Attila the Hun.

At the same time I was always very careful that my control was not usurped. That explains why I sold players who tried to undermine my control. I hesitate to say this, because it will get wrongly interpreted as callousness, but everyone is disposable. Somebody once said, 'Graveyards are full of indispensable men,' and it's a phrase worth dwelling on.

The truth is, I just could not afford to have our club revolve around either the outlook or health of one or two people. It is just too risky. Let's assume for a moment that I had never had any management issues with a player and they were not causing me the slightest bother. Imagine instead they had sustained a terrible injury, which either sidelined them for a long time or ended their playing career. In that situation I would also have had to figure out a way to prosper without them. Fortunately, in all my time at United, I only had a handful of major issues with players. When we honoured our promise to Cristiano Ronaldo that he could fulfil his lifelong desire to play for Real Madrid, I had to deal with the issue of the loss of the best player in the world, and I had to rebuild and look to a future without him. I hated losing him, and I knew his absence would be noticeable and might make our strike force seem a little gap-toothed for a while, but I also knew that if I made the right decisions then the club would continue to flourish.

It's easy to think that control begins and ends with the person running the organisation. It doesn't. People sometimes talk about me as if I was a control freak, but I don't think of myself that way. It would be impossible to run an organisation like that. I certainly wanted to be in touch and know everything that was going on at the club and that affected my job, such as the observations from training sessions or reserve games, updates from the medical staff, news from the scouting side, the weather forecast for the next game and the condition of the pitch. But I couldn't run everything. I did not need to know what brand of detergent was used in the laundry or the style of font we used in the match-day programmes. Other people had to do that. I was the puppet master, not the control freak.

## Delegation

Control and delegation are two sides of the same coin, and in my younger years my instinct was to try and control everything. I must have automatically assumed that if I did something myself it was the quickest and best way to get anything done.

Nobody had ever explained to me that working with, and through, others is by far the most effective way to do things – assuming, of course, that they understand what you want and are keen to follow. I gradually began to understand that this is the difference between management and leadership.

I never had any formal schooling to be a leader. Obviously, I'd paid attention to the way that managers acted during my days as a player but, in any football organisation, there aren't the decades-long programmes designed to produce a CEO like those at big companies such as General Electric or Goldman Sachs. No club is ever going to send an aspiring manager to an Executive MBA Program at Harvard or another business school. So I had to learn on the job and use my wits. I'd never managed a team of people, I didn't understand how working through other people allowed you to do more and amplified your reach.

The world is full of able managers. In life beyond football, corporate training schemes are designed to churn out managers by the thousand. At United we had plenty of people who could manage aspects of our activities far better than I could. The head groundsman knew far more about the technology of soil management and irrigation than I did. The doctors managed a realm whose subtleties I could not pretend to understand. The head of our youth academy knew far more than I about the abilities of each of the lads in the programme. I slowly came to understand that my job was different. It was to set very high standards. It was to help everyone else believe they could do things that they didn't think they were capable of. It was to chart a course that had not been pursued before. It was to make everyone understand that the impossible was possible. That's the difference between leadership and management.

When I started managing, my own naïveté was, to some

extent, exacerbated by the lack of resources at East Stirlingshire and St Mirren, the two Scottish clubs where I cut my teeth. There just wasn't a lot of money available to hire people. So I tried to do everything by myself. I thought I could rule the world. I was ordering the cleaning materials and grass feed, making sure we had the right quantity of pies for the games and fussing over the contents of the match-day programmes. I banned the long-time supporters from coming into the tea room to get free pies and Bovril and there was a real uproar about that. I was just acting on my instincts and what I thought was the right thing to do because I didn't know any better.

As I explained earlier, Archie Knox, my assistant manager at both Aberdeen and United, was the man who educated me about the benefits of delegation. When you're a manager, it's vital to care about the details but it's equally important to understand that there isn't enough time in the day to check on everything. Some managers are fanatics. When Johan Cruyff was managing Barcelona he'd be on the pitch the day before the game with a device to measure the moisture levels. He even insisted that the turf be clipped to a particular height. Later in my career – even when I had become much better at delegating – I would sometimes spot a detail like that. One of the things to which I always paid attention was the width of a pitch. Opponents knew that I liked wide pitches where we could outrun and outpace the competition. Once, when we were playing Manchester City at their former ground at Maine Road, I went to inspect the pitch early one morning and found the groundsman, under orders from management, was narrowing it, which is not something you are allowed to do after you have registered the dimensions with the Premier League at the start of the season. So I complained to the referee, got them to widen the pitch and we thrashed City 3–0.

These are exceptional examples. On the whole it is better to explain to the people around you that you care about little details, but that it's their job to attend to them.

When I hired someone to do something I trusted them to do it. I depended on them to get on with their job and come to me with any problems. At United that might have been the coaches or the scouts, but it was particularly true for the medical staff, sports scientists and video analysis crew. They all had the necessary training and technical background that was beyond me. I am not a doctor, dietician or computer whiz so, while it was up to me to make sure that we hired very capable people to run each of these departments, they had forgotten more about their specialties than I was ever going to know. If the doctor said that a player was not fit to take the field, I would not exert any pressure on them to change their opinion. A good number of the people in these departments started on the bottom rung of their respective ladders, but were promoted as they demonstrated their capabilities. Steve Brown was a young lad who started on a trial basis as a video analyst. He gradually progressed, flourished as he was given more responsibility, got successive pay raises and has become an essential part of that team.

As the business of football has grown, so too have the organisations. This has underlined the need for a football manager to delegate more widely and empower those around him. Nowadays all the big clubs have chief executive officers responsible for all commercial activities and making sure the books are in balance – or, for many clubs, not too far out of control. So I let David Gill worry about television contracts, securing sponsorships, finalising the niceties of player contracts, managing the finance and marketing organisations, dealing with auditors and lawyers, ensuring compliance with health and safety codes and all the laws and regulations that govern any organisation, let alone a place where 75,000 people congregate on a regular basis. I had quite enough on my hands managing the football side of the business.

There's one final example of the power of delegation that I always carried with me from early in my career. In 1972 I went down to Derby to watch a huge end of season game – Liverpool versus Derby County. Jock Stein had set me up with the tickets and Bill Shankly, the Liverpool manager, very kindly gave us a tour of the Derby boardroom. It was about 7.25 p.m. and it was a 7.30 kick-off and I asked Bill whether he should be with his players. He said, 'Son, if I've got to be with my players for the deciding game of the season, there's something wrong with them.'

When we walked into the tunnel all the players were lined up and one, Tommy Smith, the captain, was bouncing a ball on his head. Shankly said, 'Tommy, take them home, son. You know what to do.' That one sentence said everything about Shankly's style of leadership.

## Decision-making

Effective delegation depends on the ability of others to make decisions. Some people can make decisions, others cannot. It just doesn't work if you are congenitally hesitant and allow things to linger in a state of suspension. When I was a player I had a couple of managers who always changed their mind. Bobby Brown at St Johnstone would pin a team-sheet on the board and, if somebody complained about the line-up, half an hour later a different team would replace it.

Men like Bobby Brown perhaps lacked the confidence

required to stick to decisions. Others are in a perpetual quest for the last possible morsel of information, using that as an excuse not to make a decision. When you are in the football world, and I suspect in almost every other setting, you have to make decisions with the information at your disposal, rather than what you wish you might have. I never had a problem reaching a decision based on imperfect information. That's just the way the world works.

During my time at United I got rid of several people who could not make decisions. I could never deal with people who were wishy-washy or whose judgement rested on the opinion of the last person they had talked to. They just made my life harder. When I arrived in Manchester in 1986, the chief scout was Tony Collins, who had previously occupied the same position during Don Revie's successful time as manager of Leeds United. Tony was a nice man but he just couldn't give me an opinion about a player. He always used to say, 'Go see him yourself,' or 'You go and watch him.' I replaced him the next summer with Les Kershaw, one of my best ever signings.

Some characters are more suited to being second in command rather than the leader. That isn't a criticism, although it may be interpreted in that manner. I would have been a terrible number two because there is a part of my personality that needs to be the leader. It takes considerable skill to be content as a second fiddle because, even though you may work just as hard as the leader, you will never receive the same praise or financial rewards. Brian Kidd was my assistant manager for seven years, and excelled in that role. He then tried his hand as a manager, which was a taxing experience for him, and has flourished, particularly at Manchester City, as the essential assistant manager.

There is also the question of when you should make a

decision. There are probably only two times to do so – too early and too late. If I was going to err on making one of those mistakes, I far preferred to make the decision earlier rather than later. That's much easier to say than to do. After all, it wasn't until I was approaching 50, in 1990, that I fully appreciated this. I was in my fourth season at United when I finally ripped up the team – something, in retrospect, I should have done several seasons earlier.

If people wobble when making decisions about others, they can be even worse when it comes to making decisions about themselves, because these so often involve emotion and cloudy judgement. In football guys are forever taking jobs that are losing propositions. When Carlos Queiroz left United the second time in 2008 to manage Portugal, I told him he was crazy. I said, 'You're going to be judged on just two things – whether you can win the World Cup or European Championship, and tell me again: when did Portugal win the World Cup?' But Carlos's heart was set on managing his country and so he did so. It was a bad decision and turned into a disaster for him. If he had not returned to his homeland he could well have succeeded me as United's manager.

When I was young I made many more impulsive decisions than in my later years.

At St Mirren I remember taking off Billy Stark, a midfielder, after about seven minutes of play. It was a daft move. Unless he has been booked, injured and about to be arrested for burglary, it is silly to remove a player after less than 10 per cent of a game has been played, given that you obviously thought he was good enough to start a few minutes earlier. It turned out that in that game I badly needed Billy. Decades later, when United trailed West Ham 2–0, I was, as I mentioned previously, much more careful. I had started the game with Patrice Evra at left-back, but he had been on international duty and it showed. I waited until half-time, took off Evra, moved Giggs to left-back and we fought back to win the game 4–2.

I also made some ill-considered decisions when we bought and sold players that I came to regret. As I explained earlier, in 2001 we sold the Dutch defender Jaap Stam to Lazio for several million more than we had paid for him in 1998. Stam was 29 at the time, had just returned from injury and we were being offered a fat packet for him. So I sold him in a blink. Six years later he was still playing for Ajax with a Champions League final appearance for AC Milan along the way. In 2010 we bought the Portuguese winger, Bébé, even though we had not done our normal level of homework. Bébé struggled at United, never became part of the furniture and, after putting him out on loan several times, we eventually sold him.

There were some occasions where hesitancy cost me. After we signed Carlos Tévez, the Argentinian striker, from West Ham on a loan deal in 2007, we started to think about putting him on a long-term contract. Unfortunately, Tévez did not control his own destiny, because his rights – under the perverse system of third-party ownership – were controlled by third parties. This complicated any negotiations, but the real reason he eluded our grasp was because I was unsure whether I wanted him. Before Christmas 2008 we could probably have bought him for around £25.5 million, but I wanted to see how he fared in some more games. By the time I had decided, it was too late, because Manchester City had arrived with an offer for what was said to be £47 million.

I tried not to waste too much energy thinking about why, or how, other managers made decisions. There just was not enough time in the day, and it is hard to second-guess somebody's decision if you haven't been privy to their debates or are unfamiliar with the nuances of their situation. I experienced this myself throughout my career. For example, when I sold Ince, Hughes and Kanchelskis in 1995 I received a lot of criticism from people who were unaware that a hugely talented group of young players were about to emerge. Every now and again I would be perplexed if a top-tier club signed a player we had rejected and, sometimes, while privately cursing, I would admire a smart decision made by a fellow manager, especially if he had beaten us to the punch. Either way, nothing beats the lessons on decision-making imparted by the accounts of the way in which JFK handled the decisions surrounding the Cuban Missile Crisis – his calmness, his refusal to bow to pressure (whether from within or without), his willingness to contend with imperfect information while being under enormous pressure and relentless press coverage – puts everything else in perspective. Making decisions that send 75,000 people home happy at the end of a Saturday afternoon is one thing. Saving hundreds of millions from a nuclear war is another.

# 10

## THE BOTTOM LINE

# Buying

A big part of running a successful organisation is being able to convince people to join you, even if they can earn more money elsewhere. That challenge is accentuated in the Premier League because, unlike in other sports such as American football, there is no limit to the salary a club can award a player. This makes it really important for a manager and the scouting organisation to be able to sell the virtues of his club. Even at a club like Manchester United, where eventually we had access to huge transfer sums, we never wanted to get into the position where the size of our chequebook was the only route to success. It is just too risky, since there is always someone who appears with a larger pot of money.

People don't think of a football manager as a salesman. But he is. When we were trying to sign Paul Gascoigne in the summer of 1988, I pitched for my life. I went down to London and met him at his lawyer's house and argued that if he chose to go elsewhere he would be thinking in 20 years that he had made a huge mistake. Since Paul was from Newcastle, I also played up the fact that United teemed with Geordies such as

251

Bobby Charlton, Steve Bruce and Bryan Robson. I thought these appeals had worked, and then was floored to learn that he had chosen to go to Tottenham after the club bought his mother a house in Gateshead. But Gascoigne was an exception; we usually landed the players we really wanted.

Any leader is a salesman – and he has to sell to the inside of his organisation and to the outside. Anyone who aspires to be a great leader needs to excel at selling his ideas and aspirations to others. Sometimes you have to persuade people to do things they don't want to do, or to sell them on the idea that they can achieve something they had not dreamed about. Usually, this is to people who are already on the payroll. But then there is the challenge of reaching out to people who are not part of the system. In United's case, this meant three main constituencies: potential fans, possible sponsors and potential players – especially youngsters. The commercial side of United took care of the first two, while I was responsible for the third. This meant that part of my job was acting like a sales manager in a company.

Football's version of a field sales team is its scouting system. I built two of these organisations – one at Aberdeen and one at Manchester United. We incentivised the scouts like salesmen: they had a small base stipend and various bonuses if a player they spotted progressed through our system. We gave them specific territories and school teams to cover, and they understood what I was looking for in young players. Like a sales manager, I wanted to approve the terms of each 'sale', because I didn't want them signing players willy-nilly, lest I wound up with six goalkeepers, seven centre-backs and four left-wingers. The first week I was at United, I called a meeting with all the scouts and said, 'I'm not interested in the best boy in your street. I want to know about the best boy in your area. That's who I want.'

Like all sales organisations, our scouting system had people who were better than others. It requires real talent to see something that is unpolished and imagine it as a shiny gem that fits within a tiara. The star scout at Manchester United was Bob Bishop, who was responsible for covering Belfast. He was like a pied piper. He was the scout best known for spotting and signing George Best, but he spotted a raft of good players.

When I was young I picked up some selling tricks from watching other scouts. Bobby Calder was a scout from Aberdeen who I first met when he tried to sign my brother, Martin. He came to our house and brought my mother a box of chocolates, my father a carton of cigarettes and gave me a ten-bob note. Bobby wore a wee pork-pie hat and used to sit like a little, gentle angel. Later, when I was managing Aberdeen, he and I went to try and sign John Hewitt, a boy at a local school whom Manchester United, Celtic and Rangers all wanted to sign. We met with his parents and I went into a big sales pitch about what I was trying to do for Aberdeen and how it was going to be a big club. As we were leaving, Bobby said to the player's mother, 'Mrs Hewitt, I'll come up tomorrow and tell you the true story about the silver city by the sea.' I was furious with him. I thought he was going to screw up our chances. But he was right, and he taught me a very valuable sales lesson. He taught me to identify the decision-makers who influence any sale. In the case of young players, it isn't the player. It also isn't the father because, generally, he only wants to live vicariously through his son. The decision-maker is the mother. The mother wants to know what's going to be best for her son. After that experience, I always told scouts to concentrate on the mothers.

Our pursuit of David Beckham might have demanded a bit more effort than our quest for other youngsters, but, on the whole, it was fairly characteristic. Malcolm Fidgeon, who scouted for us in London, spotted him when he was 12 years old. It helped that David's father had been a diehard United fan and that David had inherited this zeal. But it was also obvious that other clubs would be pursuing him, particularly Tottenham. So we kept very close tabs on him. I got to know David's parents and siblings, partly because it pays to understand someone's background, but also as a way to ensure that they felt we cared about their son. We invited David to Manchester, he attended summer training sessions and we would send him United kit; we invited him into the first-team dressing room when we were playing in London. It made him, and his entire family, feel that we cared – and we did.

If you work for any successful organisation, it's easy to get sloppy and complacent with sales. When I got to United they took it for granted that any young boy in Manchester would migrate towards them, but instead they were going to Manchester City. Even Ryan Giggs was training at Manchester City. You cannot expect to triumph if you expect the world's most gifted to be standing outside your door with a job application form in their hand. The world doesn't work like that. You have to go and hunt for talent. At times, while our scouts would be scouring fields on weekends looking for the most talented young players, I would try to make the first overture to a player, or to his agent, who was part of another club, because the player obviously wants to measure the enthusiasm of his potential manager. When it came time to hammer out terms, I would turn things over to David Gill. This worked well for everyone because it kept me away from some of the tougher conversations that could potentially taint a relationship with a player.

# Frugality

Throwing money at a problem has never produced a solution for me. From time to time it might provide a short-term fix – such as the excitement brought by Robin van Persie in 2012 when he was added to our striking line-up, but I cannot think of a single example in football where an open chequebook turned a club into a long-term winner. We also added a lot of fizz to the club with the arrival of Eric Cantona in 1992 – but he only cost us £900,000. Money doesn't suddenly create a club with breadth and depth; it doesn't provide a lineage and history; it doesn't fill stadiums with fans prepared to endure icy rain, and it doesn't make young boys dream.

While I enjoy a flutter on the horses, I have always had an aversion to wasting money. It drove me mad when players got into the habit of regularly exchanging their shirts with opponents or sending them to relatives and friends. Each of those shirts was expensive, and the club had to pay for new ones after exhausting the stock supplied by the sponsor. About six years before I retired, Albert Morgan, our kit man, told me we were going through several hundred strips a season. Most of these shirts wound up in the hands of souvenir traders or, these days, on eBay. I told the players they could keep swapping shirts but that they would have to pay for them out of their own pocket.

The sceptics might point at some of my signings and say that I squandered money. The examples usually trotted out are Dimitar Berbatov, whom we bought for £30.75 million from Tottenham, of which we recouped only about 10 per cent when he was sold to Fulham; Juan Sebastián Verón, bought for £24 million, went for £15 million, and poor Louis Saha, a striker dogged by injuries, was sold for virtually nothing even though we had bought him for £12.4 million. However, if you take a closer look at all of my signings – over many years – the money was well spent. Even the very worst are not in the same postal code as some of the biggest blunders in the Premier League, such as the £50 million that Chelsea impulsively paid for Fernando Torres in 2011, which turned into a handful of dust when they traded him in 2015 to Atlético Madrid.

Some of my churlishness about spending comes from my upbringing. My parents made sure that my brother and I never wanted for anything, but there wasn't a lot of spare money sloshing about our tenement flat in Govan. The same was true when I became a player and a manager. Put it down to my Scottish roots, but I always tried to treat club money as if it were my own.

My first salary as a footballer came at Dunfermline in 1964, as my first club Queen's Park had an amateur status, so there were no wages. During my time at Dunfermline, I was on £28 a week (about £524 in today's money), but because I quit my job as a tool-maker, my guaranteed weekly income dropped from £41, because I lost my £13 a week tool-maker's pay packet, so it was very important to me to get bonus money for wins. When I went to Rangers I was paid £60 (£998) in the summer and £80 (£1,331) during the playing season. When I joined St Mirren as its manager, our first home game was against Hamilton, and we played in front of a crowd of 3,000 in a ground that could house 25,000. Everything about the club was run down. The players, who were part-time, were paid £12 a week during the season and £7 during the summer while the club was in the Scottish second division.

At Aberdeen, the owner, Dick Donald, would keep a close eye on all outlays. He wanted to own a successful club, but was happy with a successful small club, and was always insistent that Aberdeen should operate in the black. He had no tolerance for red ink. He always wore the same tie and he also refused to buy new shoelaces. When one got frayed and snapped he'd just knot it back together. When Aberdeen reached the Scottish League Cup final in 1984, I realised that nobody had ordered any champagne, and so I phoned the club secretary, Ian Taggart, to make sure we took eight cases on the bus (most clubs would order about 20). Taggart panicked and said, 'I can't. Mr Donald will go off his head.' Donald saw the cases and Taggart had to tell him that only two were going on the bus while the rest were going into stores. We ended up hiding the extra champagne in the bus toilet and, on the journey home, after the Cup had been won and the champagne was flowing, Dick turned to me and said: 'Mr Ferguson, how many cups did we win today?'

If I wanted to buy a new left-winger, he'd say, 'Don't we have another left-winger?' And I'd answer, 'Yes, but he's only sixteen and he's barely good enough to play in the reserve team.' He'd always be grumbling about the wages and bonuses I'd award the players and he'd ask, 'Why do you keep giving them raises?' And I'd answer, 'Mr Chairman, we're in the world of football. You don't go down the way, you go up the way, and the only way you're going to keep your best players is by giving them big bonuses when they win things.' Dick was afraid of complacency creeping in and, before the one final, he said, only half-jokingly, 'It wouldn't be a bad idea if we lost this game so the players don't get too big for their boots.' He used to say, 'I never want to see the colour red in this football club's finances.' The most I spent at Aberdeen was £300,000 in 1985 for Jim Bett, and we used the sale of a player to defray part of that cost.

Oddly enough my frugality was part of the reason I got offered the United job. In one of my first sessions with Martin

Edwards, when we were discussing the importance of developing our own pipeline of talented youngsters, I said to him, 'I've never been a buying manager.' He said, 'That's one of the things we thought about when we decided to go for you.' I cannot believe it's attractive to any employer to think he is hiring a big spender.

When I wanted to buy my first player at United, I could only get about £1 million from Martin. All the money had to come from the sale of season tickets or game tickets, or from the transfer of other players. There was no sugar daddy with more money than sense, ploughing money into the club. The very first player I bought was Viv Anderson – a defender. We bought him for £250,000 and then we bought Brian McClair for £850,000. After we did a fire sale of six players – including Jesper Olsen, Gordon Strachan and Paul McGrath – in 1989 I spent about £8 million on five players – the most expensive of whom was the defender, Gary Pallister.

It took about £60 million to build the squad that took United through the 1990s and culminated in our Treble – the League championship, the FA Cup and the Champions League – in 1999. It took just over £320 million in transfer fees to furnish us with the firepower required to compete at the highest of levels for the following decade – but those are only the outlays and do not take into account that over £256 million was received from the sale of players. My largest signing between the time I joined United in 1986 and 2008 was the £29 million we paid for Rio Ferdinand, then aged 23, when we bought him from Leeds United in 2002. Rio then played 12 seasons and 455 games for United and 54 games for England (during his time at United), before moving to Queens Park Rangers a year after I retired. Even though Rio's price was out of the ordinary, it was very good value. Amortised over the time that he was at United, Rio's transfer fee cost the club about £2.5 million per year. But it is also worth bearing in mind his cost was largely offset by the £25 million we received from Real Madrid in 2003 when we sold David Beckham, who had cost us nothing.

Beyond Rio, we built our defence on virtually nothing – £5.5 million for Patrice Evra and £7.5 million for Nemanja Vidić, both of whom we signed in 2006. We signed Rafael da Silva and his brother, Fábio, in 2008, before either of them had turned professional. We solved the goalkeeping problems that had plagued me for six years following the departure of Peter Schmeichel, with the signing of Edwin van der Sar from Fulham in 2005. Van der Sar was 34 years old when we signed him for £2 million. Compare that to the sum spent by Chelsea in the same period. Between the time we signed them and my retirement, Evra, Vidić, the Da Silvas and Van der Sar played a total of 1,049 games for United.

When I was thinking about buying a player, I'd always be assessing his speed, balance and technique. But I also always wanted to know about his reliability. It's one thing to buy a player who is available for selection every week. It's quite another to fork out a king's ransom for someone who is injured every third game. There's no point in buying that player.

Our emphasis on youth produced two things: the pipeline of talent for the first team, and a very healthy sideline business. In my time as United's manager we raised well over £100 million from the sale of players, spotted as youngsters and developed through our youth system. This includes not only the likes of Beckham and Butt but also Gérard Piqué and Giuseppe Rossi who were brought into our academy from overseas. We had spotted them, developed them, and wanted to be paid for our efforts, particularly since most were capable of playing very high quality football for ten to 15 years. Fraizer Campbell, Robbie Brady, Ryan Shawcross, Danny Higginbotham, David Healy and John Curtis are just a few examples of the youngsters who left United to go and play elsewhere. If a lad looked promising at one of our Schools of Excellence, it created little financial risk for us if we signed him. We signed Keith Gillespie as a 16 year old and he played a handful of games at United before we received £1 million for him as part of the deal that brought Andy Cole to Old Trafford. The biggest risk was that we had erred in our assessment of a particular boy and could have used his slot to work with a more talented youngster. We had to wait a little longer to see the real potential in some boys, because not everyone's physique develops at the same rate. If we elected to sell them, we were hard-nosed about negotiations.

If these boys progressed through various levels and eventually got into the youth team or, better still, the reserve team, we had a variety of options. The best players, like Danny Welbeck and Adnan Januzaj, had the talent to make the leap from the youth team to the first-team squad, but the jury usually remained out on the rest of them. It takes until the age of 20 or 21 before you know for certain whether some players will make the grade. If we were still uncertain, we put them out on loan to another club so that they could get blooded in a first team. We did that with Tom Cleverley, lending him to Watford, Wigan, and Leicester City. We lent Jonny Evans to Royal Antwerp and Sunderland twice and Welbeck to Preston and Sunderland. Sometimes it didn't produce the results we hoped for, such as when we lent Giuseppe Rossi to Newcastle and Parma or Federico Macheda to Sampdoria and Queens Park Rangers. They played so few games, their development was halted.

On occasion we might have waited too long before we sold a player who was not going to make the grade yet, or whose value tumbled due to injury. There were only a couple, such as James Chester, on whom we might have lost money. James had a number of knee injuries over a long period, and we ended up selling him to Hull City for £300,000 in 2011. He went on to play over 170 games in the next four and a half seasons and turned out to be an absolute steal.

We were always on the lookout for bargains but, in football, as in life, you get what you pay for. Unless there is an element of luck as there was with Eric Cantona, who we signed after Leeds United had approached us to buy Denis Irwin. The same was true of Peter Schmeichel who was somehow still playing for Brøndby at 28. I still can't believe a big club hadn't bought him. In 2008, a friend of Carlos Queiroz was scouting for us (for free) in Angola and happened upon Manucho. We gave him a try-out and he had a good left foot. We signed him for £250,000, because it was such a small sum, and when it became clear he did not possess the necessary talent, we sold him to Real Valladolid for £2.5 million.

Some clubs – Real Madrid and Manchester City come to mind – have used the chequebook to build a winning team. Real Madrid have long paid big sums to buy wonderfully talented players, the 'Galacticos', at the peak of their careers – Zinedine Zidane, Luís Figo, Kaká, Cristiano Ronaldo, Gareth Bale and James Rodríguez. It has worked for them, which just shows that there is more than one way to go about things. However, my upbringing always inclined me towards building rather than buying. I suppose I was more of what my son Mark, in his line of work, would call a 'value investor'.

I always liked the idea of signing talented players who were in the twilight of their careers. We didn't expect to keep them on the books for a long time, but we knew that, from time to time, we could land a player for a negligible amount of money who could help us fill a need. We signed Laurent Blanc from Inter Milan in 2001 as a free transfer. Blanc was 35 years old, but he was an accomplished and experienced player and we needed a backup in the defensive part of the squad. We used a similar tactic when we signed Michael Owen, the former England striker, in 2009, to add occasional spark to our attack. He had trained as a boy in the United system and was available on a free transfer. So I invited him to my house, made a proposal where he would be paid on a performance basis, and he was over the moon. Even though he was dogged by injuries, it worked out well for Michael because he scored the equalising goal during the first time he appeared at Wembley as a player in a Cup final, when we beat Aston Villa for the League Cup in 2010, and the following year he got a Premier League title medal, his first in 13 years of playing in the top ranks.

We made one exception to our rule about keeping an eye on the bottom line, and that was when it came time to sell players who had done sterling duty for the club. They might have played for ten or more years and reached the point where they were getting injured, unable to maintain a regular place in the first team and could count the seasons that they might still hope to play football on the fingers of one hand. In these cases we leaned over backwards to try and help them on their way by either offering free transfers (so that the acquiring club could justify giving them a larger wage packet), or a testimonial game, or both. The only one that did really well after he left us was Phil Neville, whom we sold to Everton for just over £3 million. In retrospect it was a great deal for Everton because we could clearly have got more for Phil; we also did not antici-pate that he would continue to play for another eight years. Players like Denis Irwin, Steve Bruce, Mick Phelan and Brian McClair were all given free transfers. When Peter Schmeichel wanted to quit we allowed him to go on a free transfer with the one condition that he should not play for an English club. He went off to Sporting Lisbon, but within a couple of years he returned to England to play for Aston Villa and then went to Manchester City. We did not question either move, although we would have been perfectly within our rights to do so. Treating players like this was just the right thing to do.

## Compensation

I'm sure nobody thinks of football managers as pricing experts. Pricing is usually considered the realm of brand managers, who decide how much a tube of toothpaste or bottle of vodka should sell for. It's true that, unless I got complaints from fans, I didn't worry about the price of season tickets or merchandise, but I did spend a lot of time dealing with the pricing of players – how much we would be prepared to buy them for and what salaries we'd be prepared to offer.

When you see the large sums paid for players headlined in the newspapers, it's tempting to assume that football clubs spend money willy-nilly. That's only true for a handful – those controlled by owners or ownership groups for whom money is no object. In Europe, that list has been limited to Chelsea, Manchester City and Paris Saint-Germain (PSG). For almost every other club, even in the top leagues, money and budgets matter, and for clubs like Peterborough United, a League One club in the east of England who were managed by my son, Darren, every penny counts. I just don't think you can buy success. You have to earn it.

There's never been as much money in Scottish football as in English; early on in my career I got used to making the most from a little. I happen to think that's a useful discipline for any business or organisation, because it's so easy to waste money. Also, I have always had to answer to owners who wanted to know how their money was going to be spent.

At Aberdeen, I had a cavalcade of players, starting with the captain, Willie Miller, coming into my office demanding pay hikes. The best wages were between £250–£300 a week and Miller wanted £350. Dick Donald, the chairman, wanted to sell him, but I persuaded him that this would only start an exodus. Then his team-mate Alex McLeish showed up with his wife and eventually I got him to accept a £50 rise. Finally, Doug Rougvie appeared, and I told him, 'Doug, I've got this big cake and there's a cherry on the top. Willie Miller is taking three-quarters of it and the cherry. I have a quarter of the cake left for everyone; what do you want me to do?' He was dissatisfied with our offer so we let him go to Chelsea.

As the decades ticked by, pay became more of a topic in football – at least for the press, in the main because of the huge escalation in the gap between an ordinary worker's weekly 'wages' and the salaries amounting to tens of thousands of pounds per week that were now being paid out to top football players.

'Wages', or a 'pay packet' was what we usually called our compensation when I started as a player. This term was not a coincidence because, at the time, almost every player came from a working-class background. The father of Stanley Matthews, then the best-known player in England, was a boxer. Bobby Charlton comes from Ashington, a mining town in the north of England. When I signed for St Johnstone, the fathers of the other players all had working-class jobs. In Britain, football was the sport adopted by the working class, played by young men from working-class families, and this was reflected in the employment terms. If I had not been a footballer, I would probably have been a tool-maker and my team-mates would have worked in the nearby shipyards, steel mills or car factories.

There were more than a few vestiges of *Upstairs, Downstairs* in the way that players were paid. Until 1961, the Football League had put a maximum limit on a player's weekly wage which, at the time, during the playing season, was £20. Understandably the players, who were little more than indentured servants, felt abused and underpaid. There were no negotiations over pay. You took what the manager offered and, frequently, this meant one rate that applied during the season and another – either a lower rate, or no pay whatsoever – during the summer. Any player who took issue with his wages was likely to be sidelined. It was one thing to stage a strike at a factory when the machines would be sitting there on your return, it was quite another to miss a game that would never be played again. Even after the rules, on both wages and the freedom of transfer between clubs, were loosened at the start of the 1960s, some clubs, including Manchester United, tried to enforce an unofficial lid on wages. Eventually, though, market forces prevailed.

I don't mean to suggest that players were indifferent about their pay, or that it was entirely uniform, but in an era that did not include lawyers, agents, accountants, business managers and publicists, it was not the subject of much debate or rancour. Before the Bosman ruling, clubs had all the power. It was primitive. Strikers used to get paid more than defenders and the club captain would usually receive a bit more than everyone else. When I signed for Queen's Park in 1957, it was an amateur club, so I did not receive a wage. At the peak of my playing career between 1967 and 1973, this had risen to £80 a week, and in my last season at Ayr United, I got £60.

Though these days the numbers have more zeroes attached to them than 50 years ago, human nature has not changed much. Like other people, the players of my youth wanted to be paid what they were worth. Throughout my management career I always felt that there was a happy medium. Obviously the club did not want to be taken to the cleaners by some preposterous demand but, on the other hand, I always felt we should be paying players what they deserved. I know it sounds simple, but I found that, if you adhere to that approach, things work out fine.

When I got to Aberdeen the players were being paid £120 a week, which I thought was too low, so I got their wages raised. (Bear in mind the first £100-per-week player was the England and Fulham captain, Johnny Haynes, who had reached that level in 1961.) Beyond the normal haggling, the first time I had to confront serious compensation issues was after Aberdeen won the European Cup Winners' Cup in 1983 by beating Real Madrid. This was, in a way, both the best and worst thing that happened to the club, because it shone a spotlight on the players. The players all wanted more money and every other club wanted to sign them. So within two years we had lost half the team to bigger clubs offering them far more money. We upped the salaries of our best players to £350 a week, adding bonuses for wins or League and Cup victories. Dick Donald was always guarded about using all our money to pay the first team and forgetting about everyone else. He was always eager to make sure we were paying the younger players properly.

I didn't begrudge the players a single penny. In fact, I think the best footballers are underpaid. That might seem ridiculous to someone who is working as a car mechanic or as a nurse, but I look at the topic differently. Players good enough to turn out for any team in the upper echelon of the Champions League have outshone tens of thousands of lads who would give their eyeteeth for the same opportunity. They are talented enough to entertain people all over the world – usually in numbers that dwarf the audiences attracted by music or film stars, and certainly larger than those following other sports.

One by-product of the Premier League compensation system is that bonuses have more or less died out. Top players may get a bonus if they win the League or one of the big European competitions, but the complex, multi-page bonus systems, which used to compensate players for each appearance, or each victory or goals scored, have died out in the upper echelons of the game. While nobody complains about extra money, a financial bonus does not offer the same incentive to top players as it did 25 years ago. The more powerful incentives are to appeal to their competitive instinct, the pride they have in their profession and the prospect of a winner's medal. Bonuses get spent. Medals are for ever.

When lined up against the annual compensation for people who run hedge funds, players like Cristiano Ronaldo and Lionel Messi seem woefully undercompensated. I read recently that the top 25 hedge-fund managers got paid almost £7.5 billion in 2014 – more than the combined payroll of the Premier League, Bundesliga, La Liga and Serie A, and that seems even more preposterous when you learn that many of them recorded worse returns than the stock market.

If a footballer's performance lags for any prolonged period, he finds himself on the bench or put up for transfer. The inequity seems even more pronounced when you consider that, compared to other people, a footballer's peak earning years are very abbreviated – usually about six years and almost always fewer than ten. Don't tell me that some 28 year old who can manipulate a spreadsheet (of which there are hundreds of thousands, maybe millions) deserves to be paid more than a midfielder playing for Swansea City or Southampton.

Every now and again players would get peeved when they read about one of their team-mate's contracts. Some, like Gary Neville or Paul Scholes, didn't pay any attention to what others got paid because they trusted us to compensate them fairly. Even towards the end of their careers, when Gary, Paul and Ryan Giggs were all on one-year contracts, it did not bother them. They were realists and knew we would treat them right. However, others got irked and I understand why. It doesn't matter if the compensation scheme is denominated in hundreds of thousands of pounds per week or in bags of potato crisps. It's all a matter of relative worth, because a lot of people either feel, or want to feel, that they are more valuable than anyone else.

Sometimes a player would be in a particularly strong position and know it. I encountered this with Ruud van Nistelrooy in 2003 after his first couple of spectacular seasons with United. He managed to negotiate a clause in his contract where he would have been allowed to go to Real Madrid if they offered a certain amount of money. This put him in the driver's seat and was not something we repeated. Eventually we let him go to Real Madrid, but he was one of only a tiny number of players who wanted to leave United. When he did leave, after we had enjoyed his services and goals for years, he was 30 and we received most of our initial outlay back.

I had a sharper pencil when negotiating contracts with players than I did for myself. Some leaders don't have much compunction about feathering their own nests at every opportunity. Others are too bashful about pressing to be paid what they are worth. I probably fell between those poles, particularly when the larger sums of money started to flow into football in the

1990s. Perhaps I am wrong, but I have noticed that leaders are sometimes so busy running an organisation that they do not take care of themselves properly. They will invariably not eat, sleep or exercise properly, but they also get into the habit of neglecting the management of their own financial affairs. They will spend tons of time working out remuneration details for others, and just a tiny fraction of that time on their personal arrangements. They are not careful enough about the terms of their own contracts and, if they are lucky enough to salt away some money, they will always have a tough time figuring out how to manage it properly. Maybe it is just because the best leaders tend to be missionaries rather than mercenaries.

When I started at Aberdeen I was paid £12,000 a year, or the equivalent of about £65,000 today, and in my last year in Scotland I was making £25,000, with a good bonus structure. I made a little more money on the side by doing some newspaper columns and public speaking, but it would not have bought many cases of wine. This was at a time when the highest-paid player in the team was on £15,000 a year, and sponsorship deals were tiny by the standards of today's top-echelon Premier League teams. When I started talking to United they actually offered me less than I had made, with bonuses, in my last year at Aberdeen.

After United started to win big competitions on a regular basis, I began to pay more attention to my own compensation. In 1989 Martin Edwards, the club chairman, had tried to sell United for £20 million – laughable by today's standards, but a hefty amount at the time. The deal fell through, however, after the buyer failed to raise the money. After United became a public company in 1991, there was no mystery about the value of Manchester United and I could not help but start to think about the role I had played in that. In 1998 Rupert Murdoch offered £623 million for United, which valued Martin's stake at about £87 million. Perhaps it was my Scottish trade-union heritage that gnawed at me, or maybe I just felt undervalued.

Martin was a good chairman. The club was in his bones and he cared about its welfare, but every time I raised my salary with him it became contentious. I'd go and see him in his office at Old Trafford and he used to punch my requests into this large desk calculator he kept near his phone. Years before, in order to show him I was underpaid, I even handed him the contract of George Graham who, at the time, was manager of Arsenal. I made very little headway and, in a way, I was nego-tiating from a position of weakness, because Martin knew that there was no football job I wanted more than to be manager of Manchester United. Once David Gill became chief executive, the situation was defused. David was more objective and my salary was adjusted to an appropriate level.

When the Glazers and David Gill agreed to a big increase in Wayne Rooney's salary in 2010, they wanted to know how I felt. I told them I did not think it fair that Rooney should earn twice what I made and Joel Glazer immediately said, 'I totally agree with you but what should we do?' It was simple. We just agreed that no player should be paid more than me. We agreed in less time than it takes to read the previous sentence.

For my last 15 years at United I had a rolling one-year contract and an agreement that if I was sacked I would be entitled to two years' salary, even if I turned up and started managing Manchester City the day after I was fired. That was more than enough for me.

I suspect most football managers get paid less – sometimes far less – than their star players. In the Premier League I imagine that only Arsène Wenger and José Mourinho pull down the amount of money earned by their best players. That probably explains why nothing much is written about a manager's compensation. What message does it send to a team, if most of them are being paid more than their boss?

## Negotiation

Buying and selling players provided me with an education in the art of negotiation. I got my first taste of negotiations by watching the trade-union leaders when I worked in the factories. There was a heavy Communist influence at the time, and I always felt they overstepped the mark. They'd go out on strike at the least provocation. They'd refuse to negotiate. It was always head-on confrontation. The last thing you want to do is go out on strike, but they always seemed to do it. What other weapons do you have if you are standing on the picket lines? What happens if someone calls your bluff and you are left warming yourself around braziers for three months? That image stayed with me, and so I always tried not to get myself boxed in during the tussles over players.

It's hard to remain clear-headed during negotiations and not get swept away by the passion of the pursuit or emotions. It's so easy to get over-stretched, and for a football manager it's very easy to feel that one or two new players will change the fortune of a club. If discipline slips during a negotiation it can have all sorts of ramifications. Not only does it drive the price up for a particular transaction, but it has ripple effects. In football, just as in other businesses, it means that people now expect you to pay top dollar. It also has an effect on the rest of the team because it can create unrest if your entire compensation scheme is distorted because of one new arrival or one new contract.

It would be nice to think that everyone behaved in a

gentlemanly manner during negotiations, but unfortunately that is not necessarily the case. You encounter some people with whom a handshake is sufficient to seal an enormously expensive transfer. Then there are others on whom you cannot turn your back for fear that they will try and do something underhanded. Over the years, and with dozens, if not hundreds, of negotiations under my belt, I got better at reading people. But I also learned that, no matter how many times you have been on the verge of signing a contract, there is always room for an ugly surprise.

I tried to stay unemotional and to keep a clear head when we were pursuing a player. When we wanted to sign Phil Neville, we consciously first went after his brother Gary. We knew the pair were very close, but we also knew that Phil had more natural talent and would be more sought after. However, I also knew that once we had bagged Gary, Phil would follow. There were occasions when the sellers tried to use emotion to their advantage. After a game at Old Trafford in August 2004 against Everton, David Gill, Maurice Watkins and I met the club's owner, Bill Kenwright, and their manager, David Moyes, to discuss our offer for the 18-year-old Wayne Rooney. They pulled out all the stops. After we gave them our final offer, Kenwright got Rooney's mother on the phone and she told me, 'You are not going to steal my boy.' We ended up by ploughing through the emotion and signing Wayne the following day.

I always tried to tell myself that it wasn't the end of the world if we failed in a particular negotiation and that our success was not going to hinge on the arrival of one player. If you need one person to change your destiny, then you have not built a very solid organisation. We had a chance to buy Sergio Agüero before he went to Manchester City, but eventually his agent was demanding a price we were not prepared to pay. Right towards the end of my time at United, we were pursuing Lucas

Moura, the immensely talented right-winger who, at the time, was playing in his native Brazil for São Paulo. We offered £24 million for him, which we upped to £30 million and then again to £35 million, but PSG signed him for £45 million. David and I were just not prepared to go to those sorts of levels. There were also times when negotiations to get a particular player came to naught but we wound up getting someone better. In 1989 I failed to get Glenn Hysén from Fiorentina, but wound up with Gary Pallister instead. My pursuit of the Dutchman, Patrick Kluivert, who was then playing at AC Milan, was also an exercise in futility, but it turned out all right because a bit later we snared Dwight Yorke.

Negotiations are often irrational. There are all sorts of reasons why people buy and sell things – it doesn't matter whether it is a house, a company, a stock or a football player. I found predicting the outcome of a negotiation was always challenging because, while I tried, I never knew all the cards my opponent was holding or all the pressures to which he was subject. I did know, however, that it is always good to keep as many options open as possible. For example, in 1989, after we lost to Nottingham Forest in the quarter-final of the FA Cup, I told Martin Edwards, our chairman, that we had to sell Gordon Strachan. Sheffield Wednesday had wanted to sign Strachan, but I got a call from Howard Wilkinson, the manager of Leeds United, who had got wind of what was happening. I informed Strachan of the interest from Leeds, but for some reason he was set on moving to Sheffield. I told him that out of courtesy he should tell Wilkinson of his decision, and I also said, 'You never know, he might offer you the moon. You never know what someone's going to offer you.' At the time Leeds were a rising club in what was then the second division, and their chairman, Leslie Silver, was willing to spend. That same night,

Strachan phoned me and said, 'Boss, I just wanted to let you know I've signed for Leeds United. They didn't offer me the moon. They offered me two moons.' Strachan wound up, at the age of 32, with a contract with Leeds that was far better than he was getting at United.

One of my best negotiating lessons came in August 1989 from Colin Henderson, when we wanted to sign Gary Pallister to strengthen United's defence. Henderson was chairman of Middlesbrough and also a senior commercial manager of ICI; he played us for all it was worth. I was eager, perhaps desperate, to sign Pallister so that he could play in a game two days later against Norwich City, and I suspect Henderson detected this. We even had Pallister sitting in the car with his agent outside the hotel in Middlesbrough so that we could get all the documents signed.

I'd told both Martin Edwards and Maurice Watkins, United's solicitor, that the maximum we should pay for Pallister was £1.3 million. In 1989 that was a huge sum, particularly because – prior to that – the largest amount United had ever paid for a player was the £1.8 million we had spent on Mark Hughes in 1988. Maurice and I spent a long night haggling with Henderson and had started the bidding at around £1.3 million. Eventually, we shook hands at £2.3 million, a British transfer record, and no sooner had I breathed a big sigh of relief when Henderson said the payment had to be up front. This was a shocker because, in those days, it was customary to pay big transfer sums in instalments.

I always appreciated the need to strike early during the two annual transfer windows, which were introduced in 2002–03. Other managers would complain about the transfer windows, but I liked their introduction because it meant I did not have to deal with agents for six months of the year. The last thing you want is to have your back up against the wall with the clock ticking while everyone knows that you are on the prowl for a particular type of player. But I would trade that time pressure for the freedom it created for such a large period of the year. In the summer, we would try to make up our minds about who we wanted to pursue before I went on holiday in June, even though the transfer window did not close until the end of August. We would make our intentions known early when David Gill made contact with the chief executive of the club from which we wanted to sign a player. It was just important for us to be in the mix early so that we did not get blindsided. There was a notable occasion in May 2007 when David Gill, accompanied by Carlos Queiroz, who spoke Portuguese, went to Portugal and signed Nani from Sporting Lisbon and Anderson from Porto in the course of 24 hours. That very same month, incidentally, a full ten weeks before the end of the transfer window, we also signed Owen Hargreaves from Bayern Munich.

The setting for negotiations can also play a role and, as I said earlier, I found that the hotel in the south of France where Cathy and I go on holiday was a great spot at which to convince players to cast their lot in with United. It is far away from the madding crowd and, with its view over a sunny Mediterranean, is far more conducive to the notion of a bright future than a small conference room in a stadium or a hotel suite on a rainy day in London. Phil Jones was just one of the players who brought his parents and agent to our hotel; we had a nice little chat in this delightful spot and the deed was done. Sometimes I would also use the aura of Manchester United to help seal a deal by walking a prospect out on to the pitch, or showing him around our Carrington training facility. The players would always be star-struck when they saw the gymnasium.

Contrast that relaxed approach with the problem of negotiating under pressure. Daniel Levy, chairman of Tottenham, nailed us to the flagpole in 2008 when he took us all the way to the last day of the transfer window before agreeing terms for Dimitar Berbatov, Tottenham's talented Bulgarian striker, in whom we had long had an interest. When we got wind of the fact that Levy was trying to sell Berbatov to Manchester City, we stuck in our oar, chartered a plane and flew the player to Manchester, agreeing on terms with the player and, as I thought, a transfer fee with the club. Then Levy came back to us and said he needed Fraizer Campbell, one of our young strikers, as part of the deal. David Gill demurred, so Levy then upped Berbatov's transfer fee a little. Finally, in order to get the deal over the line, and to add insult to injury, we sent Campbell on loan to White Hart Lane and paid the increased fee. We were up until midnight signing and faxing papers to make sure all the paperwork went through before the deadline expired. That whole experience was more painful than my hip replacement.

## Brokers

Agents have become like tsetse flies. These days they are everywhere in football, and almost all of them do nothing but feather their own nests and mess up the relationships that players have with their clubs and managers. They have turned many players into merchandise; a conversation with most agents is like trying to arrive at a deal in a souk.

As a result I've developed a pronounced aversion to any middle-man who gets between me and the players with whom I want to have a close relationship. Brokers have their own agendas and both player and club suffer the consequences. I was struck when I read *The Snowball*, the biography of Warren Buffett by Alice Schroeder, to learn of his distrust of investment bankers. I feel about football agents the way Mr Buffett feels about bankers – they are what he calls 'money shufflers'.

Before the introduction of the Bosman ruling, we always used to deal directly with the players and their families. Any boy good enough to play for Manchester United would, almost inevitably, have attracted the attention of other clubs, which meant that our offers would be determined by the forces of the market. Word would always get around and we would usually have a keen sense for what we were up against.

The truth is these days few players have a need for an agent, either because their lives are straightforward or they have little interest in becoming celebrities. If all their income comes from their club contract and they either aren't the type, or don't have the charisma, to attract the interest of sponsors and advertising agencies, all they need is a lawyer and an accountant. A few, and there aren't many of them, have more complicated lives, become mini-business conglomerates and do need someone to take care of all their relationships. Both Gary and Phil Neville signed seven-year contracts in the summer of 1997 in 15 minutes. I loved their father's response to the question of why they had done so – 'Because they wouldn't give us ten years.'

Agents cleverly, and slyly, insert themselves between the player and the club and try to up the ante. They claim to represent the interest of their clients but their ultimate motive is to maximise the amount of money that flows into their own pockets. Players, particularly the youngsters, have been bamboozled into thinking that it is impossible to obtain a fair deal without an agent, and they have also been fooled into thinking that the only route towards a fair deal is to play monkey games during negotiations that can take an eternity. The opposite is true, because few players calculate the amount that they are forking out for these agents over the course of their careers. The sums can be staggering. An agent will expect to receive 5 per cent of his client's basic salary from a contract negotiation. So, in a transfer where a player signs a five-year contract worth £100,000 a week, the agent will receive £1,300,000. Staggering. Harry Swales, who represented Ryan Giggs, Bryan Robson and Kevin Keegan for many years, would always refuse to take a percentage of the player's income from the club. Instead, he just took a percentage of any commercial contracts in which he was involved.

I frequently tried to use a respected player as our contract negotiator. Youngsters and their parents tended to view players as their natural allies, rather than someone like David Gill or myself, who would, inevitably, be viewed as management and, at least when we were in the thick of a negotiation, as their adversaries. I have already mentioned that, in their role as captain, both Bryan Robson and Steve Bruce were very helpful in this regard, as was Brian McClair. The same goes for Gary Neville, although I have to say there were occasions when I dreaded his appearance almost as much as the arrival of an agent. We took to calling him 'Arthur Scargill', the long-time leader of the National Union of Mineworkers, who was known for his uncompromising position on almost everything. Gary was similar. He would come into my office with a player and announce, 'I think your offer is rubbish.' He would be genuinely offended by some of our offers and would let us know that in very colourful language. But Gary was fair and he was good for the player and good for the club. I would rather deal with Gary at any time of day or night than with an agent.

There are some decent agents, but you don't need all the fingers of one hand to count them. Jorge Mendes is one. He represents some of the best players, including Cristiano Ronaldo, Ángel Di María and Diego Costa. In dealing with Jorge, especially when I was working to keep Ronaldo at United for another year in 2008 when he was pining to go to Real Madrid, I always felt that he was trying to represent the player's best interests. But Jorge is a rarity.

Many agents have no qualifications beyond the ability to ingratiate themselves with the player and his family.

I did not have a problem so much with Carlos Tévez as with his advisor, Kia Joorabchian. I always felt he was engineering another move for Tévez and, as a result, never had the feeling that the player belonged to United. It just seemed like we were renting him until Joorabchian could cut a better deal elsewhere.

There are one or two football agents I simply do not like, and Mino Raiola, Paul Pogba's agent, is one of them. I distrusted him from the moment I met him. He became Zlatan Ibrahimović's agent while he was playing for Ajax, and eventually he wound up representing Pogba, who was only 18 years old at the time. We had Paul under a three-year contract, and it had a one-year renewal option which we were eager to sign. Raiola suddenly appeared on the scene and our first meeting was a fiasco. He and I were like oil and water.

From then our goose was cooked because Raiola had been able to ingratiate himself with Paul and his family and the player signed with Juventus.

This sort of atmosphere makes it hard to establish a close relationship with a player and massively complicates life for a manager. If I felt these people genuinely had the players' interests at heart, I might feel differently. Players do not understand that their lives would be better – both financially and emotionally – if they paid a lawyer on an hourly basis to help them with their contracts. Paul Scholes was represented by Grant Thornton, the accounting firm. He paid them a simple fee and the job was done.

Agents have just become an unsavoury part of football life. I wish guys like Paul Scholes and Ryan Giggs, some of the very best players of recent times, would help educate youngsters and their parents that there is no need for them to employ agents. They would be doing the boys and football a tremendous favour.

# 11

# BUSINESS DEVELOPMENT

# Innovation

Between 1986 and 2013, the commercial side of United changed almost beyond recognition. In my final year at the club the turnover had risen to £363 million. While success on the field provided the foundation for this growth, I had little involvement in the details associated with making the cash registers ring. The commercial growth was the responsibility of the chairman and CEO. They had to worry about dealing with the sponsors and negotiating the sponsorship contracts; expanding our catering, hospitality and events activities; organising the pre-season tours, and assembling the tools for the media and marketing side, including MUTV, the website, the magazine and, these days, feeding our Twitter, Facebook and Instagram accounts. They also built up the human resources function, because you need it when you are employing 800 people. All this changed as the club grew.

In retrospect, I suppose there was always the risk that I would get diverted from my job by taking on a wider set of responsibilities at the club. But there was always a natural division of responsibilities and I cannot think of any top-flight manager who runs the football and commercial activities of a club. The separation of duties in football is somewhat equivalent to what you would find at a newspaper or fashion house or advertising agency. At each you have someone responsible for putting out the product – the editor, designer, or the head of creative. And then you have a CEO who takes care of all commercial activities – selling subscriptions and advertising; opening shops and selling dresses; soliciting clients and making ends meet. Either way, I had enough on my plate keeping the team in contention, and staying one step ahead of all the changes that crept into the game.

In the past 40 years, advances in technology and the amount of information that is available have helped transform football in the same way it has changed other sports. If you compare the Formula One car that Lewis Hamilton drives today with those that Stirling Moss used to guide around circuits in the early 1950s and early 1960s, the bicycles that Chris Froome has used to win the Tour de France with what Eddy Merckx rode in the 1970s, or the tennis rackets used respectively by Rod Laver and Roger Federer, the equipment and training approaches are very different.

Innovations in a variety of fields have been applied by football clubs. Everyone is always looking for the edge that will make them better than their opponents. As soon as you have fastened on that advantage, there's always a desire to keep it under close wraps although, inevitably, word leaks out and others emulate advances. At United, innovation and information have marched side by side for the past 30 years.

Diet has improved; players' careers have lengthened; the pitches – thanks to soil technology – have better drainage, underground heating and stronger varieties of grass that no longer disintegrate into muddy quagmires after the first rainfall;

footballs no longer absorb water the way they used to do; players wear kit made of synthetic materials compared to the cotton and wool of yesteryear. Today's top-flight football game is played at a much higher pace than 30 years ago – helped, in part, by the back-pass rule, which was introduced in 1992, but largely because of the massive improvement in the pitches. These have given today's players spectacular stages on which to perform. As a result, I would wager today's players run 15 per cent more than those who turned out in the 1960s.

Nutrition, sports and medical science, data and video analysis and, of all things, optometry have each played a part in the evolution of football. When people used to approach me and suggest that it was essential we adapt some new technique, I was invariably sceptical. Any number of peddlers used to approach us with the latest gimmick or fad. Some of their sales pitches would make you wonder whether they had bottled healing water from Lourdes. I always wanted someone to prove why a new-fangled idea would help us, and perhaps I sometimes came across as a bit old-fashioned. However, when it made sense and offered United a way to improve, I was eager to embrace it. I didn't want United to get left behind because others had stolen a march on us. I absolutely did not want to miss the future. So we added sports science and nutrition programmes to our repertoire and made massive improvements to the quality of our medical care and staff. We also developed our video analysis systems.

Nobody used to pay any attention to a footballer's diet. The normal lunch before a game consisted of three courses. In Scotland it was usually soup, a pot roast or mince and potatoes, and a treacle sponge for dessert. I don't know who came up with that menu – perhaps it was someone who wanted to guarantee a nice Saturday afternoon nap. It was definitely too heavy for me, so Cathy used to make me two slices of lemon sole followed by toast and honey for dinner on a Friday, and for a pre-game lunch on the Saturday.

Diet was very much on my mind when I took my first job as a manager with East Stirlingshire. We were due to play against Falkirk (a team I was eager to beat because I had played for them) and I wanted to change habits. I informed the board that I would start taking the team to lunch before games as part of our preparation. There was complete uproar because the lunch was going to cost £28, and in those days players were expected to buy their own lunches. I went to the hotel in Falkirk the day before the game, talked to the chef and instructed him to serve each player with two slices of lemon sole and toast and honey. The chef told me the players would be starving and I said, 'Good.' We won 2–0. The same thing happened when I went to Aberdeen, where the team had been in the habit of holing up in a hotel and having a fillet steak before a game. The hotel owner had been friendly with Billy McNeill, Aberdeen's previous manager, and, after hearing about my request for a menu change, predicted to the club chairman that I wouldn't last long as manager. So we changed locations in a hurry and thereafter the team always had lunch at the Ferry Hotel, where the menu consisted of protein, carbohydrates and sugar – or two slices of lemon sole, toast and honey.

Top-flight clubs in England began to take notice of the beneficial effects of diet in the 1990s. Most of the youngsters who came into the game in the early 1990s had just subsisted on a steady diet of pie and chips; for them, the idea of a nutritious regimen was as foreign as a bowl of spaghetti bolognese. The approach to diet has gone through different phases. Bananas were popular for a time, and then somebody thought carb-loading, with large helpings of spaghetti, would be helpful. At

United we began to take it seriously in 1990–91 when I hired Trevor Lea, a nutritionist from Sheffield. It was odd, but earlier in his life he had owned a newspaper and magazine shop that sold sweets and chocolates, which was hardly the background you would expect for a nutritionist.

Trevor understood that laying out healthy foods at the training centre only addressed part of the issue. So we called a meeting one evening with the players' wives and girlfriends. Trevor explained to the partners what he was seeking and emphasised the need for the players to reduce their consumption of fatty foods on the days leading up to games. There was a severe aspect to his approach, and he had no time for people who wouldn't comply with his regimen. This even extended to me during one of my attempts to lose weight and lower my fat levels. Every now and again I'd falter until he said, 'Either you do it all the time with me or not at all, because you are wasting my time.' He was right to admonish me. Under his guidance we lowered the players' fat levels from 14–15 per cent of their body weight to about 8 per cent. We also had sunbeds installed at Carrington to help boost the Vitamin D levels of players who had grown up in sunnier climes than the north of England.

Most footballers have very good eyesight and I had never thought much about the issue until Dr Gail Stephenson wrote to me out of the blue in the 1990s. She was a diehard United fan, but she was also a vision expert at Liverpool University. We had adopted a grey strip for away games and lost four of the five games in which we wore them. She wrote and told me that the drab colour made it much harder for the players to pick out their team-mates than our regular kit. We changed the strip and started to win. So Gail had my attention. I invited her in for a meeting, was impressed, and she became a valuable member of our back-room team. She then made the case that players' performance could be enhanced if their peripheral vision was improved. Like lots of others, I had always assumed that peripheral vision was some natural trait, like hair colour or height. Players who spend most of their time roaming one side of the field (a left-back or a right-winger) will have good peripheral vision in one direction and poor in the other. Some of Gail's work was based on research done with ice hockey players who were recovering from concussions, and our players came to benefit from her training.

The same went for sports science. At United we started taking this seriously in 2007 when we hired Tony Strudwick as our first director of sports science. He massively improved our approach to conditioning and the benefits of mobility and flexibility and indoor warm-up sessions. Our gym, which previously had lots of weightlifting equipment, suddenly had rows of exercise bikes and treadmills and big television screens so that the players could watch their favourite shows while exercising. He taught us how to measure the intensity of workouts so we could monitor which players were taxing their cardiovascular and muscular systems. Instead of running for miles, as we did when I played, the emphasis turned to interval training – short, explosive (and gruelling) surges of speed. The furthest the players were made to run was about 200 metres. It amounted to a revolution in the way we approached fitness. Tony also emphasised core body work, and that too was a big help. When it became clear that compression socks helped players recover from games we added this detail to our physical preparation.

It's amazing to think that 40 years ago we'd do a training session and then run 8,000 metres or clamber up and down the endless stadium steps of Hampden Park. It was no wonder we were wiped out for days. When I played for Rangers, the training was pathetic. Every morning was the same. We'd go on to the running track and run a lap and walk a lap. Then we'd go behind the goal and do exercises and finally we'd have a game on the training ground. There was no technical training. The only time you'd see a ball was during the game. There was never any discussion of tactics. Our health checks were also primitive. We did not measure lung capacity, or muscle mass, and there were no stress and blood tests, CT scans or electro-cardiograms and echocardiograms.

In retrospect, even at Aberdeen I was, unwittingly, torturing the players. We'd run them up and down hills and around a golf course. It was all quite old-fashioned but I didn't know any better. At United new training techniques and fresh data allowed us to make sure players didn't burn out. After each training session, Tony used to give me a summary sheet that would show how hard each player had worked. It was quite illuminating. We also started doing this during games – every now and again the reports were quite damning. All of these elements, and more, brought Manchester United into the 21st century.

## Data Overload

Today there is so much information available that it can drown you. When I started in football I had the opposite problem – too little information. The clubs didn't employ statisticians and data scientists; the players didn't wear heart-rate monitors to measure their intensity during training, or GPS devices to track the distance covered in games. There were no televised record-ings of opponents, let alone tightly edited clips. As a young manager the way I gathered information on players and teams was to go and watch dozens of games every season. I'd travel throughout Scotland, in all sorts of weather, every day of the week, to watch teams like Partick Thistle, Motherwell, Hibernian and Heart of Midlothian. In an average year I would put tens of thousands of miles on my car.

When I sought information on players, I'd always try and keep it simple. I was very interested in understanding the character of the player and the sort of upbringing he had received. Apart from that I wanted to watch his speed, his balance, his ball technique, and get a sense for his enthusiasm. We never used stopwatches to see how quickly a player could cover 50 or 100 yards. We could just tell whether they were quick or slow, and for me quickness was vital. It is easy to make things too complicated. If you looked at Brian McClair and Carlos Tévez in training you would never guess that, during a game, they would run all day. If some computer had relied on data from their training sessions to predict their performance, it would have reached the wrong conclusion. With Ruud van Nistelrooy we knew he excelled at short sprints and that was his forte. So we sought to improve that, rather than his overall stamina.

There have always been data hounds in football, just as there are in any sport. However, everything changed after Sky started blanketing the airwaves with football games. Prior to that, the only information a viewer would receive would be the result, the names of the goal-scorers and the times of the goals. These days the television coverage is drenched with possession percentages, assists, shots on goal – and what your dog had for lunch on Easter Sunday ten years ago. A manager receives all that information and a whole lot more. The statistical information was always important and I always looked at the data, but this did not determine how I picked a team. The data was more of a tool to ensure that standards were being maintained.

The coaching staff, in particular the goalkeeping coaches, tend to get fixated on analysing the way in which opponents take penalties, particularly if a game heads towards a sudden-death finish. They will be poring over this data for hours and will be full of predictions about whether the ball will be struck to the left or right or into one of the top corners. I always thought this was useless, and kept telling our goalkeepers to stay in the middle rather than go sprawling to one side. I had no idea until recently, when a friend pointed it out to me, that in 2005 some Israeli economic psychologists, after analysing 286 penalties, had published a paper titled, 'Action bias among elite soccer goalkeepers', which arrived at the same conclusion: the best way to save a penalty is to stay in the centre of the goal.

Television coverage spawned another speciality: video analysis. These days every club worth its salt has a video analysis room and a team of people responsible for compiling clips from games. Maybe because I had managed for years without video analysis, I never used it as a crutch. It was a helpful aid, but it's easy to spend too much time watching hour after hour of footage. For the most part I relied on my eyes. No machine is going to tell you whether a player is lazy or has the right attitude. The evidence was always right in front of me: not on a screen but on the football pitch. I would always glance at the data, but it almost never told me anything I hadn't already concluded. Sometimes I completely disagreed with the data. In 1987, the United chairman, Martin Edwards, came to see me while I was watching a reserve game to tell me that Steve Bruce had failed his medical as we were concluding his purchase from Norwich City. I said, 'He's hardly missed a game for about five years, so how can there be a problem?' And we went ahead with the deal.

One piece of information that I did find useful crept into use during the 1980s. This was the data gathered during pre-season 'bleep tests' – a series of short, 20-metre sprints used to gauge the players' fitness. The bleep tests were brutal but accurate – and always useful for me and my staff. We used to measure a player's fitness level at the end of one season and then, when we regrouped for pre-season training, we would test them again, so that we immediately had a sense for whether they had taken care of themselves during the summer break.

Years ago, the only way you could take a look at a player or team was by travelling to watch him play. There's still nothing that beats that sort of inspection, but today's video coverage is coming closer. At Aberdeen we had primitive video analysis. It consisted of VHS tapes of the handful of televised games that were usually shot with a couple of cameras. These tapes were of a low quality and we had no equipment and no people to edit the tapes. They were better than nothing – but not by much. Nowadays they seem to have cameras at every game, filming from all sorts of angles. At United our video analysis team reduced endless hours of tape to their essence.

We first installed specialised video analysis systems at United in the early 2000s. These allowed us to show players what they needed to improve and changed the way we planned for the future. It also gave us a lot more information and data about opposing teams and players. It's a very important part of the planning process, and really shines when the calendar gets packed and Premier League games start to pile up, with Champions League, FA Cup and League Cup fixtures.

The videos illuminated the system of play employed by an opponent, the substitutes they were likely to use in particular situations, and their approach to corners and free kicks. It helped me pick the right teams because I always had to be planning several games ahead – knowing that I had to field our strongest XI for a particular fixture. In my later years at United I worked even harder to do this and would rest players for two games so that they were primed for the most important.

The sports science and video analysis crews would forever be coming up with new ways to measure things, which was fine by me since I was always curious about fresh insights. However, I had grown up in an age before computers could generate heat maps of a player's performance or tell you how many yards he ran during a game, so I always relied more on the accumulated expertise garnered from watching tens of thousands of players compete in thousands of games, rather than on a computer printout.

As time went by we were sitting on top of a heap of information that kept growing in size. The immediate and natural impulse of any competitive person is to keep information private. However, I always thought of information in two buckets: what I was willing to disclose and nuggets I wouldn't tell my grandmother.

One mark of a leader is his willingness to share information. A great leader is happy to share his knowledge – or, at least, a portion of his knowledge. Bobby Robson, when he was the manager of Ipswich, introduced me to the notion of sharing information before Aberdeen played his team in a UEFA Cup match. Bobby invited me to watch the Ipswich training drill and I actually picked up a wee passing drill that I used for a while. I'm sure Bobby knew that I was already familiar with all his players, because I'd either seen them play or watched them on television, and all I was doing was watching a training session. I thought this was a generous gesture and a mark of the man and it is something I took away with me.

People used to be surprised how willing I was to let coaches from all over the world come to our training ground and take notes. Maybe they thought I was teaching them how to make an atom bomb using cornflakes, ketchup and two cups of flour. Once Ernst Künnecke, the manager of Waterschei, had come to watch Aberdeen play before the 1983 semi-final of the European Cup Winners' Cup. He was staying over a few days and I invited him to come and watch us train. He was flabbergasted but all we were doing was running a normal session emphasising possession, crossing and finishing. Nonetheless, I'm sure he went away thinking, 'Bloody hell. That's some club. They let you watch the training.'

In 2011 Bayern Munich let us check out their medical centre when we were thinking about improving our own. Steve McNally, United's senior doctor, and I nipped across to Germany to take a look. They let us inspect everything. They ran their medical centre like a hospital; we were massively impressed and borrowed a lot of their ideas. They also had a video analysis centre with amphitheatre seating, where the videos came up with subtitles for foreign players who didn't have a good command of German. I would have loved to have that at United for the players like Carlos Tévez and Juan Sebastián Verón who didn't understand English.

We did the same when we built the medical centre at Carrington. Word got round that it was the best in England and immediately all the other Premier League clubs wanted to inspect it. I just didn't see what the fuss was about. Everyone knew that we had a sizeable medical staff with physiotherapists, doctors, dentists and chiropodists. They knew the sorts of machines we had bought and I'm sure the various manufacturers would have been happy to send them the brochures.

I'm sometimes amazed by how people get fixated on information. It's like standing in a hospital room staring at the numbers on the bedside monitors while the patient chokes to death on a chicken sandwich. You have to consider the human element of life and the way that circumstances and chance can upset everything – even the most accurate and clearly reported data. Knowing the heart-rate of a player and doing all the video analysis in the world of his opposite number isn't going to help you if he loses control and gets sent off in the first minute.

## Confidentiality

While I like to think that I'm quite open and willing to share experiences, there are some things I've always been very careful about because in any intensely competitive pursuit, maintaining secrecy and confidentiality is a potent weapon. There is no benefit to be gained by telegraphing your moves or declaring your intentions to competitors. I would always try to keep a cloak of secrecy over anything we considered important – the amount of money we had at our disposal for new signings, the players we fancied, or injuries. My mantra was, 'Tell them nothing.' I'd never give anyone any inkling of who I wanted to sign and I had no interest in letting my fellow managers know the fitness levels of my players.

In the 2009–10 season, after Wayne Rooney got injured during the first leg of the Champions League quarter-final, I ordered him to keep wearing his rehab boot so that Bayern Munich would not expect him to turn out for the second leg. The subterfuge worked well enough, but unfortunately we failed to make the semi-finals. Stealth and secrecy are two valuable weapons for any organisation.

I used to announce the complete team line-up to the players a day before the game, but then it kept getting leaked to the newspapers. So I changed my approach and told each individual whether they would be playing but I was careful to ensure that I didn't disclose the complete team-sheet to anyone until the morning of the match. When Paul Scholes returned from his first experience with retirement to play against Manchester City in an FA Cup game in 2012, even the other players were unaware of his pending appearance until he removed his tie and jacket and put on his strip.

Agents always badgered their players for this sort of inform-ation, which they would then leak in order to curry favour with journalists. They would sit in their cars outside the training ground, waiting for their clients to emerge. They would phone the players and barrage them with questions such as, 'How are things today? How was training? Who is injured? Are you playing tomorrow? What did the manager say?' A minute later they would be distributing this feed to their favourite journalists.

There was a period during which United's secrets kept popping up in one newspaper written by the same journalist. It drove me bonkers. I couldn't figure out how this was happening, and then I discovered that the reporter lived in Alderley Edge, a village on the outskirts of Manchester, as did some of our players. It turned out that he would have drinks with some of the players on Saturday nights and, being a good reporter, he had a knack for getting them to say things that they should have kept secret. As soon as I cottoned on to what was happening, I gathered all the players who lived in Alderley Edge and told them in no uncertain terms, 'If I see one more story that includes facts I don't want to read, all of you are done. I don't care who leaked the information, you are all going to be fined.' That did the trick.

Graeme Hogg, a defender at United in the mid-1980s, was

another player who struggled to understand the concept of secrecy. We were due to play Everton in 1987, the season they won the League, and had spent the entire week working on an approach where I played with just three defenders to counter their two strikers. On the morning of the game I picked up the newspaper and Graeme Hogg had helped fashion a column titled, 'How we will beat Everton'. I couldn't believe it. I told myself I had to wait to calm down so that when I got hold of Hogg I would only commit serious assault rather than premeditated murder. Hogg started that game, but he only played a handful more games before we sold him to Portsmouth in 1988.

All things considered, I had it easy compared to anyone in politics. I had dinner with Tony Blair in Manchester before the 1997 election, and we talked about how hard it would be to keep his Cabinet ministers on the straight and narrow because they were all after his job and would leak nuggets to their favourite journalists in order to gain favourable coverage. I said to him, 'If you can keep them all in the same room, every day, you won't have a problem. But they will want to fly the nest.' He laughed and said, 'You're probably right.' I said, 'I am right. Don't worry about it.'

My circle of confidants was very small. I would confide my real feelings to Cathy and my brother, Martin, and Bridget and John Robertson, my in-laws. Beyond my family members, I knew that close pals from my boyhood and two from our time in Aberdeen, our lawyer Les Dalgarno, and our family friend, Gordon Campbell, could be relied upon to be discreet.

After Archie Knox headed back to Scotland, I gradually developed close relationships with Carlos Queiroz and Mick Phelan. But, much as I trusted them implicitly, I never was as close to Carlos and to Mick as I was to Archie. But then again, Archie and I had spent hundreds of hours together when we were earning our stripes, and that forms a different, deeper sort of bond. Among managers, I always felt close to John Lyall, and to Bobby Robson, the former England manager, whom I admired greatly, and Sam Allardyce.

But as I say, the inner circle of confidants is really quite small. Perhaps it is just very difficult to have more than a few close friends because these sorts of relationships build over a long time and lots of shared experiences. As my father always said, you only need six people to carry your coffin and, as I have got older, I have become ever more appreciative of that remark.

# 12

---

# THE RELEVANCE OF OTHERS

# Rivalries

Football is littered with great rivalries. Many of them are rooted in parochialism and are the outcome of times when travel was far more difficult than it is today. Remember, it was not until the 1950s that British clubs began to venture into Europe, and so in those days everything tended to be far more local. Newspaper journalists got into the habit of headlining local derbies and that remains true. It does not matter whether the game is between Celtic and Rangers, Everton and Liverpool, Tottenham and Arsenal, or Manchester United and Manchester City. A rivalry, particularly a local one, adds spice and bite.

Some fans, for whom football is bigger than religion, even inherit family rivalries. Their father, or grandfather, might have supported a particular team and those are the colours they will root for until their dying day. I cannot tell you how many photographs we used to receive of a newborn baby, clad in a Manchester United strip and named after a player. These babies were born into tribes, whether they liked it or not.

I don't remember a time when I was not thinking about

rivalry and competition. In Glasgow the great divide was – and still is – between Celtic and Rangers (the Old Firm). For many decades this had a deeply sectarian edge because Celtic tended to field players who had Irish Catholic roots, while Rangers drew their teams from Protestant Scotland. At Aberdeen our longest rivalry was with Rangers, but during my time at the club a new rivalry developed with Dundee United.

At United I inherited rivalries that had accumulated over decades. These varied a little, depending on the era, but a few were perennial. For United the tussles with the Merseysiders, Liverpool – whose stadium is only 32 miles from Old Trafford – and Manchester City always loomed large. The same applied to Leeds United, during the era when they were playing in the top flight. From time to time this had a vicious edge, such as the time a Leeds fan attacked Eric Harrison, our youth coach, thinking he was me. In the past 15 years, the dates of fixtures against Chelsea and Arsenal have also tended to be circled in diaries months ahead of the actual game.

Football was tailored for my personality because winning and losing is so clearly defined and measured so often. Ever since I was a boy, I've never wanted anyone to beat me. It might be because of my Glasgow upbringing, or because of my working-class roots (that's for the psychoanalysts to decide), but in Govan there were always kids who wanted to pick a fight and were natural enemies.

The spectre of contending with a rival helped goad teams towards higher performance. In Aberdeen I'd portray a visit from one of the big Glasgow clubs as an assault on our manhood. I would tell the players, 'Rangers and Celtic come up here and think they're going to walk all over us.' The implication is obvious.

Early on during my time at United, I was quoted as saying that my greatest challenge was knocking Liverpool off their perch. Somehow this quote became folklore and it was repeated endlessly. The odd thing is that I don't remember ever uttering the phrase. Either way, it was helpful, because it captured the century-long rivalry between United and Liverpool and, of course, during the 1970s and 1980s, Anfield was always a furnace. In the 26-year gap of United's League titles between 1967 and 1993, Liverpool won the League 11 times, the FA Cup three times and, most gallingly, the European Cup four times. Liverpool's success during this era was unprecedented because no other club had ever dominated English football in a similar manner. I am not sure whether United's players ever consciously thought about topping Liverpool's victory record, but I certainly always thought of it as the bogey I had to beat. The spectre of all that silverware heading to Liverpool was an intolerable prospect.

Once, in 1988, we left Anfield after a 3–3 draw marked by some appalling decisions by the referee. I said to a radio interviewer, 'It's no surprise managers have to leave Anfield choking on their own vomit, biting their tongue, afraid to tell the truth.'

There were obviously some theatrics associated with the way I stirred the competitive juices of our players when we were due to meet a long-time foe, but there were very few examples of either occasions or people (other than referees or linesmen) that made me livid for months. It is healthy for football clubs to have rivals and foes because it spurs them to perform to the best of their abilities, but I'm not so sure it pays to have bitter feuds or real enemies. I cannot think of a manager – even in the midst of our fiercest battles – with whom I would refuse to dine. I just tried to keep my thoughts to myself because the secret is not to put your own weaknesses on display. The best way to get even is to make sure you beat them. I had some well publicised spats with other managers such as Arsène Wenger but these disputes don't last for ever and he has been very helpful with our work at UEFA.

You cannot define yourself by your rivals and competitors or change your strategy and approach because of something they do. For years Manchester City, the other club in Manchester, tried to define themselves by what we did. Their chairman, Peter Swales, regularly referred to us as 'Them across the road'. He couldn't get Manchester United out of his head. Instead of seeking to improve Manchester City, and concentrate on what was under his control, he worried about us. It made no sense. On the other hand, we had one supporter, Norman Williams, who watched every home game and travelled to many away games. However, in a lifetime of supporting United, he never went to City's stadium. I asked him once why he refused to do so. His answer: 'I'm afraid of what I might catch.'

Nonetheless, you can learn from your competitors and, more importantly, you can raise your standards by trying to match or outperform them. Between 1994 and 1999 Juventus, the Italian club, served that role for United, when they were managed by Marcello Lippi and played at the level I wanted to attain. I greatly admired Lippi. He had such a sense of style and, with his silver hair, leather coat and small cigar, reminded me of Paul Newman. Eventually, I enjoyed one of my greatest nights as a manager there in the 1999 Champions League semi-final. We went two goals down after 11 minutes and came back to win 3–2, to knock them out and reach the final in Barcelona.

It's hard to keep your head when competitors do irrational things. In business, if a competitor lowers prices or splurges on an expensive television advertising campaign, it's easy to auto-matically assume that's the correct course. I suspect it requires a steely nerve to avoid following suit. In football, while I was managing, there was a similar phenomenon when other clubs and owners were prepared to pay a king's ransom to buy their way to success. In Scotland, that was Rangers. In retrospect I might have been a bit fortunate with the timing of my departure from Aberdeen, because it coincided with the arrival of Graeme Souness at Rangers, and the start of a big spending spree as they imported players from England and the Continent. Yet, if I had stayed at Aberdeen, I would not have been tempted to chase Rangers and to resort to spending willy-nilly. I would have stuck to my guns.

In England, the kings of spending were Chelsea and, in more recent years, Manchester City. Obviously, United have spent heavily since I retired, but that's over a shorter period. The success that José Mourinho achieved in his first season at Chelsea in 2004–05, when he won the Premier League and League Cup, was mainly due to his stubbornness, the determined manner he scratched out victories and draws and the fact that he had his players believing he was the Messiah. It also did not hurt that he spent almost £100 million during his first season at the club. However, he is a great leader and spectacular manager who has achieved major triumphs in four different countries. It's hard to think of anyone else who has done that.

When Manchester City was bought by Mansour bin Zayed Al Nahyan in 2008, I never for a moment thought, 'This is going to make it hard for us.' I just considered it another in a long line of challenges with which we had to contend. I didn't expect City to do the things that they've done in the last few years – some of which have been directly aimed at challenging United, but some of which have also been good for the economy of Manchester. Who could have imagined that they would build 6,000 new homes in some of Manchester's more rundown areas as part of their development plans? However, my attitude remains the same, despite the fact that they have spent in excess of £700 million from 2008 until my retirement. It's completely in United's power to beat them, no matter how much money they spend. There's no doubt that City's spending spree and their effort to create an instant history has caused jealousy around the Premier League, but I always tried to reinforce the message that, no matter how many players they bought for huge amounts of money, they could only start a game on a Saturday with 11 men.

## Global Markets

I have never studied economics, but football gave me a bit of an education in the subject. Though I've always been sympathetic towards trade unions, mainly because of what my father and his generation endured in the Scottish shipyards, I have become a big believer in free markets that provide everyone an equal opportunity to compete. Immigration may cause all sorts of social and political issues, but it has transformed the standard of play in the Premier League.

When I started in football, the sport was parochial. The British clubs had all been brewed in neighbourhoods, towns and cities. Many of the players could walk from their homes to the grounds and this continued for a long time. In 1967, when Celtic became the first British club to win the European Cup, it did so with a team entirely composed of players born within 30 miles of Glasgow. When United won the European Cup under Matt Busby in 1968, it was with a team of seven Englishmen, one Scotsman, one Northern Irishman and two who represented the Republic of Ireland. There had only been one or two foreign players in England prior to the late 1970s, when Tottenham bought Ossie Ardiles and Ricky Villa after the 1978 World Cup.

When I arrived at Aberdeen, there were no foreign players (and in this case 'foreign' includes English, Welsh and Irish). Every player was Scottish. When I went to United we had just two foreign players – John Sivebaek and Jesper Olsen – and both came from Denmark. Half a generation later, everything had changed. Chelsea were the first top-division side to field a starting XI without a British player when, in December 1999, they selected two Frenchmen, two Italians, and one Uruguayan, a Dutchman, a Nigerian, a Romanian, a Brazilian, a Norwegian and a Spaniard. In 2005 Arsenal, in a game against Crystal Palace, became the first team in the Premier League to select a complete match-day squad without a British player. The first time I fielded a team without a single English player was on 10 May 2009, at Old Trafford, in a 2–0 win against Manchester City, when we had players from the Netherlands, Brazil, Serbia, Northern Ireland, France, Portugal, Scotland, Wales, South Korea, Argentina and Bulgaria.

The arrival of overseas players occurred in two phases. Prior to 1995, when the European Court of Justice rendered its 'Bosman ruling', European players were still partially imprisoned by their clubs. In England, tribunals run by the FA had been used from the early 1980s to settle disputes about transfer prices. Once the European Court of Justice ruled that clubs no longer had to pay transfer fees after the expiration of a player's contract, all hell broke loose. Suddenly it was a free-for-all. There was increased pressure on the clubs to renegotiate contracts long before they expired, and the players – or at least the good ones – had much more negotiating power.

In Britain the trend towards foreign players accelerated in

the 1980s, when we gradually stopped producing a disproportionate share of the best players in the world. One simple
measure is the way that British teams have stopped qualifying
for the World Cup. Wales hasn't qualified since 1958, Northern
Ireland since 1986, Scotland since 1998 and the Republic of
Ireland last qualified in 2002. This happened for two reasons
– Margaret Thatcher and BSkyB.

I don't know whether Margaret Thatcher consciously sought
to destroy British football, because obviously (and correctly)
she was vocal about her disdain for hooliganism and crowd
violence, but that's what she managed to do. Following an
industrial dispute with the government, many teachers stopped
organising extra-curricular sports activities. It had disastrous
consequences. My experience was that young boys paid careful
attention to their schoolteachers, and many of them became
acquainted with the need to train and acquired substantial skills,
discipline and youthful experience playing in front of critical
and demanding eyes. Much of that evaporated, as schoolteachers
were replaced by fathers, uncles and grannies. I'm sure they
were all well meaning, but gradually, under their tutelage, the
level of high-school football started to deteriorate. Competitive
school football, which was the spawning ground of footballers
for so many generations, was replaced by boys' club football,
where there was far too much emphasis on playing a very high
number of games each season. For example, Ryan Giggs, as a
14 year old in his last year as a boys' club footballer for Salford
Boys and Deans FC, played well over 100 games.

This trend was exacerbated by rules introduced as part of
the new academy system by the Football Association that forbade
clubs from coaching boys in their youth academies for more
than an hour and a half per week. It was absolute nonsense.
This was the equivalent of telling a child who liked to play the

violin or piano that they could still aspire to join one of the world's best symphony orchestras but they could only practise for 90 minutes a week. Great footballers and great artists aren't made on 90 minutes a week. As a boy, prior to the Second World War, Stanley Matthews used to play with a ball for six to eight hours a day. George Best perfected his skills in Belfast during the 1950s by spending a childhood with a ball never far from his feet, and the same went for Cristiano Ronaldo when he was growing up in Madeira during the 1990s. Then we had to face the restrictive changes to the rules that meant we were only permitted to sign players to our academy who lived within one hour's travel of Old Trafford. Had this been in place in 1991, we could never have signed David Beckham. The change in the law had a pronounced effect on our ability to develop players born throughout Britain and immediately forced us to look overseas for players who were not covered by this regulation. This has been a boon to fans because it means that all the best European clubs have widened their scouting funnels and the global competition for talent has led to a rise in the quality of the game.

In 1992, at the beginning of the Premier League era, an avalanche of money began to pour into the game, with the signing of BSkyB's television five-year contract, which was worth £304 million. (By contrast the latest TV contract, signed in 2015, is valued at £5.13 billion.) The foreign players arrived in several waves. The first came from northern Europe, and were followed by several superb players, in the twilights of their careers, who were attracted by the wages offered by Premier League clubs. Then there were the French speakers recruited by Arsène Wenger at Arsenal. Roman Abramovich's purchase of Chelsea in 2003 marked the beginning of an unprecedented spending spree. The lengths to which clubs would go in order to sign players was exemplified by the case of Benito Carbone, who played for Sheffield Wednesday and Aston Villa before going to Bradford City. When Carbone moved to Bradford, he joined a team fighting for its life in the Premier League. In 2002 the club eventually claimed that continuing to pay Carbone's wages of £40,000 a week would force it into bankruptcy. So Carbone forfeited £3.32 million and returned to Italy.

The first non-British player I signed for United was Andrei Kanchelskis from Shakhtar Donetsk in March 1991. Peter Schmeichel followed in August 1991 from Brøndby in Denmark. The man who made the most waves was Eric Cantona. Eric was born in Marseilles, had played for Marseille, Bordeaux, Montpellier and Nîmes before crossing the Channel; he spoke little English when he joined us. Cantona had a huge impact on United, most of which emanated from his talent and drive, but some from his attitude towards training and fitness. The young players thought of him as the king and hung on his every word and he captained the team in 1996 and 1997. As Cantona started to blossom at United, other clubs all wanted their own version of Cantona. By the time Eric retired in 1997, foreign players had become the backbone of top-flight football in England.

Gradually the complexion of United started to change. We were as avid as ever about identifying boys from Manchester or elsewhere in England, but our scouting system had expanded. We now trawled for players in many more places, and our scouting system became truly global. In the latter part of the 1990s we put scouts in Italy, Spain, France, Germany, the Netherlands and Portugal to supplement our network of contacts in those countries. Then in 2000 we began hiring scouts in South America, notably John Calvert-Toulmin in Brazil and Jose Mayorga in Argentina. Now United has also got a good base of contacts in Mexico and Chile. This gradually started to pay off with the signing of Diego Forlán, the Da Silva twins from Brazil and Chicharito, who became our first player from Mexico.

The arrival of the foreign players presented new challenges. They were catapulted into a strange country where everything was different: food, weather and language. We did our best to make sure they settled in by finding them houses and arranging for schooling. We also tried to ensure they could eat their favourite foods. Barry Moorhouse, who was United's player liaison officer, was responsible for this. Many of the English players had trouble with my Scottish accent, but that was nothing compared to the trouble it created for the foreign players. Anderson, a Brazilian, and Nani, a Portuguese player, who both arrived in 2007, were two for whom language, at first, was a formidable barrier. To their credit both players took the time to improve their English, and it became easier to communicate with them.

Some players had an enviable ear for language. Patrice Evra speaks several, Nemanja Vidić picked up English within weeks, and Chicharito, who grew up in Mexico, and the Da Silva twins, who were born in Brazil, understood that their football would improve if they brushed up on their English. The standout was Diego Forlán. He had a great ear for language and could have been a translator at the United Nations because he could shift with ease between Spanish, Portuguese, Italian and French. When, in 2014, he signed for the Japanese club, Cerezo Osaka, he astonished his hosts by speaking in Japanese during his inaugural press conference.

Beyond the language barrier, I think too much is made of the difficulties of integrating foreign players. I came to welcome what they brought to the club, and the multiculturalism enriched

315

everything. Dwight Yorke, for example, who was born in Tobago, brought a lovely warmth and carefree sense of joy to the club after we bought him from Aston Villa in 1998, and that was good for morale. The gap between the home and foreign players was most evident at dinner at The Lowry, the hotel where we stayed prior to home games and where we always always had a buffet dinner. The staff would tend to congregate at one table and the British players at another, where they would all be solemn and speaking to each other in low voices. The table that was always the most raucous and alive with laughter was where the Serbs, Dutch, French and Portuguese sat.

The foreign players also set an example for some of the English players. For one thing, they tended to stay away from alcohol. Some did this for religious reasons but it mainly stemmed from the fact that they had grown up in places where getting drunk on Friday and Saturday nights is not a matter of habit. They did not feel compelled to explore their body's capacity for alcohol at Christmas parties or after we brought home a trophy. The majority of them would be very careful about their diet and dedicated about training. One of the other traits that distinguished the foreign players was their physique. The medical scans of the players who hailed from climates warmer than Britain tended to reveal much healthier joints. Their knees and hips didn't have the telltale signs of early arthritis that you would tend to find in the British players who had grown up in the damp and the cold. They also tended to be wiser about listening to their bodies. Unlike the British players, they would not try to play through injuries and risk turning a bad knock into a recurring aggravation. They just do not try to prove they can beat the pain.

About the only issue I had with the foreign players was when they got homesick or had gone to play international games and wanted to extend their stays in their homelands. Eric Djemba-Djemba, the Cameroonian midfielder, who played for United between 2003 and 2005, often returned late from leave.

For United there were only positives about extending our reach, mining new countries for talent and importing these players. When we won the Champions League in 1999, we did so with five players from outside Britain on the field – if you excuse the Irishmen – but our successes in the ensuing 14 years were only made possible because we travelled beyond our pre-existing borders.

Commentators frequently remark on the number of foreign players in the Premier League, but they often ignore the nationality of managers. In the 2014–15 season, there were eight foreign-born managers at the helm of Premier League clubs. Like the foreign-born players, they have enriched the game, although the first to arrive from outside the United Kingdom or Ireland, the Czechoslovak, Dr Josef Vengloš, did not appear until 1990 and only had a brief stint at Aston Villa. But, since then, foreign-born managers have become a staple of the Premier League, and the fact that many played for, or managed, first-rate European clubs, where they were schooled differently, has added layers to the game. (I'm referring to more than just the style of dress you see on the sidelines, though they look mighty dapper. Just look at the turnout of managers like Roberto Mancini, Roberto Di Matteo – during his brief time at the helm of Chelsea – or Roberto Martínez. Fortunately, José Mourinho proves that style is not just the preserve of managers named Roberto.)

Injecting these foreign sensibilities into the Premier League has made it a better sport for the fans, even if, from time to time, I might have objected to some of the tactics. The only managers who ever took the Premier League away from me have been from outside England: Arsène Wenger (France), Roberto Mancini and Carlo Ancelotti (Italy) and Kenny Dalglish, who was managing Blackburn Rovers at the time (Scotland). One small, yet startling, point: the last time an English manager won the English League was in 1992, when Howard Wilkinson was at Leeds.

It's actually remarkable how many Scotsmen have done well as Premier League managers – it's one of those rare statistics to which I do pay attention. Believe it or not, when Paul Lambert was sacked by Aston Villa in 2015 it was the first time since 1984 that there had been no Scottish manager in the Premier League. Just four years before that, seven of the 20 teams in the Premier League were headed by managers who had been raised in the Glasgow area. I know I am hopelessly biased, but I think managers like Kenny Dalglish, David Moyes, Paul Lambert, Owen Coyle, Bill Shankly, George Graham and, of course, Matt Busby just have, or had, a dour grit, stubbornness and determination about them that equips them well and is part of their heritage.

# 13

---

# TRANSITIONS

# Arriving

Leaders who are new to an organisation are often far too eager to stamp their imprint on everything. I know there's a widely held belief that a leader only has a chance to make his presence felt during his first 100 days, but it is not something to which I subscribe. There is a right and wrong way to arrive in a fresh setting – especially when you are the new sheriff in town. It is very tempting to appear with a fresh posse of trusted lieutenants and all guns blazing. In football, some of this behaviour occurs because of the inordinate emphasis on short-term results. A new manager knows that he has a limited lifespan if he does not generate quick results, even with a multi-year contract in his pocket and an owner promising to be patient.

I made this mistake when I became the manager of St Mirren. I was 32 years old, with all of four months of management experience, a bit too cocky for my own good and determined to shake things up. Instead of taking time to get my bearings and assess everything, I arrived with too many preconceived ideas. I was hot-headed, very passionate about my job, and did not want anyone to make me look like a fool. I'm sure some of that had to do with my own insecurity and inexperience. I was wondering to myself, 'What are they all thinking? What are they going to do? How are they going to react?' Then, of course, there are the periods of self-doubt when you are wondering whether you are making the right decisions. I was too eager to show that I was the boss and too quick to make decisions. Quite frequently I made decisions that I regretted.

Steve Archibald, a fantastic striker at Aberdeen, drove me nuts shortly after I arrived. He had an opinion on every subject, and was not bashful about sharing them. He should have been a professor and he did not make my arrival at Aberdeen easy. He was constantly questioning everything. But he was stubborn, wanted to win, and I just found a way to deal with his personality.

When I arrived at United in November 1986, I was only accompanied by Archie Knox. Cathy stayed in Aberdeen with the boys so that they did not interrupt their schooling which, in a way, was a blessing for me, because all I had on my plate was work. Archie and I had been together for three years at Aberdeen and I wanted him with me at United because we looked at the world in a similar manner, which gave us a unified consistency. He excelled at his job and was hard-working and trustworthy. I did not consider it a handicap to work with the United staff that had worked for my predecessor, Ron Atkinson. I actually thought it was helpful because, unlike me, they knew the club and were familiar with the players and our competitors in what was then the first division. In a way it is a little bit similar to what happens when a new prime minister arrives in Downing Street. He does not change the people who run all the Civil Service departments, but he does set out his own agenda and make his priorities clear.

I was more than happy with the backroom staff and coaching

team that I had inherited at Old Trafford, with the exception of the chief scout, whom I asked to leave at the end of my first season. All of them were good, solid characters, and they had an interest in seeing that the new manager did well. Not only was it in their self-interest, but it was also a matter of professional pride.

I knew that it would take time for me to take stock of everything at United, and I also wasn't about to make foolish promises about what was possible. I knew there was a lot to address, but I knew too that I couldn't do everything immediately. I immersed myself in the club; looked carefully at their performance history; examined the way they approached the pre-season; investigated their youth and scouting system; and gradually started to understand each of the players. I developed a keener sense for how much the club's heritage relied on attack. United had embraced an attacking style of football from its earliest years as a club, and this was a tradition that threaded its way back through the eras before and, of course, after the Second World War. Today's generation still knows the names of Bobby Charlton, George Best and Denis Law, but others such as Willie Morgan, David Pegg, who died in the Munich air crash, Charlie Mitten, who played in the early 1950s, and Billy Meredith, who played at the start of the 20th century, are only known to the diehards. This heritage, which had worked so well for Sir Matt Busby, fitted me like a glove, since attacking was my natural instinct.

All this took time. And then there were the surprises. For example, I would never have guessed that the undersoil heating at Old Trafford did not work. It had gone on the blink during our first FA Cup third-round tie against Manchester City, and we discovered that rats had chewed through the underground cables. It had been repaired in time for the fourth-round tie, three weeks later, against Coventry City but, again, on the morning of the match, we found out that half the ground was frozen and the other half was a swamp. You cannot anticipate things like that; it just shows that, when you are trying to build the pyramids, some guys will always drop or break some stones. I'd wager that no winning organisation has ever been built in the first 100 days. If you want to build a winning organisation, you have to be prepared to carry on building every day. You never stop building – if you do, you stagnate. I always used to say, 'The bus is moving; make sure you're on it, don't be left behind.' Manchester United was always a bus on the move.

There is no point suddenly changing routines that players are comfortable with. It is counterproductive, saps morale and immediately provokes players to question the new man's motives. A leader who arrives in a new setting, or inherits a big role, needs to curb the impulse to display his manhood.

If I were given the chance to replay my arrival at United, I would do two things differently, because in one respect I moved too quickly, and in another too slowly. Before I arrived at Old Trafford, I had been alerted to the fondness that some players had for the pub, and I was well aware of the fact that alcohol is one of the enemies of high performance. I wasn't about to let it fester, and so I tried to stamp out the drinking immediately. The Monday after my first game in charge of United, I gathered everyone in the club into the gymnasium. There were around 40 people in the place – players, coaches and backroom staff. I just told everyone plain and simple, 'Look, all these stories I'm hearing about your drinking habits have got to change. You have got to change because I'm not going to change.' I'm sure that a lot of the audience were thinking to themselves that they had heard it all before. It was not as if any binges had occurred in the few days that I had been in charge, or that I had any firm evidence that a player had crossed the line. I was just working from hearsay, and that's not wise.

Knowing what I know today, I would not have held that meeting but, instead, made an example of one or two players after they had crossed the line, rather than cast aspersions on everyone. It was too early for me to force a confrontation on an issue, but in the long run it didn't hurt. It is all well and good, as a new arrival, to feel the impulse to issue your own version of the Ten Commandments, but actions speak so much louder than words. My message about alcohol would have been more effective if I had just quietly gone about getting rid of one of the players who had the wrong priorities. In the end it took a long time to eradicate the drinking habit at United, but after I sold some of the main culprits, people could see I was not just full of hot air and things slowly started to improve. Eventually, the drinking stopped, apart from the occasional outings.

The second mistake I made was to wait too long to reshape the team. Some of this was out of my hands, because we had a limited budget for transfers and our pool of talented young players was thin. Nonetheless, I let the prospect of what was possible, rather than what was probable, cloud my judgement. In my heart I knew that I would never be able to turn some of the players into the sort of performers required to consistently win trophies. I gave some of them too much benefit of the doubt and, had I moved a bit more quickly, I suspect we could have become a winning club a couple of years earlier.

If you are a new boss, there is always a fine line to walk when you first appear. You want to eliminate as much uncertainty as possible because that can paralyse an organisation. Yet you also do not want to make promises you know you might not keep. At United, I hope I made it clear to people – particularly the non-playing staff – that they were secure and I wasn't about to put them in front of a firing squad. All I sought was performance and, as long as they performed, they were going to be part of the journey ahead.

When a former player, who is new to management, asks me for advice, I usually tell him not to seek confrontation. Whenever you show up in a new role, it will not be long before you have to face trouble and a clash over something. There is nothing to be gained by stirring it up yourself. Trouble will find you quick enough.

## Leaving

Leaving is complicated, and almost impossible to get right. Gallons of ink have been spilled on how David Moyes became my successor as manager of United. I understand why critics, particularly in light of the results of the 2013–14 season, say we should have handled the transition better. That season was a real disappointment, which culminated in the failure to qualify for the Champions League for the first time since 1995. It was not a happy time. But not much has been said about the challenge of picking a manager at a top-tier football club. It is not an easy undertaking.

At United the issue was complicated by the length of my tenure. I do not want to sound vainglorious, but no manager in the post-Second World War era has led a team for as long as I led United. Sir Matt Busby managed United (in two spells) for 24 seasons, Bill Shankly was at the helm of Liverpool for 15 seasons, and Arsène Wenger has been at Arsenal since 1996.

I'm sure the length of time I had been in the role made things trickier. I know it did not make them easier. Picking a successor was never going to be a piece of cake.

I'm sure football clubs could learn a lesson or two from companies that have a successful history of navigating management transitions. For example, I was never asked the question that I have since learned is commonly posed to the CEOs of many companies: 'If you get hit by a bus, who takes your place?' It is a good question, because it forces people to pay attention to the issue. However, I am not sure that it would have changed anything at United because, without trying to make any excuses, there are peculiarities associated with picking a Premier League manager.

Like other organisations on the prowl for a leader, United's board of directors had the freedom to survey the field. We had the opportunity to look within the club or cast our net further afield. Either way, we had far fewer candidates than a normal company. The trouble with football clubs, particularly those in the top tier of the Premier League, Bundesliga, La Liga or Serie A, is that there are not many candidates qualified to become their manager, and owners and boards of directors invariably find that their choices are further limited by the men who are available and not bound to another commitment from which they cannot extricate themselves.

It's not as if any of the clubs in these leagues have hundreds, let alone thousands, of employees in their coaching ranks. If the criterion for the search for a successor to a United manager is limited to those who have managed a Premier League club in the previous five years, there are probably around 50 candidates; if the desire is to find someone who has managed a club that's finished in the top six, then the number dwindles to 12; and if you add the hardest criterion of all – a consistent history of winning – then you are left with about 3 who are already at top clubs. Managers just have a very tough time maintaining a winning record. David O'Leary was manager of Leeds from 1998 till 2002, when he reached the semi-finals of both the UEFA Cup and Champions League and secured a fourth-place finish in the Premiership. For a brief time he was on the top of every club's list. Then Leeds faded, O'Leary's lustre was tarnished, and he hasn't managed a top-tier team since 2006.

We obviously had a preference for a manager with experience of top-flight football, who had persevered through hard times and demonstrated that he could handle the pressure of the press coverage and the relentless trickery of agents. Personally, I have a bias that favours managers who have been solid players. Even though there are a handful of examples of managers who either did not play much professional football or did so at mediocre clubs (José Mourinho and Gérard Houllier being the two prime examples), I have a bias towards candidates who have done well on the pitch. They just have more experience and greater credibility with players.

At United we didn't have an obvious internal successor, though it was not for want of trying. Even before the Glazer family arrived in Manchester, I had been thinking a lot about potential successors. During my entire time at United, the only real internal candidate for the manager's role was Carlos Queiroz. Unfortunately, he spoiled his chances by leaving United twice – first for Real Madrid and then by going to manage Portugal. I was always encouraging some of the best United players – Ryan Giggs, Gary Neville, Darren Fletcher, Nicky Butt, Dwight Yorke and Andy Cole – to earn their coaching credentials, yet it was unrealistic to expect any of them to switch from being a player to immediately becoming manager of the club for which they had just finished playing.

United tried that once when Wilf McGuinness succeeded Matt Busby in 1969, having retired from playing in 1959. It was a disaster. Forget about the tensions caused by the fact that Sir Matt kept his office and was a daily presence at the club, McGuinness – or anyone else for that matter – was always going to have a tough time managing his former team-mates. Ryan Giggs is eventually going to be a great manager – he has intelligence, presence and knowledge – but there was no chance that I would ever have asked him, or any other player, to consider being my successor while he was still fortunate enough to be playing. A footballer needs to squeeze every last possible moment out of his playing career. There is more than enough time for management later in life. Had Ryan Giggs retired in his mid-thirties, rather than when he was 40, there is every chance that he would have been my assistant in my final five years at Manchester United, alongside Mick Phelan. He would have had to start at a lower coaching level, but he would definitely have been alongside me and Mick, learning the trade.

But, assistant managers can get itchy feet. It is very hard to keep them, particularly if they know their boss has no intention of retiring. Former Manchester United coaches and players are all over the place. Mark Hughes has flourished, although – because he is such a retiring and quiet man – I had always wondered whether he had the personality to pull it off. He did a good job as the Wales manager, followed that with a stint at Blackburn before going to Manchester City, where I thought the new owners treated him unfairly when they sacked him. Now he is at Stoke City and in his element.

Assistant managers who stay in the role for a long time do so because they aren't cut out for the top job. René Meulensteen, who was United's technical skills coach for the youth academy between 2001 and 2006, wanted to manage a club; against my advice he departed for Brøndby in Denmark. After about six months it wasn't working out for him, so I brought him back to United as a first-team coach. He then left again, but he had bad experiences as a manager at Anzhi Makhachkala and Fulham. I think he now understands his forte is as a wonderful first-team coach.

We also always kept track of what was happening in management circles elsewhere. For example, I had dinner with Pep Guardiola in New York in 2012, but couldn't make him any direct proposal because retirement was not on my agenda at that point. He had already won an enviable number of trophies with Barcelona – two Champions Leagues, three La Liga titles, two Copa del Reys (Spanish Cup), two UEFA Super Cups and two FIFA Club World Cups – and I admired him greatly. I asked Pep to phone me before he accepted an offer from another club, but he didn't and wound up joining Bayern Munich in July 2013.

Life is such that the best of theories, or the best of intentions, sometimes don't translate into practice. Believe me, the United board wanted nothing more than to select a manager who would be with the club for a long time. All of us knew the history of the club and the success and benefits that come from stable leadership. When we started the process of looking for my replacement, we established that several very desirable candidates were unavailable. It became apparent that José Mourinho had given his word to Roman Abramovich that he would return to Chelsea, and that Carlo Ancelotti would succeed him at Real Madrid. We also knew that Jürgen Klopp was happy at Borussia Dortmund, and would be signing a new contract. Meantime, Louis van Gaal had undertaken to lead the Dutch attempt to win the 2014 World Cup.

We could obviously have taken the risk on a young manager who had not been tested, but eventually, as everyone knows, we selected David Moyes. Many people seem to have forgotten his performance at Everton where, despite being under severe financial constraints, he achieved strong League performances.

Sadly, things did not turn out for David as he and we all wished. Despite what people might think, the board of directors at United wants nothing more than for its manager to succeed. If the manager succeeds, the club succeeds, and the virtuous cycle is renewed. When David was appointed to a six-year contract, it was done with the best of intentions. Everyone hoped he would have a very long run at United. But it did not work out like that. I also know the Glazers well enough to understand that removing David was the last thing they wanted to do.

I'm sure there are some things that David would do differently if he had the opportunity to relive his time at Old Trafford, such as keeping Mick Phelan, who would have been the invaluable guide to the many layers of the club that Ryan Giggs is to Louis van Gaal today. The results were obviously disappointing, but it is difficult to imagine what it is like to walk out of the tunnel into a packed stadium knowing that every person is wondering about your future. I had experienced that feeling once or twice and it is very lonely. It is obviously fair to ask whether the transition at United could have been managed better. But the club did a good job, working through a discreet process in a professional manner. Right now, I hope that Louis van Gaal stays for a long time and, obviously, with Ryan Giggs at his side, there is a path towards a healthy, long-term succession plan.

About the only manager transition in top-flight English football that has gone well for the club was when Bob Paisley succeeded Bill Shankly at Liverpool. Shankly had rebuilt the club, gaining promotion back to the top division, winning three top division titles, two FA Cups and a UEFA Cup during his tenure, and Paisley, who managed the club between 1974 and 1983, topped it by winning three European Cups. As an outsider, I would never have guessed that Paisley would pull off what he eventually accomplished. In fact, when Shankly recommended Paisley, he initially refused the job. He had been the physiotherapist and then first-team coach prior to assuming the role; he was as quiet as Shankly was ebullient. He kept Shankly's team intact, understood the system, and gradually improved his squad by adding quality players and continuing the principles put in place by Shankly. Whoever selected Paisley deserves a lot of credit.

I had two attempts at retirement as a manager. I botched the first one – which is, perhaps, why I did a better job of it the second time around. My first run at retirement was a textbook case for how not to do it. I was turning 60, which in my father's time was a watershed age, but these days has far less significance. Nonetheless, I found myself contemplating my age. I was also irritated with the club who, in response to questions from the press, had announced that there would be no position for me in the organisation after retirement, lest there be a repeat of what happened after Matt Busby retired.

I could not help but think of what happened to Jock Stein and Bill Shankly after they had retired from Celtic and Liverpool, and I was determined that would not happen to me. I made matters worse by not having a plan for what I would do after I retired and by announcing my intention prior to the start of the 2001–02 season, which made the players go to sleep. It was as if I had put chloroform over their mouths. I knew when I made the decision and announced it to the players that I had made a mistake.

By Christmas 2001, Cathy and my boys persuaded me to change my mind. I was relieved they did so because, left to my own devices, I'm not sure that I would have summoned up the courage to phone Maurice Watkins, the club's solicitor, and announce my change of heart. He just said, 'I told you that you were stupid.' In retrospect, it all worked out well enough. It was as if I had inadvertently given myself a half-time breather. After 15 minutes, I was raring to get back on the field.

Had it not been for the death of Bridget Robertson, Cathy's sister, in October 2012, I would have continued managing United. I really wanted to win another Champions League and I had been planning for the future. In my last summer as manager of Manchester United, when I met Robin van Persie during the process of signing him from Arsenal, one of the questions he asked me was, 'How long are you going to carry on for?' I told him the truth. Retirement was not on my agenda. We'd tied down a number of our squad to new deals and, with an eye on the future of the club, signed Powell (18), Henríquez (18), and Zaha (20), as well as agreeing contracts with some of the most promising youngsters. It was business as usual. Also, I had already started work on a couple of new signings for the following summer. It would have been interesting, if I had stayed on, to see if we could have got those deals over the line. But Bridget's death was the watershed moment. It is hard to conjure up a more tangible reminder of mortality, and I felt that, after all those years during which Cathy had put me first, it was time that I took care of her needs. Bridget had not just been Cathy's sister but also her closest friend. When I decided to really retire, I just went with my instincts.

There were no demons in my mind about the horrors of not going to work. I also had a list of things that I wanted to do, so I could not imagine that I was going to be bored. Maybe things had just run their course and 39 years of management had been enough. I just sensed it was time to go. I knew that I would miss the players and the staff, and I was not quite sure how I would adjust to not going at full tilt, but I also felt a great sense of relief about not having to do certain things – particularly contending with the press and dealing with agents. Once I made the decision, I found myself looking forward to retirement.

I was fortunate because I got to retire as a football manager. Most football managers do not have that opportunity. Some lose a few games, get fired and never find another management job. They just disappear and are never heard from again. Or there are people like Bill Shankly who, after his retirement from Liverpool, discovered that the audience that used to lap up his stories had vanished. He was a lost soul. He used to go and watch the training sessions at Tranmere Rovers and Everton. He was only 68 when he died.

I imagine that some people thought I would have trouble letting go and ceding the authority that I had enjoyed for so long to others. But I was not confused about the difference between the role of being a United director and ambassador and the club's manager. After anyone retires from a position of responsibility and remains associated with the same organisation, it is unfair to your successor to try and retain the authority you once possessed. You have to let go and let the new man and the new regime do what they think is best.

I had heard the stories of what happened after Matt Busby had retired. He stayed in his office at Old Trafford, continued to show up at the club most days and was the power behind the throne. That was all a bit far-fetched, but I did not want to intimidate my successor with my presence in his day-to-day working environment. This is why I cleared out my office at Carrington straight away and, apart from attending games, and activities with sponsors, I maintained my distance. Carrington was off-limits and I chose not to join the other directors when they went to the dressing room after games; that remains the case today. I was not about to meddle in somebody else's business. I realised that when I watched a United game, the television directors kept a camera trained on me to gauge my reaction. I think they hoped they would catch me acting like Statler or Waldorf, the two curmudgeons in *The Muppets*, who are always criticising what is happening on the stage. I just wanted David and United to win – just as I do these days with Louis van Gaal. When the club made the decision to remove David, there were some who wanted me to return to the sidelines. But I was not tempted for a moment. I had made my decision to retire. My time was over.

Obviously I had a great run at United and accumulated a lovely set of trophies. But when I look at my name on the stand that's opposite my seat at Old Trafford, I wonder, from time to time, whether I deserve that recognition. This is not an attempt at false modesty, but sometimes I think that, with the teams and players I had at my disposal, we should have done more.

My most acute disappointment is with the Champions League. We lost three Champions League semi-finals and two finals. When I retired, United had won the trophy three times, but we really should have won it five times. Real Madrid has won it ten times (including five in a row), Bayern Munich has won it five times (including three in a row) and Barcelona, AC Milan and Ajax have taken it home more often than United. But the comparison that really hurts is with Liverpool, who have won the Cup five times. It is not much consolation that they only won it once during my time at United. It still stings.

I could argue that for three years the regulations were stacked against us, but every club faced the same restrictions about the number of foreign players that were permitted. After we won the Double in 1994, we had a strong squad, but the rules – until they were changed in late 1995 – allowed teams to field only three players born outside the country in which they were employed, plus two 'assimilated' players who had come through their youth set-up. Unfortunately our squad included Brian McClair (from Scotland), Denis Irwin and Roy Keane (from Ireland), Peter Schmeichel (from Denmark), Andrei Kanchelskis (from Ukraine/Russia/Soviet Union), Eric Cantona (from France), and Mark Hughes and Ryan Giggs (from Wales).

We were also unlucky on a couple of occasions – but that's football (and life). We should have won when we played Borussia Dortmund in the Champions League semi-finals in 1997 but we lost our goalkeeper the night before the game and against Bayer Leverkusen in 2002 we went out on the away goals rule at the semi-final stage of the Champions League, having drawn 2–2 at Old Trafford and 1–1 in Germany. We could have won both the 2009 and 2011 finals against Barcelona. The first was played in Rome and, through poor planning, we stayed in a lousy hotel and several players felt groggy after uncomfortable nights. At Wembley in 2011, Barcelona were very clever and rattled us by maintaining a lot of possession. Instead of staying patient and sticking to our plan, a bit of panic set in and our attacking impulse became our undoing. We were overcome by primal instincts.

## Fresh Challenges

But those are the yesterdays and now, after a lifetime of getting ready for work at six in the morning, I like waking up at eight, having breakfast with Cathy (which I had not done for 30 years), reading the paper, and going to have lunch in the village. I suppose retirement, for some people, can be like bereavement.

Immediately after you retire, there are lots of things to do and plenty of people around. Normally, after the players had disappeared at the end of the season, I would be in my office at Carrington every day until we left for our annual holiday in France in early June. In 2013 I found there were other things that filled my time. There was a fair amount of press attention after I retired, and I was helping to put the finishing touches to my autobiography. After that the summer got chewed up, with a pair of notable firsts, one more pleasurable than the other: a boat trip up the coast of Western Scotland, and a stint in hospital for a hip replacement.

The first reminder that I had retired came when we were on holiday in France that June. In previous years I would be on the telephone several times a day, usually dealing with players we wanted to buy or were willing to sell. David Gill would make frequent visits, and the club was never far from my mind. I would also have to meet players, and sometimes their parents, when we wanted to convince them to stake their futures to United. It was always the arrival of the fixture list for the upcoming season that would jolt me out of any propensity to put all cares aside. In 2013, for the first time in my life, my most pressing need, as I relaxed by the Mediterranean, was to beat my brother-in-law, John Robertson, at Kaluki.

When I recovered from the hip surgery and started going to games at Old Trafford, it felt a little odd. I had never had lunch in the directors' lounge before a game, and for the first time I also really noticed the noise of the crowd. While I had been managing, I had usually been able to block out the sound from the stands, and it rarely ever registered with me.

It is only now, a couple of years into this new chapter of my life, that I really have come to appreciate the change in circumstances. While I was working I had never fully appreciated that I was not in control of my life. I know this will seem peculiar, given how much I value the virtues of control and discipline, but when you sit atop any organisation, you are imprisoned by the calendar and the relentless needs of others. It doesn't matter if you work 24 hours a day, there will always be something or someone that demands your attention.

It was no wonder I always sensed – though I am not complaining – that the hamster wheel never stopped spinning. I was always looking at my watch – and not just in the closing minutes of games. So after I retired, for the first time in my life, I was in charge of my life in a way that I had not been since the school holidays of my childhood, when the only thing I needed to do was be home for lunch and dinner. It was a liberating and refreshing experience and has allowed me to do things that I could never have done while I was at the helm of United.

I have tried to balance things so that I stay vital and engaged, while also leading my life at a different pace. Apart from Manchester United games, the regular fixtures in my diary are appearances for the club in my role as a board member and club ambassador; the classes that I teach at Harvard; and the work I do as a UEFA coaching ambassador. In the UEFA role, I chair the annual Elite Coaches Forum in Geneva. In advance I will meet Ioan Lupescu from UEFA and we will structure the agenda. The forum itself is attended by the coaches of the teams competing in the Champions League and Europa League, as well as experienced coaches like Gérard Houllier, Roy Hodgson and UEFA president Michel Platini and his committee. The retired Italian referee, Pierluigi Collina, also attends, and we discuss with him the performance of referees but, in general, we cover the issues related to the previous season's competitions and look at ways we can continue to improve the game. I'm also a member of the technical study group of the Champions League and the Europa League; we meet the day after the finals to analyse the trends and tactics from the previous night's game.

During the horse-racing season, barely a week goes by without some kind of activity. Together with a few pals, I have owner-ship interests in a number of horses. We buy them usually when they are two year olds. I have enjoyed watching What A Friend winning two Group One races, or going to race meetings at York or Doncaster, and being able to linger at the track without feeling the need to bolt back to Manchester.

I like going through the sales catalogues and trying to under-stand the bloodlines and pedigree of the horses. Every now and again, when one of these horses turns into a winner, we have made some decent money – although this is the exception. I don't kid myself: horse racing is a pastime; it is not a way to build a durable investment. I always try to either watch or listen to a race when one of our horses is running, and invariably get a chuckle when the phone rings, or the texts arrive, at the end of the races.

I found myself getting absorbed by *The Brothers*, Stephen Kinzer's account of the lives of the Dulles brothers who were the US Secretary of State and head of the CIA in the 1950s. This was not a subject I knew much about, and the litany of their endless interference in countries all around the world during the Cold War kept me riveted. Coincidentally, at about the same time, I also picked up Ben Macintyre's *A Spy Among Friends*, another study of the Cold War era, which explains the way the double-agent, Kim Philby, betrayed his closest friends, as he spent decades leading a treacherous life in broad daylight. I'm glad the Dulles boys and Philby weren't working for United. Though I don't read many books about football, I have found myself going back to my roots and enjoyed two works about the sport north of the border. The first, *Black Diamonds and the Blue Brazil*, is an affectionate portrait of Cowdenbeath FC written by a long-time fan, Ron Ferguson, who, despite the name, is not a relative. The second is a biography of Sean Fallon, *Celtic's Iron Man*, by Stephen Sullivan. Fallon was Jock Stein's right-hand man at Celtic for many years, and this book is a detailed account of the life that, to all intents and purposes, they led together.

Retirement has presented the opportunity to indulge myself in trips and excursions that I would not have taken while at United. I fulfilled one ambition in 2014 when I attended the Oscars in Los Angeles. The Kentucky Derby horse race and the US Masters golf are also on the wish-list.

There have also been some really special experiences, like the tour I received of the vast State Hermitage museum in St Petersburg, which has the largest collection of paintings anywhere in the world. Mikaël Silvestre, who was a stalwart of United's defence for many seasons, was kind enough to line up a dinner, while Cathy and I were visiting Paris, at Le Taillevent, one of Europe's gastronomic treasures. Mikaël ensured that we were spoiled rotten, but he also couldn't resist playing a practical joke; he had instructed the sommelier to tell me that, unfortunately, he could not serve us any wine, because we had chosen to dine on Tuesday – the one day in the week when the restaurant did not offer alcohol. I also spent a couple of pleasurable days at Notre Dame, the university just west of Chicago, where Bobby Clark, the former Aberdeen and Scotland goalkeeper, is the football coach. Bobby gave me a tour of the Notre Dame campus, which has a staggering collection of stadiums and gyms that are better than those of most Premier League sides.

Sharing stories and memories with Mikaël or Bobby reminds me of what I miss about my old life. It isn't the open-top bus tours, the pleasure of spotting a youngster with great talent or the thrill of a closely fought game. Rather, it is all those shared experiences and the camaraderie that emerges between people who live and work together for a long time. I miss talking to Mick Phelan; seeing Albert Morgan, our kit man, every day; giving stick to Tony Sinclair and Joe Pemberton, our head groundsmen at Old Trafford and Carrington. I also used to relish the daily exchanges with the laundry team and Carol Williams and Rita Gaskell from the canteen. But most of all I miss being around the company of young people eager to take on impossible challenges – whether they were the players or the eager crew of video analysts. Just thinking about all these people and the scenes inside a winning dressing room makes me chuckle. But, as I said, those are the yesterdays and right now I keep remembering a short piece of advice about tomorrow that I was given before I retired. It was, 'Don't put your slippers on.' The line has stuck with me. It's why I put my shoes on right after breakfast.

# EPILOGUE

## SIR ALEX FERGUSON – THROUGH ANOTHER LENS

Since his retirement, match days for Sir Alex Ferguson have brought a fresh ritual. Gone are the times when he would leave The Lowry Hotel, where the Manchester United squad often stay on the night before home games, for the ride in the team bus to Old Trafford. Instead he arrives in one of the Chevrolet SUVs supplied by United's largest sponsor, and makes his way to the executive suite for a pre-game lunch.

These days, when Sir Alex watches a game, it's no longer from the manager's seat but rather from the directors' box – a perch that would have seemed inconceivable to a child growing up, as he did, in 1940s Govan. At kick-off he takes his seat – among the eight inscribed with 'Reserved for Sir Alex Ferguson' – opposite the triple-decker North Stand, the largest football stand in the United Kingdom, which, since 2011, has borne his name in large red letters. He no longer chews gum throughout the game, but instead repeatedly clears his throat. He keeps his thoughts to himself, particularly on days when United are not at their best, but every now and again, when a player in red is on the attack, he will mutter, 'Take him on, son. Take him on.'

After the game, he will retreat to his own suite, which has few of the trappings of the luxury boxes found at American stadiums or new football grounds like the Emirates, Arsenal's London home. It is the size of a windowless railway carriage: three black couches line the wall, a small bar stands at one end, a television is mounted near the ceiling and, occasionally, after the end of a game, the door opens and a security guard ushers in a new visitor.

Sometimes the door opens and a familiar face appears – a talk-show host, a film star or a former player. There might be a couple of people, dressed smartly in suits and ties, who have won a prize at a charity auction to watch a game with Sir Alex. People come to obtain an autograph, shake his hand or pose for a photograph. Drinks are passed around, glasses are raised and Sir Alex genially introduces everyone – urging them all to try the steak pies.

Eventually, the crowd thins down to a smaller group, most of whom have known Sir Alex – or Alec, as his Scottish relatives and friends call him – for the better part of a lifetime, and are now in their sunset years. At this point in the proceedings, it is hard to believe that the man on the receiving end of much good-natured teasing managed Manchester United for 26 years – first as Alex Ferguson OBE, then as Alex Ferguson CBE and, finally, as Sir Alex Ferguson, during which time he won 38 trophies, including 13 Premier League and two Champions League titles.

For those in the suite, the facts that, under his leadership, United won their 20th League championship, eclipsing the record set by Liverpool, or that, by the end of a truly remarkable career (although he would be the last person to mention this fact), he had become the most successful manager in the history of football, are beside the point. His career, an extraordinary mix of personal stamina, willpower and leadership, is not what draws these people to Old Trafford. There may be a friend, who tells how, when he was lying despondently in a hospital bed receiving life-saving treatment, Sir Alex came and spent several hours lifting him out of his gloom. There might be the wife of a former player, glowing with the satisfaction that comes from knowing she and her husband are sitting there because Sir Alex answered her letter and invited them to spend the afternoon with him.

Manchester United's long-time kit man, Albert Morgan, proudly wearing his club blazer, will sit quietly and act as the occasional straight-man. Ferguson's brother, Martin, invariably introduced as 'the greatest scout in history', might be there, along with one or two of Sir Alex's grandchildren. John Robertson, Sir Alex's wry brother-in-law, who was a compositor for the *Glasgow Herald*, will be muttering amusing and sardonic asides. Then the good-natured jousting begins and the conversation enters familiar stomping grounds, with stories, the comfort of recycled jokes and past embarrassments plucked out of the air. There will be prolonged discussion over whether St Patrick was Welsh. Somebody will try to remember the starting line-up for St Mirren in the early 1970s, and soon everyone is pitching in until the faded team-card is complete.

It's hard to imagine anyone less qualified than me to fill out a musty team-card or to write a book about football with Sir Alex Ferguson. As a ten year old in Wales in the 1960s, my peak footballing accomplishment was to stand on the touchline as the 'physio', holding a sponge and a bottle of water, lest any of my schoolmates might get injured, and to guard the Thermos and slices of oranges that served for their half-time refreshments.

Though I had followed Manchester United since the team

won the European Cup for the first time in 1968, and, like every British schoolboy, knew the names of its troupe of players, I don't qualify as a diehard fan. Manchester United's former captain, the blunt and confrontational Roy Keane, would dismiss me as a member of the 'prawn sandwich' crowd. When I moved to the US in 1980 to become a journalist at *Time* magazine, I kept half an eye on the team, but it wasn't until the late 1990s that I began to follow the club more closely – partly, no doubt, because more games were being broadcast in the United States. The other reason I was drawn back to the game was because of a fondness for the theatre and gossip that surrounds the Premier League: the big-ticket transfers, the rash managerial sackings, the intensity of the local derbies and, more often than not through this period, another trophy for Sir Alex Ferguson's United team.

As a journalist at *Time*, before, in 1986, joining Sequoia Capital, the California-based private investment partnership, I wrote two books about companies dominated by strong leaders. The first was an account (written with Barry Seaman) of Lee Iacocca's turnaround of Chrysler almost 40 years ago. The second, published in 1984, was a study of the very early years of Apple and the influence of its co-founder, Steve Jobs.

As the years slid by, I became increasingly interested in the ways one person can shape and influence an organisation, particularly the handful who maintain their hunger for success and can coax others to perform at high levels for prolonged periods. When, in the mid-1990s, I found myself *primus inter pares* among Sequoia's partners, I became even more aware of the challenge. Like any organisation, Sequoia Capital has to constantly fight for its place in the world. While we have an affinity for winning, I don't pretend for a moment that we resemble Manchester United. For a start, our lineage is nowhere near as long. We only came into being in 1974 when Don Valentine, a veteran of Silicon Valley's semiconductor industry, organised our first investment partnership. We operate beyond the glare of public scrutiny, although that has changed to a modest degree in the past few years, since Silicon Valley is now awash with journalists and bloggers. There is now even a popular HBO series titled *Silicon Valley*.

While few know the names of Sequoia's principals, that is not the case for some of the founders or companies with whom we have been involved since their inception. The most successful of these – Apple, Cisco, Google, Yahoo! and PayPal – have become every bit as visible in the business pages as United is on the sports pages. The same is true for some of our more recent investments, such as LinkedIn, Airbnb and Dropbox or, in China, VIPShop and JD.com. The combined market capitalisation of companies that received their first investment from Sequoia Capital is about $1.5 trillion.

After the Premier League arrived on American television and I was able to watch Manchester United regularly, my curiosity about the skill it takes to become a successful leader eventually led me to Sir Alex. I was intrigued to know how he had accumulated more trophies than any other manager in the world's most competitive and popular sport. Thanks to the good offices of Charlie Stillitano, one of the founding members of the US Soccer Foundation, I was introduced to the man himself. In a London hotel room, on the eve of a United game against Arsenal seven years ago, we polished off a bottle of wine and – interrupted a couple of times by players who needed some private words with Sir Alex – began the first of many conversations that eventually helped form this book.

The list of leadership topics that Sir Alex and I started to chew over soon stretched the length of a football field. How had he been able to inculcate the benefits of teamwork above the role of an individual – particularly among young, highly paid, intensely competitive characters? How had he managed to instil hope of a better tomorrow and the desire to win in a club that, prior to his arrival in 1986, had failed to win an English League championship for almost 20 years? How did he find and develop talent? How did he retain them? How did he set targets? How did he make people aspire to achieve the impossible? When did he give up on young players? How did he balance different levels of compensation? How did he cope with distractions, mete out punishment and instil discipline? How did he bounce back from setbacks or deal with press criticism or maintain balance in his life? How did he think about competitors and deal with changes? How did he set aside his personal feelings for particular individuals? How did he prevent complacency from setting in? How did he prepare, plan and communicate? How did he maintain his enthusiasm and hunger?

Many of the habits and approaches that hold true for the best football teams are also germane for any organisation that seeks to excel – even an investment partnership housing multiple businesses and active on several continents. There are plenty of parallels between life in the English Premier League, the most fiercely contested sporting competition in the world, and the stretch of land that lies between San Francisco and San Jose – which is little farther than the distance between Old Trafford and Anfield. Yet it is also easy to make too many trite analogies between Manchester United, an organisation that, 50 to 60 times a year, confronts a worldwide television audience, most of whom consider themselves qualified experts, and the world of large companies and government agencies, or of local hospitals, boy-scout troops and community centres.

For Sequoia Capital, lessons drawn from leaders in other fields or organisations can be applied in two ways. The first is to our own, internal investment partnership, where we deal with many of the organisational challenges that bedevil any company or institution seeking to perform at the highest possible level. Like any other organization, we contend with issues around recruitment, team-building, setting of standards, questions of inspiration and motivation, avoiding complacency, the arrival of new competitors and the continual need to refresh ourselves and purge under-performers. The second is towards the companies in which we invest, and where we are often the first, serious business partner for talented entrepreneurs, frequently still in their early or mid-twenties, setting out on a path that, sometimes, turns an entire industry upside down. In the first case, after internal wrangling and jawboning, we can usually apply what seems relevant. In the second, where we are minority shareholders in companies started and run by people of great wit, imagination, drive and, often, emotional fragility and temperamental dispositions, we need to rely on powers of persuasion, motivation, sensible counsel and, more often than not, good humour, to help someone do something, or make a decision, the wisdom of which might not be immediately apparent.

There is no other place in the world where companies wreak so much havoc on existing industries as Silicon Valley, the world I have inhabited since the early 1980s. Here new technology companies are formed almost every day. Most of them either fail or are quickly subsumed by others. Only a handful, far fewer than all the Silicon Valley spin-masters would have you believe, are great in the way in which Manchester United, Bayern Munich, Real Madrid or Barcelona are great and have dominated football since the Second World War. In the past

40 years, the list of technology giants is surprisingly short; the only qualifiers, at least in my book, are Apple, Cisco, Oracle, Google, Facebook, Intel, Microsoft, Amazon, Qualcomm, Alibaba and Tencent (though the last five are based in Seattle, San Diego and China rather than Silicon Valley proper).

Any student of business, management or economics knows there are very few groups capable of excelling for a long time. Just think of all the restaurants, hotels, bars, bakeries and toy shops on the High Street that once commanded a devoted following, only to founder as their standards fell or tastes changed. The same is true in the corporate world, and in the United States a quick look at the Dow Jones 30 index shows the vicissitudes of time. Only seven companies that were in the index in 1976 are still present. Some, like steel mills and ship-builders, were slaughtered by offshore competition; retailers, like Sears, clung too much to their heritage; while once powerful companies in a wide range of industries – newspapers, cinema, radio and television broadcasting, advertising, real-estate brokerage, printing – have been upset, transformed or gutted by advances in technology. Many, of course, were felled by managers who made the wrong choices, thought themselves invulnerable and were undone by a combination of ineptitude and vanity.

For firms like Sequoia Capital, this cycle of growth and decay is of keen interest because our business depends on it. The technology world is far less forgiving of leadership failures than other industries, because a sudden, underlying change can quickly catapult a young company into a position of prominence and spell trouble for an industry leader. The floor of the technology world is littered with the butchered carcasses of high flyers that once could do no wrong: Digital Equipment, Compaq, Data General, Cray Computer Corporation, Silicon

Graphics, Lotus Development, PeopleSoft, Novell, Sun Microsystems, Wang Laboratories, Siebel Systems, BlackBerry, Nokia – the list is endless. So we've always been eager to learn about what leadership characteristics differentiate the so-called 'academy' companies from the true giants, particularly since I have always felt that a vast gulf separates a great leader from a very good manager. Accomplished and skilful managers can be hired by the truckload. Leaders are the rarest of commodities. So, here is what I learned about the character of one leader – the man who used to wear a jacket bearing the initials 'AF'.

When the teenager, later identified as 'AF', started as a professional footballer, he and his fellow players were treated little better than oddly gifted manual workers, employed by local business people who, in addition to a football club, also owned steel mills, shipyards, a chain of shops or, in the case of Louis Edwards, Manchester United's chairman and principal shareholder between 1965 and 1980, a meat distribution business. The class barriers, reinforced by archaic structures laid down by the Football Association's rule-makers in their London headquarters, reinforced this divide.

Sir Alex played his first League game in 1957 – when, despite the date, the game was still lodged in its interwar mode. Players selected for international teams would often only discover they had been picked after seeing their name on a team-sheet in the newspapers. Floodlights were just starting to appear; the handful of fixtures that received television coverage were broadcast in black and white; commercial hoardings were absent from most British stadiums; fans stood on terraces (with the seats reserved for VIPs and season-ticket holders); the footballs were made of leather and became painfully heavy when wet; boots covered the ankles; players' shirts and shorts were made of cotton and the pitches quickly turned to mud. It was still an intensely local game. In the United Kingdom international fixtures were often interpreted to mean games between England, Scotland, Wales and Ireland. European football – the European champion- ship and the European Cup Winners' Cup – had yet to be launched and the European Cup was only two years old; the majority of players were born within a couple of bus rides of their club ground, and a salary cap that existed until 1961 meant that football workers were paid like factory hands. It was also a game played by white men; it was not until 1978 that a black footballer first appeared in the English national side.

Sir Alex himself attributes much of his success to his working-class roots on the banks of the River Clyde. The memory of the grit and perseverance his father displayed as a shipyard worker – working 60-hour weeks in cold, dangerous conditions – looms large. Beyond this ingrained disposition for hard work, and a touching inclination to appear early for appointments, Sir Alex has always seen himself as something of an outsider, a rebel without being a firebrand, irritated by pompous people in positions of authority and happiest when surrounded by family and the friends he has known since childhood. While he is intensely competitive and doesn't easily forget past slights, he is not a man who harbours malice. He has a natural sympathy for those who are struggling and an affinity with his fellow managers, partly because all of them had a common challenge: the unpredictable behaviour of club owners who could dismiss them at a moment's notice. It was entirely characteristic of him, in remarks to a packed Old Trafford following his final game as a manager, to mention the United midfielder, Darren Fletcher, who for the previous five years had been battling ulcerative colitis, and the retirement of the midfielder, Paul Scholes, after more than 700 appearances for the club, whose dislike of the spotlight was inversely related to the influence he wielded on the pitch.

He might blanch at the label, but Sir Alex, a lifelong supporter of the British Labour Party, is, at heart, a conservative – with a small 'c'. He is self-made, keenly appreciates loyalty (which is returned in spades), doesn't tolerate slackers, poseurs and braggarts, and cannot hide his disdain for high-profile free-loaders who show up with an entourage for an important game and demand a clutch of free tickets for the best seats in the ground. Even though he's worked hard all his life, Sir Alex feels he's had it easy compared to miners, farmers, fishermen, oil-field workers, steelworkers and shipbuilders – manual labourers who have often faced difficult and dangerous conditions at work. He is, by nature, an optimist, and though he has the jovial characteristics of the pub owner he once was, he is not inclined to embrace complete strangers with bear hugs as his brother, Martin, is prone to do.

Though he is fond of the good things in life and is wealthy by most people's standards, Sir Alex isn't avaricious, and has never felt the need to own the largest house (or collection of homes) or a stable of exotic cars. Compared to today's footballing stars, he and his wife Cathy live quietly and modestly. Though she never attended games at Old Trafford, Cathy – whose instinct is to protect her husband from the overtures of strangers – has always been keenly aware of whatever duel is being fought on the field.

Sir Alex has a chess master's memory for numbers, deals and people, which lends additional authority to his observations. Ask him the score of football games played decades ago, and he'll remember not just the final score and most names on the starting team-sheets but also the critical substitutions and the build-up to many of the goals. He will reel off the entire Premier

League fixture list for the weekend that lies ahead with the same quiet confidence with which other people complete *The Times* crossword in ten minutes. He will remember with precision what price he paid and gained for a player (wincing when recalling occasions on which the latter was less than the former); the amount he contributed for his share of a horse – like Harry the Viking or Chapter and Verse – and how much he paid for a 1986 Pétrus or 1993 Sassicaia, though his face will suddenly harden and his lips will purse when recounting an investment over which he feels he was duped. It is easy to see how, if destiny and circumstances had been different, he probably would have succeeded at whatever he had turned towards: leading a trade union, operating a chain of retailers, commanding an aircraft carrier, or – if for some reason Silicon Valley had developed between Glasgow and Edinburgh in the 1940s and 1950s – founding a company.

Unnervingly he can recite the names of the hotels that he and Cathy have visited and, without guile and almost reflexively, will name each of the children of their friends. He is reticent about asking others for special treatment and will cringe when recounting an experience or pleasure that came his way due to the kindness of others. Long-time football fans might remember his emotional outbursts on the sidelines, and journalists who covered him throughout his career might recall being subjected to the occasional stream of profanities and abuse, but most people aren't aware of his patience and innumerable acts of kindness: the good-natured way he will pose for photographs or sign autographs, politely say a few words to someone who interrupts his dinner at a restaurant or who stops him in the street. Little wonder that, for years, he has welcomed the relative anonymity of New York, where he has an apartment.

He likes winning whatever card game (such as Kaluki) or

snooker challenge he plays. He prefers red wine and has never drunk whisky, the pride of his homeland. For the past 15 years, his summers have been spent in the same hotel in the south of France, where he knows all the staff by name, and thoroughly admires the way the owner is up at dawn meticulously inspecting his property.

Sir Alex is a card-carrying member of several tribes – his own family, the memory of the tenements of Govan, Glasgow, Scotland and Manchester United. Most of all he still feels he belongs to the working-class tribe, and remembers, with a shiver, the cold Scottish mornings when, as an apprentice tool-maker, he had to tie rags around the end of the lathes to keep his hands warm.

Sir Alex Ferguson was United's manager from 1986 to 2013, but never held the title that, in the business world, applies to the most senior person in the organisation: chief executive officer. From 1980 to 2000 that role belonged to Martin Edwards, at the time the club's principal shareholder, from 2000 to 2003 to Peter Kenyon and from 2003 to 2013 to David Gill, whom Sir Alex came to view as a blood brother.

This may sound odd, but Sir Alex, unlike so many other people who experience success at the head of an organisation, was not confused about his position. He knew he was a hired hand. He did not delude himself into thinking that he was the man who built Manchester United; he was well aware of the fact that he had come to a club with a rich heritage that had enjoyed much success due to the work, sacrifices and perform-ance of those who had preceded him. Sir Alex never imagined when he joined United that his image would one day be cast in bronze and be placed, for all to see, outside the stadium. I would be surprised if he ever thought, even in his most private moments, that he was bigger than the club. He has the sort of moral compass that is not found among leaders who award themselves a disproportionate share of the spoils; talk about themselves and their accomplishments in the third person; don't have the humility and inner decency to recognise that they are standing on the shoulders of those who came before; or understand that they are merely custodians, charged with leaving the organisation in better condition than it was when they arrived.

Ferguson ruled everything that occurred on the pitch, was responsible for the lion's share of the club's spending and was in charge of the majority of the club's payroll. Generation of revenue (negotiation of television rights, sales of sponsorships, setting of ticket prices, international tours) and management of advertising, promotions, stewardship of financial systems and human relations were the preserve of the club's 'commercial side', which fell under the purview of the CEO. But of course the 'commercial side' hinged on a first-rate performance on the field, and the growth in the value of the club – from £20 million in 1989, when Martin Edwards first thought about selling his stake, to £1.93 billion today – is irrevocably associated with Sir Alex. While he had plenty of frustrations during his managerial life, his control over what is colloquially called the 'dressing room' – the players, coaches, groundsmen and the medical and sports science staff – was as complete as that of any absolute monarch. The way that former players, now in their fifties or sixties, still address him as 'Boss' is freighted with meaning. In the words of Reggie Jackson, one of the kings of American baseball during the 1970s and 1980s, Sir Alex was the straw that stirred the drink.

Other business organisations split executive responsibilities in a similar way to Manchester United. Think of an advertising agency or fashion house, whose inspiration and following comes from the inventiveness and imagination of a creative director, but where the commercial affairs are run by a CEO. Consider the newspapers and magazines of yesteryear, where the editorial coverage was the preserve of the editor and the sale of subscriptions and advertising of the publisher or the CEO. Look at movie companies where directors are always at war with the men (and now women) who used to be called 'suits'. In the arts there are orchestra conductors, museum and theatre directors responsible for artistic repertoires, shadowed by a CEO, whose name is usually unknown to the public but who is responsible for maintaining a going concern. If Manchester United were a Silicon Valley company, Sir Alex's title would probably have been chief product architect or chief designer, and David Gill's would have been chief commercial officer.

Some – particularly from the business world, large public agencies or the military – will look at Manchester United and conclude that this footballing enterprise would be straightforward to run. If so, they are underestimating the challenge of constantly buffing a global entertainment brand that relies on the unpredictable physical condition and mental state of a changing collection of absurdly talented live performers. While United's reputation is vast (and, thanks to the explosion of satellite television and mobile computing, it now has fans in faraway places such as Bhutan, Djibouti or Belize), its business and payroll, measured alongside some of Silicon Valley's companies or some of the world's larger companies, is surprisingly small and pedestrian. The club's revenues in its last fiscal year were £433 million, which is what Apple and Google do in 30 hours and four days respectively. It only operates one line of business and it does this in one time zone rather than in separate locations scattered across different continents. The club's expansion opportunities are circumscribed. The Old Trafford stadium has 75,731 seats and is already the largest club ground in Britain. It is hard to squeeze more games into a year when, in a busy season, the most heavily worked players already take the field 38 times for Premier League games as well as FA Cup, League Cup and European competition fixtures, not to mention the pre-season exhibitions, friendlies, international matches, testimonial and charitable games that find their way into the calendar. United's share of television revenue, which was non-existent before the formation of the English Premier League, fluctuates with the team's performance, as do its other sources of revenue: ticket sales, rental of luxury boxes, and sponsorship and merchandising opportunities. Like most sports franchises, Manchester United would not meet any of Warren Buffett's investment criteria – its performance is unpredictable, it requires large capital outlays and there is no lid on costs.

And yet a huge gulf exists between Manchester United, and the other top-ranked clubs in the Premier League, and every other football team in Britain. The vast difference in crowd size is illustrative of the way that in football, as in almost every other organised activity, the fruits of triumph are concentrated in a few hands. Manchester United might fill their stands with 75,000 people for every game (as befits a stadium that is as much an international house of worship as a 'theatre of dreams'), but drop down 15 teams to West Bromwich Albion, and average attendance is 25,000; drop down to the league below, the Championship, and the crowds can dwindle to under 15,000. So, while Manchester United may appear easy to operate, it is, as with other organisations, another matter entirely to operate it well. It is even more of a challenge to keep it operating at a very high standard for a protracted period. Maintaining that standard of excellence is no fluke.

That same disparity, between the winners and the also-rans, exists in the technology world. Here, the market-leading company will sweep up the lion's share of the spoils – measured in customers, profits, free cash flow and market value. Think of IBM at the peak of the mainframe business; Intel, when the demand for microprocessors was unstoppable; Microsoft, as personal computer software spread into every business and home; eBay, when online auctions were all the vogue; Google, as it became synonymous with 'search' and Facebook with its hammer-lock on social networking. Then of course there is Apple which, without the monopoly characteristics of these other companies (making its accomplishment even more staggering), has outstripped them all.

The rivalries that exist in the English Premier League, while heated and often profane, seem quaint and gentlemanly compared to the competition that exists between the founders of technology companies where vicious barbs, lawsuits, theft of trade secrets and targeted assaults on one another's payroll are the order of the day. Perhaps this is only natural since the winner in technology races (where so often the leaders are monopolies in all but the eye of the law) mops up not just a share but the equivalent of all of the Premier League's television, ticket, merchandising, beer and hot dog money (including the ketchup and mustard). Microsoft, Intel, Amazon, Bloomberg, Google, Apple, Facebook, Oracle, Qualcomm, Alibaba, Baidu, Tencent, Cisco and eBay all illustrate this point, and if anyone thinks the competitive atmosphere in California is hot, they should go to China to sample the invective with which technology CEOs greet a rival's move. The founders of many of these technology companies would sooner share a pint of turpentine with one of their arch-rivals than sit down and mend fences with a glass of Tignanello, one of Sir Alex's favourite red wines. Larry Ellison, the founder of Oracle, was probably only half joking when he said he wanted to shoot the CEO of PeopleSoft, a company he acquired after a bitter two-year takeover battle in 2005.

Despite the difference in tone that exists between our two worlds, writing *Leading* with Sir Alex made two things apparent. The first is that a manager of a professional football team, and someone who works in an investment partnership with a fondness for the venture capital business, share the same pursuit – they are both transfixed by the possibilities of eternal youth. While both need to make sure their own house is always in order, their pursuit of success and market leadership is not constricted by the straitjacket that eventually fells every technology company – a slowing growth rate, some caused by sheer size, but most by a massive market change. We also have another enormous advantage which for a football club means fielding young players and, in the case of a venture capitalist, constantly striking up partnerships with young founders eager to make a mark with a new idea. Both manager and investor are largely insulated from the challenges posed by old products or ageing workforces. We have the wonderful luxury of always being able to stay on the young side of life.

The second point that became clear was that the principles of leadership are timeless, and that the opaque jargon found in so many management books is little more than a marketing ruse. The trick lies not in memorising some list of the rudiments of leadership (which any intelligent 14 year old can do) but, rather, having the stamina, knowledge and skill to consistently implement them. Press Sir Alex to choose three words to summarise his approach to leadership and he would pick three that begin with the same letter – preparation, perseverance and patience. Compel him to select one word and he would fasten on – consistency.

There are plenty of attributes that separate the great leader from the good manager. Both may put their work before family and friends, survive on little sleep, endure a lifetime of red-eye flights. Look more closely and you will find that the great leader possesses an unusual, and essential, characteristic – he will think and operate like an owner, or a person who owns a substantial stake of the business, even if, in a financial or legal sense, he is neither. It is extremely rare to find this trait among people like Sir Alex who are hired into a company, although in Silicon Valley this sense of long-term proprietorship is the distinctive hallmark of the best company founders. These sorts of people will never be oblivious to the pressing exigencies of their business, but they will always have a larger purpose in mind. Their attitude and approach is a world removed from that of most of the handsomely paid retainers who find themselves at the helm of an enterprise.

The great leader will embrace audacity and the unthinkable, will not shirk from making controversial and unpopular decisions, and will have unshakeable confidence in his convictions. He will have a clear sense of his ultimate goal and will be able to communicate that articulately to others. While his business may be complicated, he will be able to strip things down to their essence. The great leader will not compile endless lists of marching orders but, rather, will have a preference for keeping his followers' eyes on no more than two or three objectives. He will have the patience required to assemble something superlative while simultaneously curbing his own impatience. He will survey his colleagues with a clinical detachment and, regardless of their past contributions, will not hesitate about bidding them farewell if they miss too many beats. The great leader is prepared to trust the judgement of others, is unafraid of delegating authority, refrains from micromanagement, and will not be impelled to dominate every conversation or insist upon always having the last word in a debate. The great leader knows that most success comes from making a few large decisions correctly rather than trying to be involved in making lots of small choices. He will understand that there are others in the organisation capable of doing things that he himself cannot do or would not do as well. He will derive more satisfaction from the achievements of his organisation than from his own accomplishments, will not demand outlandish compensation for himself, will treat the organisation's money as if it were his own and will have no particular need to be singled out by the spotlight. He will probably watch and listen more than he talks, will not radiate anxiety when the chips are down, will have a keen understanding of what he doesn't know and a fetching sense of humility. If he does his job well, people will see him as being tough but fair rather than capricious and mercurial. He will definitely not feel the need to be universally loved. At the end of his tenure, knowing that his time has ended, he will relinquish authority with grace and will not sour the life of his successor.

Compare this with the capable manager who has attained his position by virtue of attrition, by being politically acceptable or by being a faithful, long-suffering servant. Having achieved the position that he has sought for many years he will concentrate on making sure that nothing goes wrong on his watch, will be wary about offending others, will shy away from making difficult decisions, will be at ease with the imperfections of compromise, will allow his strategy to be dictated by others, will find refuge in appeasement and court the affection of those around him. When he eventually retires, his organisation will be little different from the one he inherited. It will definitely not have achieved anything remarkable.

The great leader has two other traits that separate him from other helmsmen. The first is an obsession. Obsessives, those who cannot imagine doing anything else with their lives, always find their work more fulfilling than those who find themselves in a profession because it was expected of them or because they did not have a calling that tugged at their emotions. For people, like Sir Alex, who are obsessed by a pursuit, there is no separation between life and work. They are leading their life, rather than feeling compelled to seek respectability from their work.

The obsessives will find it far easier to maintain their enthusiasm for their calling than the person who clambers up an organisation and survives the Darwinism of the workplace. It is much more natural for the obsessive to achieve the consistency – of effort, determination, drive and ambition – that is the foundation of leadership. It is much easier to endure all the setbacks, reversals and frustrations of management when you deeply enjoy your work – a sense that most ordinary managers rarely, if ever, experience.

The second trait of the distinctive leader is his capacity for dealing with people. These leaders will be able to extract extraordinary levels of performance and commitment from their employees and colleagues. Some of that will just be by setting a personal example, but the bulk will come from having a keen understanding for the character of their employees and an empathy for them when they are weathering difficult circumstances. They will be able to blend intimacy with ambition.

Listening to Sir Alex, and watching him with others, made it clear that there is an uncommon resilience about him and the mainstays of his United teams. The need to succeed ran deep. This is the inner fortitude born of adversity, shaped by setbacks, reversals and the fear of failure, burnished by the sense of social inequity common to outsiders, underdogs and immigrants, by the stubborn refusal never, ever, to give up, and the personal shame associated with disappointing colleagues. These are the same constitutional underpinnings required of entrepreneurs, and have been the characteristics of the sort of people I have always admired. About ten years ago I added a piece of copy to the Sequoia website that tried to summarise the character of the people with whom we seek to work. It reads: 'The creative spirits. The underdogs. The resolute. The determined. The indefatigable. The defiant. The outsiders. The independent thinkers. The fighters. The true believers.' Reading it now makes me think it could also serve as instructions for Sir Alex's United scouts.

Silicon Valley teems with examples of these types. Jerry Yang, the co-founder of Yahoo!, is one. His father died when he was a toddler and Jerry arrived in the United States from Taiwan, with his mother and younger brother, at the age of ten unable to understand English. Sergey Brin, the co-founder of Google, and Jan Koum, the co-founder of WhatsApp, share some of the same lineage as Jerry, though they arrived from the east. Sergey and his family fled religious persecution in the Soviet Union, as did Jan and his mother when they left Ukraine in 1992. There was much poignancy to the symbolism associated with the spot where, in February 2014, Jan signed the papers to sell his company to Facebook for $19 billion. It was outside the former welfare office in Mountain View where he and his mother had queued to collect their weekly food stamps. I'm not saying that childhood privation is a prerequisite for entrepreneurial success, but the children of middle-class parents – Microsoft's Bill Gates, Facebook's Mark Zuckerberg and Snapchat's Evan Spiegel – are among the minority of successful technology entrepreneurs. The most successful start-ups will, almost inevitably, have an immigrant or first-generation American or someone who has emerged from tough circumstances in their starting line-up.

Most entrepreneurs, especially in Silicon Valley, are self-made. They are not the product of business schools, and the majority of them have not spent any time working inside a large company being fashioned by others. They are what they have made themselves. Nobody has trained them to be what they become but they are, like Sir Alex, the products of their obsessions. The reason baby-faced leaders emerge in Silicon Valley is because they trip upon their obsession before the rest of the world wakes up to its potential. For these teenagers, or 20-somethings, their areas of interest develop wickedly fast, and either have not hit the radar screens of the big companies or are dismissed as fads. That's been true of personal computer software, short-form messaging, file-sharing software, music streaming, the use of black cars in place of taxis and the rental of spare bedrooms. Like Sir Alex, these founders were learning to be leaders on the job – which, in most cases, was their very first, full-time occupation.

By contrast Sir Alex, who happened on his calling before he was old enough to wear long trousers to school, chose a field – football – where changes occur slowly and the tricks of the trade are well known. This meant that, for him (and all the top-flight managers), it took far longer to accumulate the experience and knowledge required to lead than it does for a young Silicon Valley founder who has leapt on a new breakthrough before it has aroused notice elsewhere. By the time he arrived at United, Sir Alex had already served a long apprenticeship as a professional footballer, and had earned his coaching 'badges' before going on to manage Scottish clubs for 12 years. He had spent 30 years preparing for the opportunity that he earned at Old Trafford. Yet, whether it is in Manchester or Cupertino, mastery of a particular field remains a prerequisite for leadership, because it is the breeding ground for inner conviction and the foundation on which authority, and ultimately the respect of others, comes to rest.

Like Sir Alex, the Silicon Valley founders rely on their eyes, ears and instincts. For them it tends to lead to a desire to figure things out from first principles and a disdain for all conventions. They will harbour contempt for the structure and hierarchy of larger companies though, eventually, their own companies will take on these same habits. Early on, these founders will fire a relentless barrage of questions aimed at those who know a lot about a particular topic. They will also tear through piles of books or, these days, delve into the nooks and crannies of the web and late at night fall asleep listening to TED talks. As these small companies become larger and attract attention, the boundaries of the worlds of the founders expand. Accomplished and experienced people will take their calls or meet them. Warren Buffett is famous for entertaining the founders of some of Silicon Valley's younger companies at his favourite lunch spot in Omaha. Retired CEOs are usually happy to welcome these adventurers to their vacation homes in Florida or Palm Springs. Whatever form it takes, the underlying propellant is an inexhaustible thirst for knowledge.

These characters aren't afraid of adopting what makes sense for them and ignoring everything else, which is why their companies become the corporate expression (like United under Sir Alex) of themselves: Apple a product of a ruthless, poetic perfection; Oracle of a ferocious competitor with a tendency to vacuum up assets; Google an extension of Stanford University writ large; Intel, in its heyday, a triumph of engineering precision, and Amazon an expression of mathematical prowess. Along the way, there are usually lots of mistakes, much confusion, considerable management turnover, failed products and close encounters of the worst kind.

Growing up, while simultaneously building a company and trying to develop as a leader, is a tall order. Bill Gates, Mark Zuckerberg, Larry Page, Jeff Bezos, Larry Ellison, Elon Musk – and plenty more – all became chief executive officers when they were a decade younger than Sir Alex was when he took his first managerial position at East Stirlingshire. They are the products of their childhood and the hobby that turned into an obsession and became the seed of a business. None of them had built a management team, called on customers, dealt with suppliers or negotiated contracts. Their first customer is often themselves (since many of them build a product to satisfy a personal need); their initial hires are usually friends or school-mates (since nobody with a well-polished CV is inclined to risk going to work for somebody whose voice has barely broken); their early suppliers will be wary; their landlord will demand cash up front.

For these founders, the challenge of becoming their own person is exacerbated by the demands of a young company, which will only become more taxing as it grows. Since they are rowing against the tide, these people are suspicious of those who don't share their interests, or are of a different generation. Their task is made no easier by the fact that many of them do not share Sir Alex's gregarious disposition and ease in the company of others. On Myers-Briggs personality tests, plenty will be classified as either introverts, or extreme introverts. For this cadre of founders, eye contact, public speaking and small talk are painful activities. They will prefer the companionship of a computer, a technical paper or a book to that of a fellow human being. For them, overcoming their natural reticence is the first of many accomplishments.

Like United, the distinctive Silicon Valley companies will be shaped by leaders for whom working on products is the activity they most enjoy. For Sir Alex, that meant working with the United players and shaping their style of play. In California it might mean a founder who is fixated on the elegance of a chunk of code, the speed at which bytes are transmitted, the chemical and physical properties of a piece of silicon, the space in which data is stored or the size of a typeface. Like Sir Alex they will tend to leave to others the activities that don't interest them. Hence the manner in which Steve Jobs ceded logistics and operations to Tim Cook, or the way Bill Gates spent little time worrying about the design of marketing campaigns.

The best of these corporate leaders will also shun distractions and apportion their time with great care. Not for them incessant speeches at conferences, television interviews, meetings with politicians or attendances at charity functions. For them, every moment not spent dealing with business (or, when they get a bit older, family) is a wasted opportunity. Look at the old photographs of a younger Alex Ferguson, appearing bleary-eyed after surviving on four or five hours of sleep a night, and you see the face of every young entrepreneur. The most extreme example of this blistering desire to concentrate on his business that I ever encountered was the young Bill Gates. After he had bought a television set so he could watch educational videotapes, he eliminated the temptation to watch shows or movies by disconnecting the tuner. He also removed the radio from his car, lest news bulletins or music prevented him thinking about Microsoft during his brief commutes or on trips to and from the airport. For Bill and for Microsoft, the ability to shut off the outside world paid enormous dividends. The helicopter rides that he took to save time when forced to attend social engagements, or the enforced solitary confinement when he decamped twice a year to pore over technical papers and books, both helped eliminate the noise. It took Bill until 1994, when he was 39, to partially abandon his first true love, Microsoft, and marry Melinda French.

Profiles of successful leaders invariably dwell on what is visible – the result of careful handling by publicists, staged appearances or simply the reticence of the individuals themselves. Success depends on what happens behind the scenes where the hard work – the 17- or 18-hour-long days and the seven-days-a-week ritual – is conducted. Sir Alex is a great believer in the virtues of industry and set the example with his own actions – not asking anyone to apply themselves with more resolve than he demanded of himself. Sir Alex's world was visible for millions of viewers to see, and might have seemed effortless and spontaneous from the comfort of an armchair, but it was the result of relentless preparation. Behind every trophy there were dozens of Saturday mornings standing in driving rain scouting teenagers; behind every League trophy were thousands of training sessions; behind every triumph was a large, increasingly global network of individuals, whose sole task was to funnel youngsters into a system that ten, 15 or even 20 years later would have them making a critical pass or an important tackle.

I know Sir Alex would applaud the work ethic found among California's younger companies, not to mention their counterparts in China, who sometimes make me feel that Silicon Valley is a retirement community. It's why, in their formative years, companies like Google and Facebook had 'war rooms', where tiger teams of programmers were sequestered until they had solved a particular crisis, or 'lockdowns' where coders were forbidden to leave the premises until some calamity had been averted.

Sir Alex will be the first to say that much of the success he enjoyed was made possible by the setting in which he found himself – which, I suspect, is also responsible for the good fortune of many people in Silicon Valley. Sir Alex is not referring to United's history and earlier association with success, as much as he is to the support he received from the club's owners and board of directors, the ultimate arbiters of his fate – and, to a lesser extent, to the growth in the television market.

At both Aberdeen and United, Sir Alex did not have to deal with owners or directors who wanted to meddle in football affairs, or assistant managers who usurped his authority. Sir Alex was given what every leader deserves – control to shape his own destiny and that of his organisation. Having the time to establish a solid foundation and to, gradually, build towards long-term prosperity, is not a luxury afforded most football managers or business leaders, where the pressure to win or the need to produce quarterly earnings makes the quick fix almost irresistible. This freedom from the tyranny of immediate results enabled Sir Alex to constantly work on the composition of the club several years into the future, without worrying whether he would still be there if United had a bad losing streak. He was also granted the freedom to control his own realm. In Silicon Valley the founders of companies are also fixated on the importance of control. Today, they try to enshrine their position with all sorts of legal protections, which, for the weaker ones, means that they are doing themselves and their companies a disfavour. Nonetheless, the underlying impulse remains the same as Sir Alex's – the conviction that, come hell or high water, their way is the best.

Undoubtedly some of United's success during this period rests on the way technological breakthroughs transformed the television coverage of football. United, and for that matter the rest of the Premier League, have reaped enormous dividends from a huge decline in the price of computing and communication. Satellite transmission, remote-controlled cameras, high-definition displays, flatscreen televisions, the proliferation of the internet, the rise of social networking and instant communications are what have allowed United to perform on a global stage. Sir Alex readily admits that he vastly underestimated the impact of satellite and cable transmission of football games, and the container-loads of money that trailed in their wake. Yet the crowds that began to gather in living rooms and pubs to watch United did so because of the entertainment that he helped orchestrate. Any time United slipped, or were eliminated from the final throes of the European Cup competition, it had an immediate effect on the club's revenues. The revenues that flowed to United from the expanded television coverage were inextricably linked to the team's performance. The results lifted United's share of broadcast rights from an insignificant amount in 1985–86 to £60.8 million in Sir Alex's final season.

Yet for all the tailwinds propelling technology start-ups, they too, like the Premier League teams, have to deal with cruel blows and rude reversals of fortune. I cannot think of one successful company that Sequoia has been involved with that did not, at some point, face the threat of extinction. Newspaper headlines and television anchors love to proclaim the arrival of yet another Silicon Valley 'overnight success' or announce the baptism of a young, newly minted billionaire. Set aside the fact that a good number of what today are known as 'unicorns' will fall by the wayside, the more noteworthy examples of the companies that have eventually beaten all odds have been started by people blessed (and, in many cases, haunted) by the same sort of inner drive, discipline and hunger that propelled Sir Alex and his most successful players. Look at Pixar, where it took 16 years of experimentation, corporate convulsions, dead-ends and lay-offs before the release of the company's first full-length movie, *Toy*

*Story*. Or there is Nvidia, a chip company, formed in 1993, which now underpins the video-game industry, but whose first product was an abject failure and nearly consigned the company to oblivion. Today, as each rides high, it is easy to forget that, at the dawn of this century, Amazon was running on fumes and Blockbuster refused to purchase Netflix for pennies on the dollar. LinkedIn, now known around the world for its 364 million strong online professional network, required one year to reach its first 100,000 members. In each of these cases it required extraordinary drive, self-discipline and conviction to stay true to the course.

These triumphs of force and conviction are not limited to small companies. In the mid-1980s Intel, whose original business in computer memory devices had been destroyed by Japanese competitors, was reinvented by Bob Noyce, Gordon Moore and Andy Grove as a designer of microprocessors. Lou Gerstner's astonishing turnaround of IBM in the 1990s demonstrates what an extraordinary leader can do to a company given up for dead. The greatest example of the power of conviction is the minutely chronicled turnaround of Apple by Steve Jobs – a mission given the shortest of odds by people such as Michael Dell who, in 1997, famously announced that he would shut the company down and return the proceeds to shareholders.

For each of these examples, the technology industry is littered with examples of companies that did not fulfil their original destiny, because those at the helm either lacked the combination of drive, discipline and conviction that is required to build anything great or because they were started by people who did not understand the vast gulf that separates theory from reality. For me, three examples loom large. The first, by a long measure, is Webvan, an online grocer that became our worst investment because we abandoned common sense in a haphazard pursuit of mindless growth. Another is Zappos, the online shoe retailer, which, though acquired by Amazon in 2008 for just under $1 billion (now worth over $6 billion), did not fulfil its promise because, try as we might, we failed to persuade its founder of all the things that are required to build a great, enduring company. Finally, there is PayPal, which was bought by eBay in 2002 for $1.5 billion, even though Elon Musk and I had implored the rest of the board not to sell the company. Sadly, PayPal is now worth about $40 billion – proof that conviction and patience, as Sir Alex says, are precious commodities.

Understanding what is possible, setting realistic expectations and communicating them clearly enough to bring a team along with you, especially in a setting where everyone wants quick results, is one of the hardest leadership skills. It is easy to brim with enthusiasm, establish unattainable goals and leave everyone feeling deflated if the targets aren't achieved. While at St Mirren Sir Alex learned about the consequences of making bold predictions of future triumphs, and thereafter was careful to build success one step at a time. The purposeful cadence of a relentless, disciplined march is difficult to maintain, but a long record of success is built one trophy (or one sales record, engineering release, or financial result) at a time. The consistent application of a well-tuned approach that does not shift with every passing fancy, but is supple enough to absorb and accommodate useful advances, is one of the distinctive characteristics of Sir Alex's style. It is not an accident that Manchester United (without, under Sir Alex, ever resorting to the power of an overwhelming chequebook) was quick to change the composition of its squad as the Premier League made it possible for the best footballers in the world to ply their trade in Britain.

The goals designed for a young company to serve as a rallying cry tend to be more audacious than the ones Sir Alex so carefully set for United. The more inexperienced Silicon Valley founders are unable to trot out anything beyond the limp and oft-used cries that 'We're going to change the world' or, 'We're going to make a difference'. The more thoughtful, conversely, offer something that, at first hearing, sounds completely implausible. That was certainly my reaction when I first heard Google's co-founder, Larry Page, explain that he wanted to put the internet on a hard drive. It took me a long time to figure out the depth and subtlety of his remark.

Communicating what he wanted from staff and players always seems to have come naturally to Sir Alex. Part of this was born of inner confidence, part from the gradual accumulation of victories, but much came from the absence of any confusion in his own mind about what he wanted. Listen to any of his former players and they will tell you that, once they began to master Sir Alex's heavy Scottish accent, there was no mistaking what he sought. His directions tended to be short and concise because barely anyone, whether they work in a hospital or steel mill or are part of a boy-scout troop, can remember more than three instructions. Long-winded monologues do not strike the target in the way that brief talks relaying precise and concise instructions do. I cannot begin to describe the number of presentations I have sat through where the words of the CEO have been hard to fathom, or where the message was so glib it had no credence. The best summary I ever heard of a business was from Sandy Lerner, the co-founder of Cisco Systems, who, in 1986, when the company had just eight employees, was asked to communicate her company's purpose. Her answer was as terse as a Glaswegian's: 'We network networks.' It sounded deceptively simple, but it served as the company's north star for the ensuing 25 years. Sir Alex's counter might well have been the message that he burned between the ears of every newcomer to the club, 'At United we expect to win every game.' In Silicon Valley they would call that a mission statement.

Plenty of organisations achieve one success, some notch up several, but few make it a habit of a lifetime. Manchester United, under Sir Alex, demonstrates how the taste of success gives people confidence that they can repeat the accomplishment; sets a standard that, at a minimum, needs to be matched; and, as an ever-expanding cadre of people experience triumph, begins to become self-perpetuating. Winners want to be around winners. That same formula applies in Silicon Valley, albeit with a local twist. Here it is most pertinent when young companies, during their early days, try to recruit engineers. If these fledgling enterprises attract the right calibre of engineers, the after-effects can last for ten years. Engineers tend to have a particularly acerbic view of the credentials of others and only want to make job offers to those who meet their standards. (It's an attitude faintly reminiscent of the way Sir Alex views a person on whom he bestows the ultimate compliment, 'a true professional'.) When this works, the prospects for the business explode dramatically – particularly today when well-written software can quickly touch hundreds of millions of people. If the recruiting machines sputter, or hiring standards are lowered, it is almost impossible for the company to meet the leader's original aspiration.

On the other side of the same coin is staff retention. I don't mean to belittle the way Sir Alex inspired his teams to achieve more than they thought they were capable of doing; of building tremendous bonds of loyalty with players, many of whom he first came to know as young teenagers; and of perpetually needing to ensure that he had the best goalkeeper or midfielder on his team-sheet. At United it was very rare, at least while Sir

Alex was at the helm, for an agent to convince one of his clients to try his chances at another club, and much of that was due to the fact that most of the squad, if they were appearing regularly, could not have imagined a better stage on which to perform. From time to time, there might have been posturing about a move elsewhere, as there was with Wayne Rooney in 2010 when the end of his contract loomed; but, for the most part, the last thing on the mind of a United player was a job with another club.

That is not the case in California, where people tend to work for Silicon Valley rather than for a particular company. Here there is a similar need to ensure that any business has the best possible management or engineering line-up, but the task is made significantly harder because of the hordes of recruiters who spend all their waking hours trying to prise alluring candidates from their perches. A lot of this is due to the richness of the job opportunities, since there are many more interesting slots in which top-flight people can ply their trade in Silicon Valley than there are for a star striker employed by one of the best six or seven European football clubs. The main reasons for the job-hopping tendencies in Silicon Valley are, for a minority, the dream of striking out on their own, or frustration with the ballooning size of their employer and, for the majority, the way in which stock compensation programmes are designed. At a young company an early employee is usually given a grant of stock that vests after four years. If the company is flourishing and the stock has enjoyed massive appreciation, many employees will feel that they are better off repeating the cycle by obtaining a new slug of stock granted at a low price. For the best Silicon Valley companies, it is often harder to retain people than to recruit them.

I marvel at what I learned about the way Sir Alex dealt with his players and inspired and cajoled his teams – a habit he refined as the years went by. Not many Silicon Valley CEOs, perhaps because many of them are so young, can modulate their tones with comparable dexterity. Sir Alex could simultaneously play cheerleader, motivational speaker, shrink, confessor, piano-tuner, puppet-master, choreographer, teacher, judge and lord high executioner. As he grew older he became increasingly adroit at modulating the application of these skills and figuring out how to extract that extra 5 per cent – the difference between gold and silver – from individuals and groups of individuals. He learned to bolster players' confidence when their spirits were down; he was quick to bring them down a peg or two when they were getting too big for their boots; he was bemused by some of their habits (like Eric Cantona putting salt in his socks before games, or Cristiano Ronaldo specially tailoring two pairs of socks to get the leg-coverings he desired); he stoked their hunger for repeated success and, most importantly, he made each understand (no matter how much they were getting paid or how often they appeared in advertisements or magazines) that the team was bigger, and much more important, than any individual – a cruel truth that many, in both companies and investment firms, have a habit of forgetting.

While Sir Alex, like most people, enjoys being liked, he never sought affection from his players, though neither did he want to paralyse them with fear. So while he tended to know most of them very well, particularly those that stayed at United for many years, he maintained his distance. Respect was all he sought because, once earned, it makes it so much easier for a leader to control an organisation and bend it to his will.

He also understood that one of the keys to an enduring organisation is to build from within, by helping youngsters gain their footing and become successful, rather than recruiting expensive guns for hire, like the leader of a band of mercenaries.

It is a less risky and more predictable way to build an enduring organisation. This in-house development programme requires great patience, and takes a long time, but it is a process that breeds the sorts of bonds that only years of shared experiences can provide – stability, familiarity, trust and, eventually, life-long loyalty. Some will say that this is impossible in a world attuned to immediate results. I beg to differ. Every great organisation has the ability to adopt this approach if they have the right governance structure and leadership team. It's a style of management for which I have great affection since, at Sequoia, I was the fortunate beneficiary of the same approach, and it is the one that we continue to embrace. We also have tried to do what Sir Alex did, after he fell into his stride at United, when he kept tuning his squad, making sure it was nicely balanced between the enthusiasm of youth, the strength of players in their prime, and the experience of those in the twilight of their careers. Sir Alex was careful to make gradual shifts to the composition of these squads, since wholesale change can confuse, disrupt and demoralise.

Many leaders allow habit, affection, happily shared experiences or sentiment to cloud their judgement. It is easy to fall into a comfortable routine and assume that the people who contributed yesterday will continue to make contributions tomorrow. It is easier to be tolerant or to compromise than to confront ugly situations, deliver painful news or demand changes. Partly because of his nature and partly because it is very difficult to hide shortcomings on a football field (compared to the way mediocre bumblers can survive in large companies for decades), Sir Alex never blanched at putting the team before the man, or the future before past accomplishments. Some saw this as a ruthless display of cold-blooded behaviour, particularly fans ruing the exile of one of their favourites. Sir Alex, rightly, saw it as a necessity. One of the challenges for young founders is to understand that, if their company is ever going to be hugely successful, it will – almost certainly – outstrip the capabilities of the people they first hire to manage sales, or marketing or engineering.

Leaders usually spend far too much time worrying about their competitors. That's especially true in football, where the owners in particular are prone to coveting a competitor's success. I do not mean to imply that Sir Alex paid no attention to his competitors, because he spent as much time as any manager making sure he was staying in touch with their line-ups and tactics and was perfectly willing to borrow ploys that made sense. However, he refused to allow Manchester United to be defined by its competitors, and always felt that the destiny of his club was shaped by what went on inside Old Trafford rather than elsewhere. Hence, his phlegmatic reaction to the arrival of the oligarchs, Middle Eastern princes and other well-heeled foreign owners. For Sir Alex, money never bought success, although the occasional big-ticket signing could bring a frisson to proceedings.

Precisely the same phenomenon occurs in Silicon Valley. While it is foolish to ignore developments elsewhere, no organisation ever achieved greatness by perpetually reacting to its competitors. You cannot lead by following. The businesses that are consigned to eternal mediocrity are those led by people who do not know what they want. By contrast, the few companies destined for greatness tend to be led by people with an idea of what they want, even if, at the outset, this might be outshone by far greater clarity about what they do not like. That was certainly the case for Larry Page and Sergey Brin at the outset of Google. Neither of them cared a whit for the search services provided by Yahoo!, Excite, Lycos, Infoseek or AltaVista, so they sought to produce something superior. The same was true for Apple's senior design team, when they set about trying to imagine an mp3 player they could tolerate (the iPod) or a mobile phone they would like (the iPhone).

Silicon Valley winners emerge by concentrating on what they control and by making sure that, for as long as possible, they stay off the radar screen of foes that have the firepower to blow them to smithereens. Stealth is one of a start-up's most potent weapons. It does not pay to arouse either the ire or the scrutiny of the beast – especially when those beasts are quasi monopolists capable of mounting withering attacks. Any number of companies – such as Novell, Lotus Development, AOL, Adobe, Barland, Netscape and Symantec – discovered the perils of arousing the attention of Microsoft at the height of its powers. A big part of the reason that Google became successful was the way its management maintained a low profile until it was too late for Microsoft – by then also hamstrung by government enquiries – to react and torpedo the business.

When a business or a service firm changes leader, the consequences are usually messy. The sad truth is that, irrespective of the field, there are few examples of companies pulling off smooth management successions. The best examples are organisations that just do it less poorly than others. In settings like large oil companies, airline and hotel businesses or the big consumer brands, the change at the top is invisible for several years because the product catalogue, existing clients or long-held investments don't change overnight. That's less true in the world of technology, where it is so rare for companies to successfully adapt themselves to changing circumstances and brand-new market opportunities. It is even less the case in football, where the effect of a leadership change on team performance – especially a negative one – is laid bare fairly quickly.

Just as employees and shareholders in Silicon Valley companies speculate about the implications of a change in helmsmen, so too did the fans of United when Sir Alex announced his retirement. The British newspapers accorded the changing of the guard at Old Trafford, and the arrival of David Moyes from Everton, with the coverage that usually accompanies the arrival of a new government, a signal event for a member of the royal family, or a state funeral. Yet the United team that took to the field at the start of the 2013–14 season was almost identical to the one that had played, 89 days earlier, for Sir Alex in the last game of his management career.

United's followers might console themselves with the knowledge that leadership changes in Silicon Valley are rarely flawless. Yahoo! for example, which had two CEOs during its first 12 years, riffled through a further six in the subsequent eight years. Something similar has occurred at Hewlett-Packard, which was run by its founders from 1939 to 1978, but which in the last 16 years has run through seven CEOs. As I write, the board of Twitter has found itself with the unenviable task of finding a fourth CEO and considering a sale, even though the company is not yet ten years old. About the only Silicon Valley company I can think of that grew from strength to strength as it swapped CEOs was Intel during its first 30 years. There was a special reason for this. The company's first three CEOs, the third of whom was the utterly remarkable Andy Grove (the person I most admire in Silicon Valley), also happened to be the threesome who showed up for work on the day Intel was formed in 1968. Intel's founding spirit did not get diluted by bureaucrats, chief financial officers, activist shareholders, meddlesome directors or, most importantly, people at the helm who did not have the keenest appreciation for the company's products and a deeply ingrained sense of ownership.

There's one final character trait that all great leaders share – from Intel's first three CEOs to Sir Alex Ferguson himself. It's an attribute that few leaders will readily observe in themselves and few management books will single out. In fact, this impulse is often easier for outsiders to spot and, in the case of Sir Alex, was something I gradually gleaned from our conversations and the outings that provide the backbone for this book. Great leaders are competing – not with others – but with the idea of perfection itself. It does not matter how many sales records they have broken, how many competitors they have extinguished, or how many breathtaking products they have introduced – a greater, more perfect version of their success always beckons. For them greatness is just never good enough. In retirement, Sir Alex, who is not prone to melancholy, is wise enough to relish the triumphs of his life and derive satisfaction from his accomplishments rather than allow himself to dwell on whatever trophies eluded his grasp. For the most successful leader in the history of professional sports, the 38 trophies he added to Manchester United's collection – including those that accompanied the Treble-winning year of 1999 – were milestones on a journey whose ultimate, and maddeningly elusive, destination was the seductive and tantalising notion of perfection itself.

Michael Moritz
San Francisco
September 2015

# ACKNOWLEDGEMENTS

It always takes a team, and the one fielded for this book featured Nick Davies, managing director of John Murray Press, whose shrewd eye and keen judgement sharpened the manuscript, as well as Roddy Bloomfield and Kate Miles. Other members of Hodder & Stoughton – Jamie Hodder-Williams, Lucy Hale, Karen Geary and Vickie Boff – were always available at a moment's notice. Alasdair Oliver designed the cover and Amanda Jones managed production. In the United States, Mauro diPreta, the publisher of Hachette Books, and Michelle Aielli helped make sure we received good care in a country where footballs are not round.

From his perch in Aberdeen, Colin Dalgarno provided steadfast and reliable research. In London, Jack Hagley turned numbers into pictures, and is the person responsible for the graphical illustrations in the book, while Sean Pollock shot the cover photograph.

Our literary, legal, financial and publicity squad consisted of Chris Parris-Lamb and David Gernert at The Gernert Company; Sue Knight and the team at Grant Thornton and Les Dalgarno, Ken Gordon and the team at Burness Paull in the United Kingdom and Andrew Kovacs, Sandi Mendleson, David Kass, Karen Valladao, Pete Laboskey and Joe McNulty in the United States.

Mark Damazer, Walter Isaacson, Michael Lewis, Michael Lynton, Jane Sarkin, Doug Stumpf and Judith Thurman provided advice and guidance as we gradually turned an idea into a book. Lyn Laffin and Zoe Diompy in Manchester and Tanya Schillage in California made sure that we always appeared on time. Harriet Heyman helped with the epilogue.

Jason Ferguson in Manchester and Martin O'Connor in New York prompted and nudged us at every turn. They both deserve to have their names in very large fonts on the cover. The man, without whom this would not have happened, is the irrepressible and lovable Charlie Stillitano.

## PICTURE ACKNOWLEDGEMENTS

Introduction, Sir Alex Ferguson at Harvard Business School © Anita Elberse; Chapter 1, Scotland manager Jock Stein (right) with his assistant Alex Ferguson (left) in 1985 © EMPICS Sport/PAI; Chapter 2, Manchester United youth team player David Beckham, February 1992 © Mirrorpix; Chapter 3, Sir Alex Ferguson (right) and assistant manager Carlos Queiroz (left) at Carrington training ground, 25 July 2006 © Matthew Peters/ Manchester United via Getty Images; Chapter 4, Steve Bruce and Bryan Robson after Manchester United beat Blackburn to win the FA Premier League in 1993 © David Cannon/ALLSPORT/Getty Images; Chapter 5, Alex Ferguson talks to Eric Cantona during Manchester City vs. Manchester United in 1996 © Mark Leech/Getty Images; Chapter 6, Sporting Lisbon's player Cristiano Ronaldo (right) fights for the ball during a friendly match, August 2003 © Andre Kosters/AFP/Getty Images; Chapter 7, Sir Alex Ferguson during a Champions League match against Real Madrid, 2013 © Back Page Images/Rex Shutterstock; Chapter 8, Sir Alex Ferguson at a press conference in Manchester, 2009 © John Peters/Manchester United via Getty Images; Chapter 9, Aberdeen chairman (centre) Dick Donald with Alex Ferguson (right), pre-season friendly Aberdeen vs. Arsenal, 1980 © SNS Group/Alamy; Chapter 10, Sir Alex Ferguson and David Gill © Ian Hodgson/ANL/Rex Shutterstock © PA Archive/PAI; Chapter 11, Sir Alex Ferguson in the dressing room © Sean Pollock; Chapter 12, Arsenal manager Arsène Wenger and Sir Alex Ferguson during a Premiership match between Arsenal and Manchester United, 2005 © Ben Radford/Getty Images; Chapter 13, Former Manchester United manager, Sir Alex Ferguson waves to the crowd from the directors' box at Old Trafford, October 2013 © epa european pressphoto agency b.v./Alamy; Epilogue, Sir Alex Ferguson being interviewed by Sir Michael Moritz © author collection.

The Data Room, Sir Alex Ferguson lifting the Premier League trophy at Old Trafford, 2013 ©Alex Livesey/Getty Images
The Archive, Sir Alex Ferguson at his desk in Carrington © Sean Pollock

Every reasonable effort has been made to trace copyright holders, but if there are any errors or omissions, Hodder & Stoughton will be pleased to insert the appropriate acknowledgement in any subsequent printings or editions.

# THE DATA ROOM

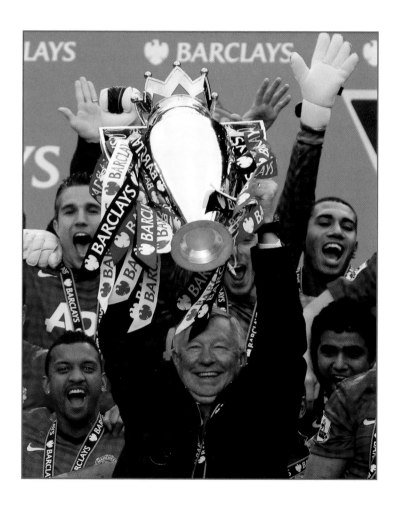

# SIR ALEX FERGUSON AT MANCHESTER UNITED 1986–2013

| | | | |
|---|---|---|---|
| **Matches** | Won | Drawn | Lost |
| **1,500** | 895 | 338 | 267 |
| | 59.7% | 22.5% | 17.8% |

| | 86/87 | 87/88 | 88/89 | 89/90 | 90/91 | 91/92 | 92/93 | 93/94 | 94/95 | 95/96 | 96/97 | 97/98 | 98/99 | 99/00 | 00/01 | 01/02 | 02/03 | 03/04 | 04/05 | 05/06 | 06/07 | 07/08 | 08/09 | 09/10 | 10/11 | 11/12 | 12/13 |
|---|---|---|---|---|---|---|---|---|---|---|---|---|---|---|---|---|---|---|---|---|---|---|---|---|---|---|---|
| **Winning %** *(bars)* | | | | | | | | | | | | | | | | | | | | | | | | | | | |
| **League** | 11 | 2 | 11 | 13 | 6 | 2 | 🏆 | 🏆 | 2 | 🏆 | 🏆 | 2 | 🏆 | 🏆 | 🏆 | 3 | 🏆 | 3 | 3 | 2 | 🏆 | 🏆 | 🏆 | 2 | 🏆 | 2 | 🏆 |
| **FA Cup** | 4R | 5R | 6R | 🏆 | 5R | 4R | 5R | 🏆 | F | 🏆 | 4R | 5R | 🏆 | | 4R | 4R | 5R | 🏆 | F | 5R | F | 6R | SF | 3R | SF | 4R | 6R |
| **League Cup** | | QF | 3R | 3R | F | 🏆 | 3R | F | 3R | 2R | 4R | 3R | QF | 3R | 4R | 3R | F | 4R | SF | 🏆 | 4R | 3R | 🏆 | QF | QF | 4R | |
| **Charity Shield / Community Shield** | | | | 🏆 | | | 🏆 | 🏆 | | | 🏆 | 🏆 | F | F | F | F | | 🏆 | F | | | 🏆 | 🏆 | F | 🏆 | 🏆 | |
| **Champions League** | | | | | | | | 2R | GR | | SF | QF | 🏆 | QF | QF | SF | QF | 16 | 16 | GR | SF | 🏆 | F | QF | F | GR | 16 |
| **Cup Winners' Cup** | | | | | 🏆 | 2R | | | | | | | | | | | | | | | | | | | | | |
| **UEFA Cup / Europa League** | | | | | | | 1R | | | 1R | | | | | | | | | | | | | | | | 16 | |
| **Super Cup** | | | | | 🏆 | | | | | | | | F | | | | | | | | | | F | | | | |
| **Intercontinental Cup** | | | | | | | | | | | | | | 🏆 | | | | | | | | | | | | | |
| **Club World Cup** | | | | | | | | | | | | | | GR | | | | | | | | | 🏆 | | | | |

## Goal Distribution by Minute

Games won or drawn by a Manchester United goal after 85 mins

**101**

Games lost or drawn by an opposition goal after 85 mins

**51**

| Goals scored | **2,769** | Goals conceded | **1,365** |
|---|---|---|---|
| Clean sheets | **625** | Failed to score | **263** |

# 1986–87

Division 1 · 11th ········· Final League Position

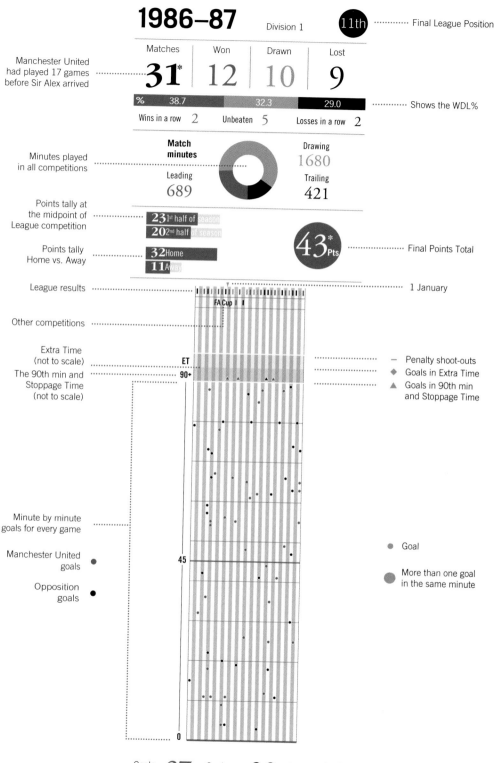

| Matches | Won | Drawn | Lost |
|---|---|---|---|
| 31* | 12 | 10 | 9 |

Manchester United had played 17 games before Sir Alex arrived ········· 31*

| % | 38.7 | 32.3 | 29.0 |
|---|---|---|---|

········· Shows the WDL%

Wins in a row 2 · Unbeaten 5 · Losses in a row 2

Minutes played in all competitions ·········

**Match minutes**

Drawing 1680

Leading 689

Trailing 421

Points tally at the midpoint of League competition ·········

23 1st half of season
20 2nd half of season

Points tally Home vs. Away ·········

32 Home
11 Away

43* Pts ········· Final Points Total

League results ········· 1 January

Other competitions ·········

FA Cup

Extra Time (not to scale) ·········

ET

The 90th min and Stoppage Time (not to scale) ·········

90+

········· — Penalty shoot-outs
········· ◆ Goals in Extra Time
········· ▲ Goals in 90th min and Stoppage Time

Minute by minute goals for every game ·········

Manchester United goals ●

Opposition goals ●

● Goal

● More than one goal in the same minute

45

0

Goals scored 37 · Goals conceded 30 · Clean sheets 12

# 1987–88 Division 1 — 2nd

| Matches | Won | Drawn | Lost |
|---|---|---|---|
| **48** | 29 | 12 | 7 |

| % | 60.4 | 25.0 | 14.6 |
|---|---|---|---|

Wins in a row 5  Unbeaten 11  Losses in a row 2

**Match minutes** — Drawing 2087, Leading 1632, Trailing 601

35 1st half of season
46 2nd half of season
47 Home
34 Away

**81 Pts**

# 1988–89 Division 1 — 11th

| Matches | Won | Drawn | Lost |
|---|---|---|---|
| **48** | 18 | 15 | 15 |

| % | 37.5 | 31.3 | 31.3 |
|---|---|---|---|

Wins in a row 6  Unbeaten 10  Losses in a row 3

**Match minutes** — Drawing 2578, Leading 1076, Trailing 666

27 1st half of season
24 2nd half of season
35 Home
16 Away

**51 Pts**

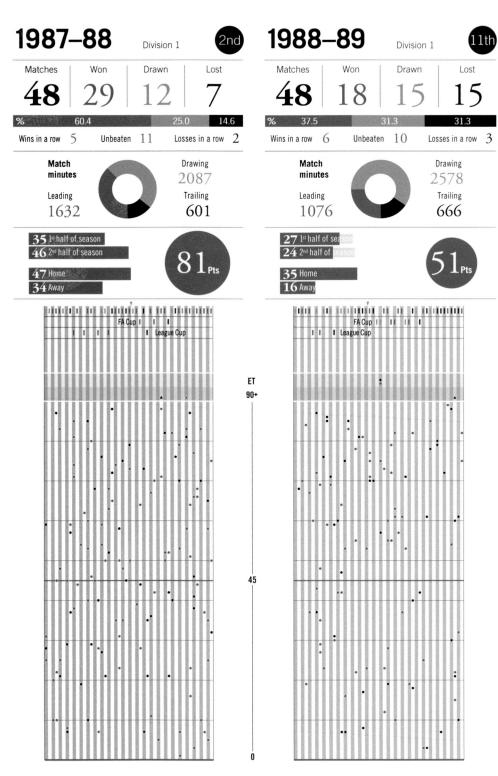

FA Cup · League Cup · ET 90+ · 45 · 0

Goals scored **86**  Goals conceded **45**  Clean sheets **14**

Goals scored **63**  Goals conceded **41**  Clean sheets **21**

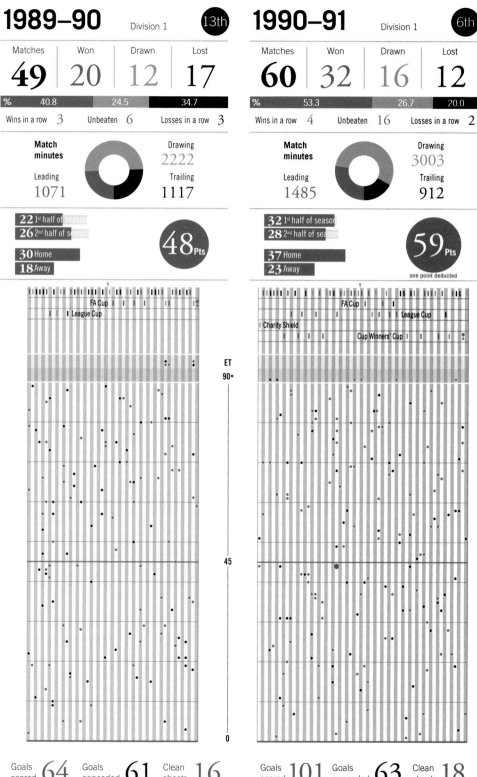

# 1989–90
Division 1    13th

| Matches | Won | Drawn | Lost |
|---|---|---|---|
| **49** | 20 | 12 | 17 |

| % | 40.8 | 24.5 | 34.7 |
|---|---|---|---|

Wins in a row **3**    Unbeaten **6**    Losses in a row **3**

**Match minutes**

Leading **1071**    Drawing 2222    Trailing **1117**

**22** 1st half of season
**26** 2nd half of season
**30** Home
**18** Away

**48** Pts

FA Cup
League Cup

ET
90+
45
0

Goals scored **64**    Goals conceded **61**    Clean sheets **16**

# 1990–91
Division 1    6th

| Matches | Won | Drawn | Lost |
|---|---|---|---|
| **60** | 32 | 16 | 12 |

| % | 53.3 | 26.7 | 20.0 |
|---|---|---|---|

Wins in a row **4**    Unbeaten **16**    Losses in a row **2**

**Match minutes**

Leading **1485**    Drawing 3003    Trailing **912**

**32** 1st half of season
**28** 2nd half of season
**37** Home
**23** Away

**59** Pts

one point deducted

FA Cup
League Cup
Charity Shield
Cup Winners' Cup

Goals scored **101**    Goals conceded **63**    Clean sheets **18**

# 1991–92  Division 1    2nd

| Matches | Won | Drawn | Lost |
|---|---|---|---|
| **58** | 30 | 21 | 7 |

| % | 51.7 | 36.2 | 12.1 |
|---|---|---|---|

| Wins in a row | 7 | Unbeaten | 16 | Losses in a row | 3 |
|---|---|---|---|---|---|

**Match minutes**

Drawing 2842

Leading 1753    Trailing 625

48 1st half of season
30 2nd half of season
43 Home
35 Away

**78** Pts

ET
90+

45

0

| Goals scored | 85 | Goals conceded | 43 | Clean sheets | 27 |
|---|---|---|---|---|---|

---

# 1992–93  Premier League    1st

| Matches | Won | Drawn | Lost |
|---|---|---|---|
| **50** | 27 | 15 | 8 |

| % | 54.0 | 30.0 | 16.0 |
|---|---|---|---|

| Wins in a row | 7 | Unbeaten | 15 | Losses in a row | 3 |
|---|---|---|---|---|---|

**Match minutes**

Drawing 2487

Leading 1328    Trailing 685

35 1st half of season
49 2nd half of season
47 Home
37 Away

**84** Pts

| Goals scored | 73 | Goals conceded | 35 | Clean sheets | 23 |
|---|---|---|---|---|---|

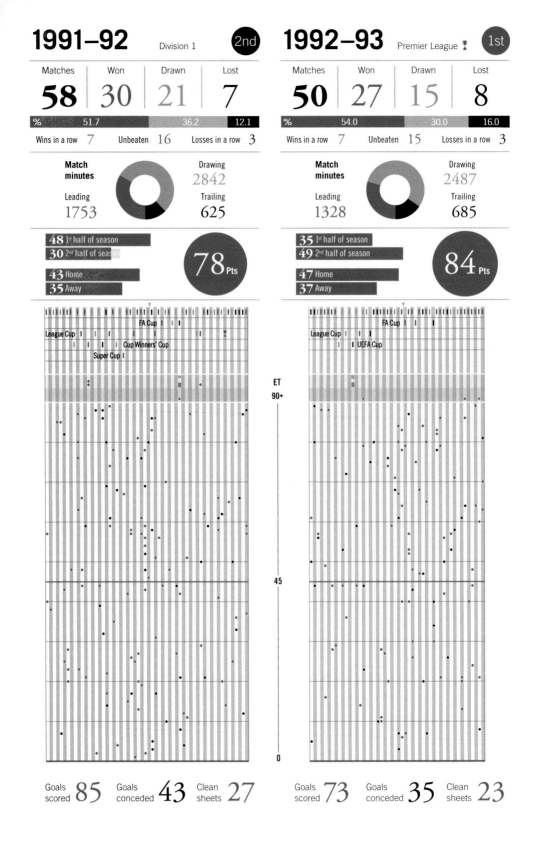

FA Cup — League Cup — Cup Winners' Cup — Super Cup — UEFA Cup

# 1993–94

Premiership 🏆 1st

| Matches | Won | Drawn | Lost |
|---------|-----|-------|------|
| **63** | 41 | 16 | 6 |

| % | | |
|---|---|---|
| 65.1 | 25.4 | 9.5 |

| Wins in a row | 7 | Unbeaten | 34 | Losses in a row | 1 |

**Match minutes**

Drawing 2505

Leading 2610

Trailing 555

52 1st half of season
40 2nd half of season
48 Home
44 Away

**92** Pts

# 1994–95

Premiership 2nd

| Matches | Won | Drawn | Lost |
|---------|-----|-------|------|
| **59** | 36 | 13 | 10 |

| % | | |
|---|---|---|
| 61.0 | 22.0 | 16.9 |

| Wins in a row | 5 | Unbeaten | 13 | Losses in a row | 1 |

**Match minutes**

Drawing 2587

Leading 1942

Trailing 781

45 1st half of season
43 2nd half of season
52 Home
36 Away

**88** Pts

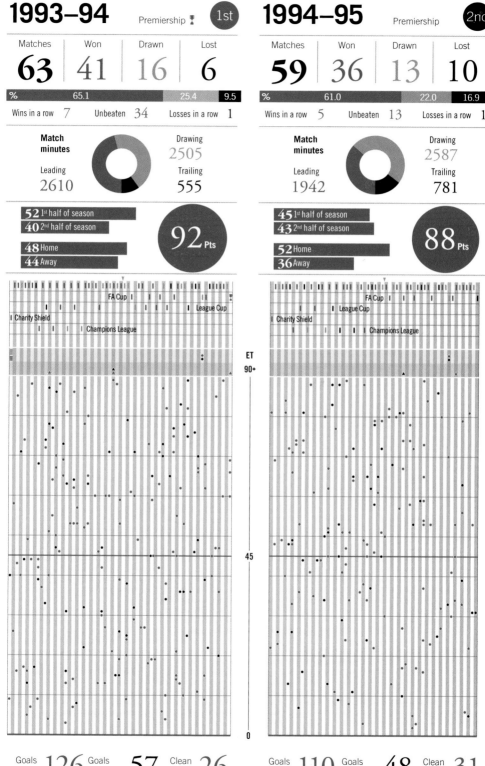

ET
90+

45

0

| Goals scored | Goals conceded | Clean sheets |
|---|---|---|
| 126 | 57 | 26 |

| Goals scored | Goals conceded | Clean sheets |
|---|---|---|
| 110 | 48 | 31 |

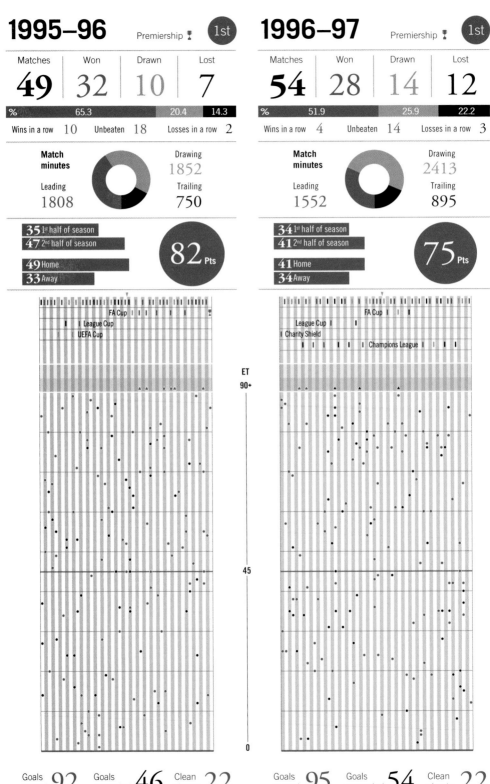

# 1995–96

Premiership 🏆 **1st**

| Matches | Won | Drawn | Lost |
|---|---|---|---|
| **49** | 32 | 10 | 7 |

| % | | |
|---|---|---|
| 65.3 | 20.4 | 14.3 |

| Wins in a row | 10 | Unbeaten | 18 | Losses in a row | 2 |
|---|---|---|---|---|---|

**Match minutes**

Drawing 1852
Leading 1808
Trailing 750

35 1st half of season
47 2nd half of season
49 Home
33 Away

**82** Pts

FA Cup
League Cup
UEFA Cup

ET 90+

45

0

| Goals scored | 92 | Goals conceded | 46 | Clean sheets | 22 |
|---|---|---|---|---|---|

# 1996–97

Premiership 🏆 **1st**

| Matches | Won | Drawn | Lost |
|---|---|---|---|
| **54** | 28 | 14 | 12 |

| % | | |
|---|---|---|
| 51.9 | 25.9 | 22.2 |

| Wins in a row | 4 | Unbeaten | 14 | Losses in a row | 3 |
|---|---|---|---|---|---|

**Match minutes**

Drawing 2413
Leading 1552
Trailing 895

34 1st half of season
41 2nd half of season
41 Home
34 Away

**75** Pts

FA Cup
League Cup
Charity Shield
Champions League

| Goals scored | 95 | Goals conceded | 54 | Clean sheets | 22 |
|---|---|---|---|---|---|

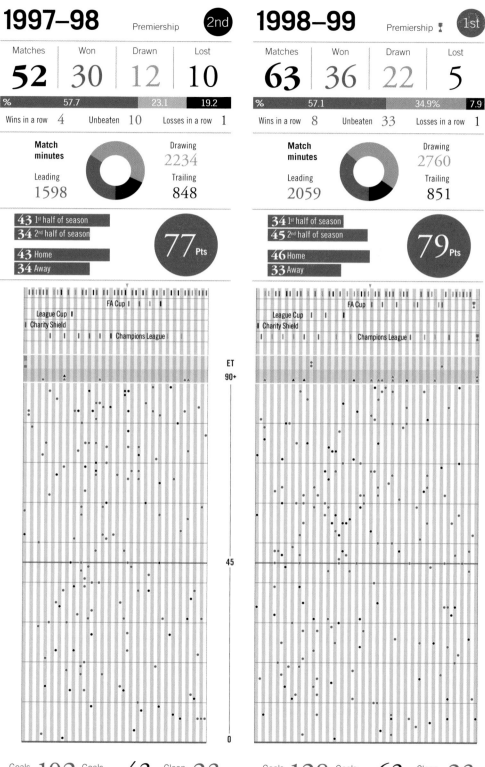

# 1997–98

Premiership — 2nd

| Matches | Won | Drawn | Lost |
|---|---|---|---|
| **52** | 30 | 12 | 10 |

| % | 57.7 | 23.1 | 19.2 |
|---|---|---|---|

Wins in a row 4  Unbeaten 10  Losses in a row 1

**Match minutes**

Leading 1598
Drawing 2234
Trailing 848

43 1st half of season
34 2nd half of season
43 Home
34 Away

**77 Pts**

FA Cup
League Cup
Charity Shield
Champions League

ET
90+
45
0

Goals scored 102  Goals conceded 43  Clean sheets 23

# 1998–99

Premiership — 1st

| Matches | Won | Drawn | Lost |
|---|---|---|---|
| **63** | 36 | 22 | 5 |

| % | 57.1 | 34.9% | 7.9 |
|---|---|---|---|

Wins in a row 8  Unbeaten 33  Losses in a row 1

**Match minutes**

Leading 2059
Drawing 2760
Trailing 851

34 1st half of season
45 2nd half of season
46 Home
33 Away

**79 Pts**

FA Cup
League Cup
Charity Shield
Champions League

Goals scored 128  Goals conceded 63  Clean sheets 23

# 1999–2000
Premiership 🏆 1st

| Matches | Won | Drawn | Lost |
|---|---|---|---|
| **59** | 38 | 11 | 10 |

| % | | | |
|---|---|---|---|
| 64.4 | 18.6 | 16.9 | |

Wins in a row 5    Unbeaten 14    Losses in a row 2

**Match minutes**      Drawing 2277

Leading 1932      Trailing 1101

43 1st half of season
48 2nd half of season

49 Home
42 Away

**91** Pts

Charity Shield    League Cup    Club World Cup
Super Cup    Champions League    Intercontinental Cup

Goals scored **124**    Goals conceded **66**    Clean sheets **20**

# 2000–01
Premiership 🏆 1st

| Matches | Won | Drawn | Lost |
|---|---|---|---|
| **57** | 32 | 12 | 13 |

| % | | | |
|---|---|---|---|
| 56.1 | 21.1 | 22.8 | |

Wins in a row 8    Unbeaten 10    Losses in a row 3

**Match minutes**      Drawing 2181

Leading 2096      Trailing 853

43 1st half of season
37 2nd half of season

47 Home
33 Away

**80** Pts

Charity Shield    League Cup    FA Cup
Champions League

Goals scored **107**    Goals conceded **50**    Clean sheets **23**

ET
90+
45
0

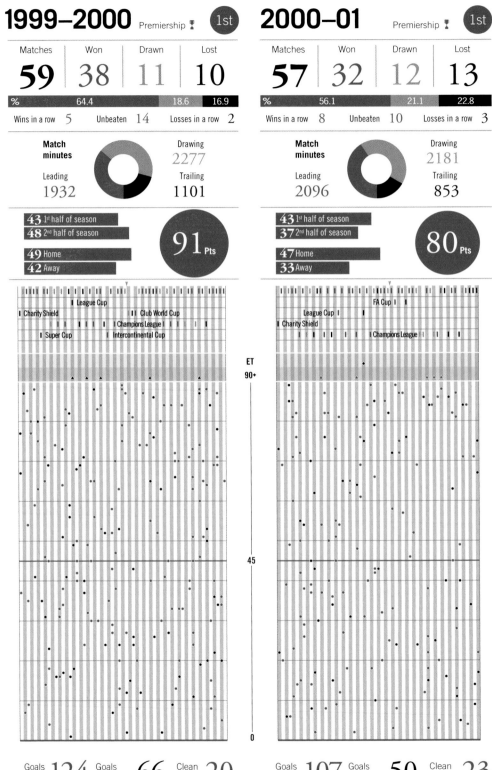

# 2001–02

Premiership   **3rd**

| Matches | Won | Drawn | Lost |
|---|---|---|---|
| **58** | 33 | 11 | 14 |

| % | | |
|---|---|---|
| 56.9 | 19.0 | 24.1 |

| Wins in a row | 9 | Unbeaten | 11 | Losses in a row | 2 |

**Match minutes**

Drawing 2314

Leading 1978

Trailing 928

**33** 1st half of season
**44** 2nd half of season
**35** Home
**42** Away

**77** Pts

FA Cup
League Cup
Charity Shield
Champions League

ET
90+
45
0

| Goals scored | 122 | Goals conceded | 69 | Clean sheets | 20 |

# 2002–03

Premiership   **1st**

| Matches | Won | Drawn | Lost |
|---|---|---|---|
| **63** | 42 | 10 | 11 |

| % | | |
|---|---|---|
| 66.7 | 15.9 | 17.4 |

| Wins in a row | 8 | Unbeaten | 11 | Losses in a row | 2 |

**Match minutes**

Drawing 2524

Leading 2200

Trailing 946

**35** 1st half of season
**48** 2nd half of season
**50** Home
**33** Away

**83** Pts

FA Cup
League Cup
Champions League

| Goals scored | 130 | Goals conceded | 61 | Clean sheets | 22 |

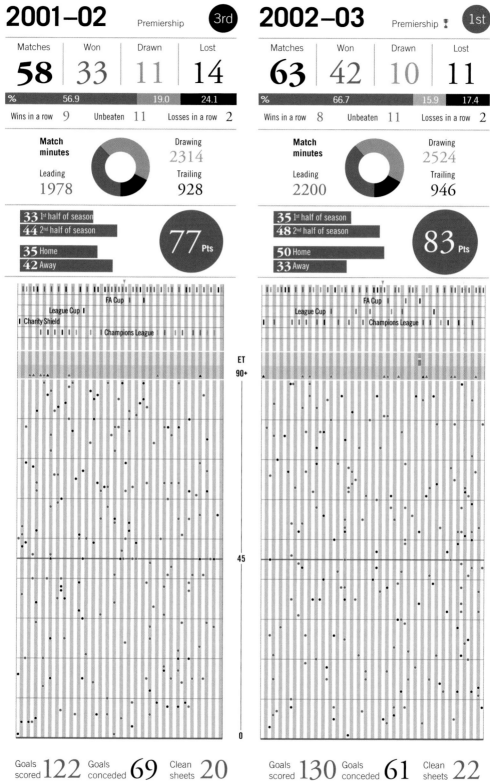

# 2003–04  Premiership  3rd

| Matches | Won | Drawn | Lost |
|---|---|---|---|
| **55** | 35 | 8 | 12 |

| % | | |
|---|---|---|
| 62.6 | 14.5 | 21.8 |

Wins in a row  8    Unbeaten  9    Losses in a row  2

**Match minutes**

Drawing **2242**

Leading **1971**    Trailing **737**

**46** 1st half of season
**29** 2nd half of season
**40** Home
**35** Away

**75** Pts

FA Cup
League Cup
Community Shield
Champions League

ET
90+

45

0

Goals scored **98**    Goals conceded **49**    Clean sheets **22**

# 2004–05  Premiership  3rd

| Matches | Won | Drawn | Lost |
|---|---|---|---|
| **61** | 35 | 16 | 10 |

| % | | |
|---|---|---|
| 57.4 | 26.2 | 16.4 |

Wins in a row  7    Unbeaten  14    Losses in a row  1

**Match minutes**

Drawing **2764**

Leading **2107**    Trailing **619**

**37** 1st half of season
**40** 2nd half of season
**42** Home
**35** Away

**77** Pts

FA Cup
League Cup
Community Shield
Champions League

Goals scored **100**    Goals conceded **44**    Clean sheets **31**

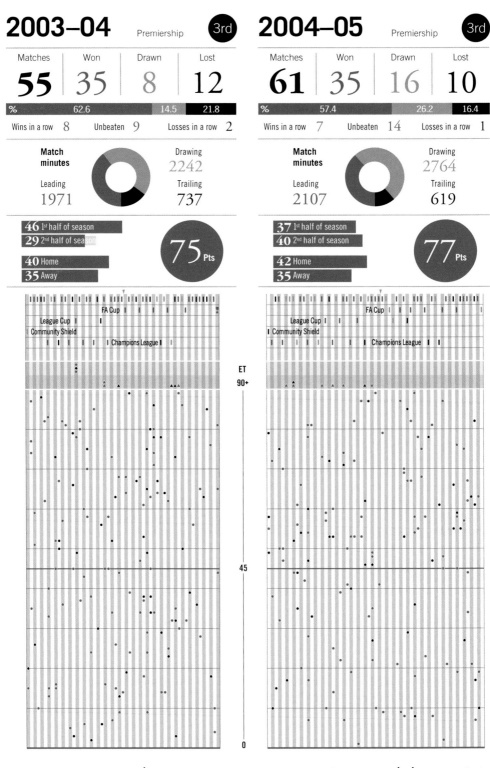

# 2005–06

Premiership   **2nd**

| Matches | Won | Drawn | Lost |
|---|---|---|---|
| **56** | 35 | 13 | 8 |

| % | | |
|---|---|---|
| 62.5 | 23.2 | 14.3 |

Wins in a row   8     Unbeaten   10     Losses in a row   2

**Match minutes**

Drawing   2300

Leading   2145     Trailing   595

**41** 1st half of season
**42** 2nd half of season

**44** Home
**39** Away

**83** Pts

# 2006–07

Premiership   **1st**

| Matches | Won | Drawn | Lost |
|---|---|---|---|
| **60** | 42 | 7 | 11 |

| % | | |
|---|---|---|
| 70.0 | 11.7 | 18.3 |

Wins in a row   7     Unbeaten   14     Losses in a row   2

**Match minutes**

Drawing   2642

Leading   2162     Trailing   596

**47** 1st half of season
**42** 2nd half of season

**47** Home
**42** Away

**89** Pts

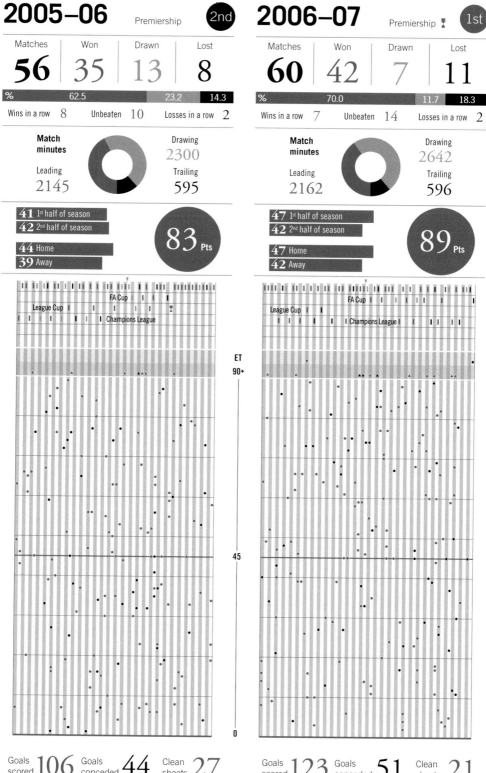

ET 90+

45

0

League Cup    FA Cup    Champions League

| Goals scored | Goals conceded | Clean sheets |
|---|---|---|
| 106 | 44 | 27 |

| Goals scored | Goals conceded | Clean sheets |
|---|---|---|
| 123 | 51 | 21 |

# 2007–08 Premier League 🏆 1st

| Matches | Won | Drawn | Lost |
|---|---|---|---|
| **57** | 39 | 11 | 7 |

| % | | | |
|---|---|---|---|
| 68.4 | | 19.3 | 12.3 |

| Wins in a row | 6 | Unbeaten | 10 | Losses in a row | 1 |
|---|---|---|---|---|---|

**Match minutes**

Drawing 2572
Leading 1999
Trailing 559

- **45** 1st half of season
- **42** 2nd half of season
- **52** Home
- **35** Away

**87** Pts

FA Cup
League Cup
Community Shield
Champions League

ET
90+
45
0

| Goals scored | 110 | Goals conceded | 33 | Clean sheets | 31 |
|---|---|---|---|---|---|

# 2008–09 Premier League 🏆 1st

| Matches | Won | Drawn | Lost |
|---|---|---|---|
| **66** | 44 | 15 | 7 |

| % | | | |
|---|---|---|---|
| 66.7 | | 22.7 | 10.6 |

| Wins in a row | 11 | Unbeaten | 16 | Losses in a row | 2 |
|---|---|---|---|---|---|

**Match minutes**

Drawing 2887
Leading 2441
Trailing 612

- **41** 1st half of season
- **49** 2nd half of season
- **50** Home
- **40** Away

**90** Pts

Super Cup
FA Cup
League Cup
Community Shield
Club World Cup
Champions League

| Goals scored | 119 | Goals conceded | 46 | Clean sheets | 39 |
|---|---|---|---|---|---|

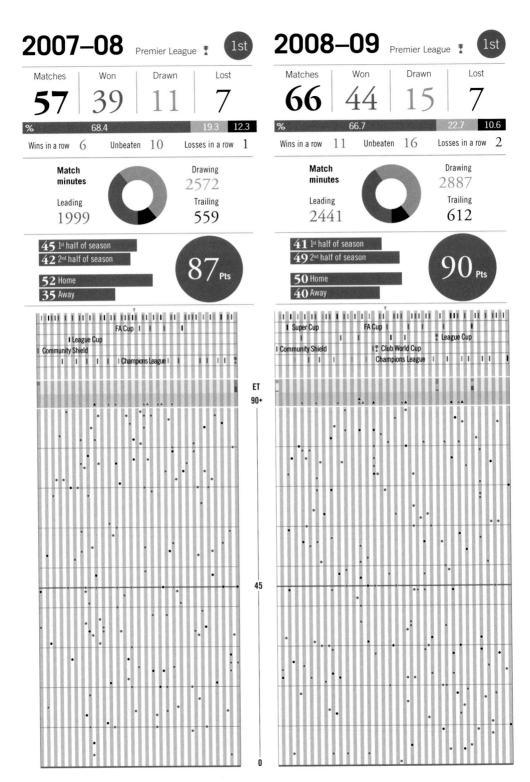

# 2009–10   Premier League   2nd

| Matches | Won | Drawn | Lost |
|---|---|---|---|
| **56** | 39 | 6 | 11 |

| % | 69.6 | 10.7 | 19.6 |
|---|---|---|---|

| Wins in a row | 8 | Unbeaten | 11 | Losses in a row | 2 |
|---|---|---|---|---|---|

**Match minutes**

| Leading | Drawing | Trailing |
|---|---|---|
| 1812 | 2450 | 778 |

| 40 | 1st half of season |
|---|---|
| 45 | 2nd half of season |
| 49 | Home |
| 36 | Away |

**85** Pts

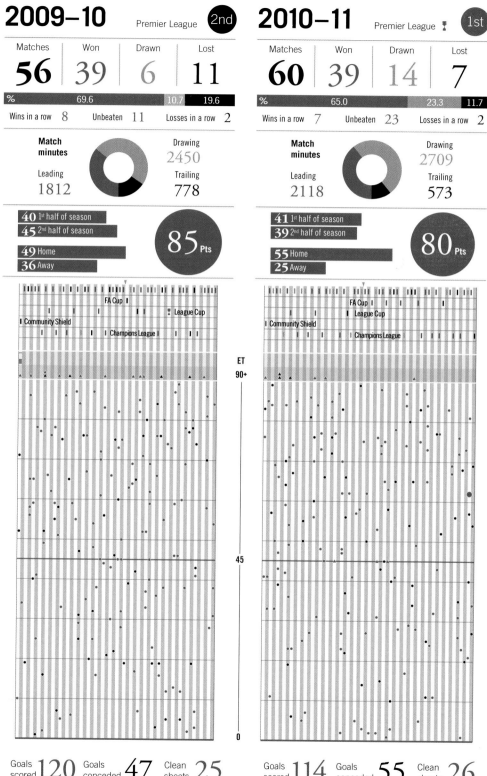

FA Cup
League Cup
Community Shield
Champions League

ET 90+
45
0

| Goals scored | 120 | Goals conceded | 47 | Clean sheets | 25 |
|---|---|---|---|---|---|

# 2010–11   Premier League   1st

| Matches | Won | Drawn | Lost |
|---|---|---|---|
| **60** | 39 | 14 | 7 |

| % | 65.0 | 23.3 | 11.7 |
|---|---|---|---|

| Wins in a row | 7 | Unbeaten | 23 | Losses in a row | 2 |
|---|---|---|---|---|---|

**Match minutes**

| Leading | Drawing | Trailing |
|---|---|---|
| 2118 | 2709 | 573 |

| 41 | 1st half of season |
|---|---|
| 39 | 2nd half of season |
| 55 | Home |
| 25 | Away |

**80** Pts

FA Cup
League Cup
Community Shield
Champions League

| Goals scored | 114 | Goals conceded | 55 | Clean sheets | 26 |
|---|---|---|---|---|---|

# 2011–12
Premier League — 2nd

| Matches | Won | Drawn | Lost |
|---|---|---|---|
| **54** | 35 | 8 | 11 |

| % | | |
|---|---|---|
| 64.8 | 14.8 | 20.4 |

Wins in a row 5    Unbeaten 13    Losses in a row 2

**Match minutes**

Drawing 2006
Leading 2262
Trailing 592

45 1st half of season
44 2nd half of season
47 Home
42 Away

**89** Pts

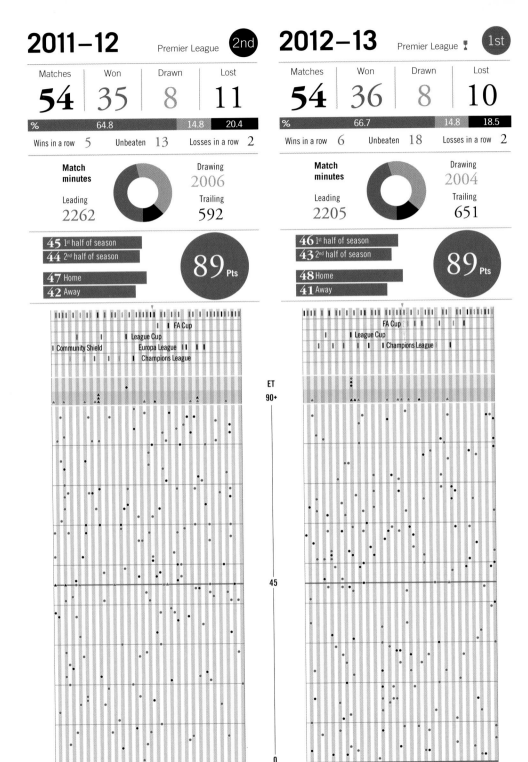

FA Cup
League Cup
Community Shield
Europa League
Champions League

ET
90+

45

0

Goals scored **120**    Goals conceded **56**    Clean sheets **25**

# 2012–13
Premier League 🏆 — 1st

| Matches | Won | Drawn | Lost |
|---|---|---|---|
| **54** | 36 | 8 | 10 |

| % | | |
|---|---|---|
| 66.7 | 14.8 | 18.5 |

Wins in a row 6    Unbeaten 18    Losses in a row 2

**Match minutes**

Drawing 2004
Leading 2205
Trailing 651

46 1st half of season
43 2nd half of season
48 Home
41 Away

**89** Pts

FA Cup
League Cup
Champions League

Goals scored **114**    Goals conceded **65**    Clean sheets **15**

# Academy Players by first-team debut season

During Sir Alex's time at Manchester United

**1986–87**
Tony Gill 14/2
Gary Walsh 63/0

**1987–88**
Deiniol Graham 4/1
Lee Martin 109/2

**1988–89**
Russell Beardsmore 73/4
Derek Brazil 2/0
Mark Robins 70/17
David Wilson 6/0

**1992–93**
David Beckham 394/85
Nicky Butt 387/26
Keith Gillespie 14/2
Gary Neville 602/7

**1991–92**
Ian Wilkinson 1/0

**1990–91**
Darren Ferguson 30/0
Ryan Giggs 963/168
Paul Wratten 2/0

**1989–90**

**1993–94**
Colin McKee 1/0
Ben Thornley 14/0

**1994–95**
Kevin Pilkington 8/0
Simon Davies 20/1
Chris Casper 7/0
John O'Kane 7/0
Paul Scholes 718/155
Phil Neville 386/8

**1995–96**
Terry Cooke 8/1

**1996–97**
Michael Appleton 2/0
Michael Clegg 24/0

**2000–01**
Bojan Djordjic 2/0
Michael Stewart 14/0
Danny Webber 3/0

**1999–2000**
Luke Chadwick 39/2
David Healy 3/0
Paul Rachubka 3/0
Richie Wellens 1/0

**1998–99**
Alex Notman 1/0
Mark Wilson 10/0

**1997–98**
Danny Higginbotham 7/0
Ronnie Wallwork 28/0
Michael Twiss 2/0
Phil Mulryne 5/0
Wes Brown 362/5
John Curtis 19/0

**2001–02**
Jimmy Davis 1/0
Daniel Nardiello 4/0
Lee Roche 3/0

**2002–03**
Darren Fletcher 342/24
Mark Lynch 1/0
Danny Pugh 7/0
Kieran Richardson 81/11
Mads Timm 1/0

**2003–04**
Phil Bardsley 18/0
Chris Eagles 17/1
Eddie Johnson 1/0
Paul Tierney 1/0

**2004–05**
Sylvan Ebanks-Blake 2/1
David Jones 4/0
Gérard Piqué 23/2
Giuseppe Rossi 14/4
Jonathan Spector 8/0

**2008–09**
Ben Amos 7/0
James Chester 1/0
Richard Eckersley 4/0
Federico Macheda 36/5
Danny Welbeck 103/19

**2007–08**
Fraizer Campbell 4/0
Jonny Evans 156/5
Danny Simpson 8/0

**2006–07**
Michael Barnes 1/0
David Gray 1/0
Kieran Lee 3/1
Phil Marsh 1/0
Ryan Shawcross 2/0

**2005–06**
Adam Eckersley 1/0
Darron Gibson 60/10
Ritchie Jones 5/0
Lee Martin 3/0

**2009–10**
Joshua King 2/0

**2010–11**
Ravel Morrison 3/0

**2011–12**
Tom Cleverley 47/4
Larnell Cole 1/0
Zeki Fryers 6/0
Michael Keane 3/0
Will Keane 1/0
Paul Pogba 7/0

**2012–13**
Robbie Brady 1/0
Ryan Tunnicliffe 2/0
Scott Wootton 4/0

50+ appearances    appearances/goals    **Total appearances:** 5,429 **Total goals:** 573

# MANCHESTER UNITED SQUAD MEMBERS, BY NATIONALITY (1986–2013)

TRINIDAD & TOBAGO

AUSTRALIA

AUSTRALIA

SOUTH AFRICA

ENGLAND

ENGLAND

WALES

REPUBLIC OF IRELAND

SCOTLAND

FRANCE

CZECH REPUBLIC

NETHERLANDS

SWEDEN

NORTHERN IRELAND

DENMARK

NORWAY

RUSSIA (CIS)

YEAR

| 1987 | 88 | 89 | 90 | 91 | 92 | 93 | 94 | 95 | 96 | 97 | 98 | 99 |

30

25

MEDIAN AGE OF SQUAD

MEXICO

CHINA   ANGOLA   ECUADOR

ARGENTINA                                        SENEGAL                    JAPAN

CAMEROON        SOUTH KOREA

URUGUAY

USA

BRAZIL

WALES

REPUBLIC OF IRELAND

SCOTLAND
NORTHERN IRELAND

FRANCE

BULGARIA

SWEDEN

POLAND

NORWAY

PORTUGAL

SPAIN

ITALY

DENMARK

SERBIA

BELGIUM

YEAR

| 01 | 02 | 03 | 04 | 05 | 06 | 07 | 08 | 09 | 10 | 11 | 12 | 13 |

# MOST SUCCESSFUL EUROPEAN CUP-WINNING MANAGERS 1974–2013

### Carlo Ancelotti (ITA)

Champions League: 3     Domestic League Titles: 3     Domestic Cups: 3

### Rafa Benítez (SPA)

Champions League: 1     Other European Trophies: 2     Domestic League Titles: 2     Domestic Cups: 2

### Vicente del Bosque (SPA)

Champions League: 2     Domestic League Titles: 2

### Fabio Capello (ITA)

Champions League: 1     Domestic League Titles: 7

### Johan Cruyff (NED)

Champions League: 1     Other European Trophies: 2     Domestic League Titles: 4     Domestic Cups: 3

### Sir Alex Ferguson (SCO)

Champions League: 2     Other European Trophies: 2

Domestic League Titles: 17

Domestic Cups: 14

### Louis van Gaal (NED)

Champions League: 1    Other European Trophies: 1

Domestic Cups: 3    Domestic League Titles: 7

### Raymond Goethals (BEL)

Champions League: 1    Other European Trophies: 1    Domestic League Titles: 4    Domestic Cups: 1

### Pep Guardiola (SPA)

Champions League: 2    Domestic League Titles: 6    Domestic Cups: 3

### Jupp Heynckes (GER)

Champions League: 2    Domestic League Titles: 3    Domestic Cups: 1

### Guus Hiddink (NED)

Champions League: 1    Domestic League Titles: 6    Domestic Cups: 5

### Ottmar Hitzfeld (GER)

Champions League: 2

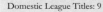     

Domestic League Titles: 9    Domestic Cups: 6

## Marcello Lippi (ITA)

Champions League: 1    Domestic League Titles: 5                    Domestic Cups: 1

## José Mourinho (POR)

Champions League: 2              Other European Trophies: 1

Domestic League Titles: 8                    Domestic Cups: 7

## Bob Paisley (ENG)

Champions League: 3              Other European Trophies: 1

Domestic League Titles: 6                    Domestic Cups: 3

## Arrigo Sacchi (ITA)

Champions League: 2              Domestic League Titles: 2

## Giovanni Trapattoni (ITA)

Champions League: 1    Other European Trophies: 4

Domestic League Titles: 10                    Domestic Cups: 3

# THE ARCHIVE

# The Manchester United Football Club plc

18 August 1997

Dear Eric

Some months have passed since we last spoke and I felt that I should write to you as a mark of respect and esteem in which I hold you.

When we re-started training, I kept waiting for you to turn up as normal but I think that was in hope not realism and I knew in your eyes when we met at Mottram your time at Manchester United was over. Although, I still feel you should have taken both your Father's and my advice and taken a holiday before making such a major decision.

One thing, I would like you to remember is to remain active and fit. I always remember when I finished at 32 and I started management, I was more concerned about organising training and the coaching of players that I forgot about my own fitness and then when I realised about six years later what was happening, I started to train again to recapture my fitness and it was murder, so you do need to keep your fitness.

I am sure you have been keeping an eye on our results and as you can see we are
doing quite well as you know we have signed Teddy Sheringham to replace you but at the moment he is finding it difficult to find the space he got at Tottenham and is playing deep so we have some adjusting to do. Players sometimes don't realise how difficult it is to play at our level as every game is a Cup Final for our opponents so I just hope he can do it for us.

Our pre-season tour wasn't too bad. The Far East tour was better than expected and our games against Inter Milan were very good. The Charity Shield wasn't a great performance but we were better than Chelsea and deserved to win, even though it went to penalties.

I still feel as we discussed at the end of the season that a top class striker is what is needed and that is always going to be the problem at our club as the financial restraints will always stop us getting the best because of our wage structure and it is such a pity because when you are at the top you should buy the best to stop the others getting to you. If I was younger, I suppose I would look at it differently, but from a personal point of view, I have not won the European Cup and it does get to me at times. However, I just have to carry on and not put up a mental barrier and I have always had that belief and trust in my players and wish to continue to do so. I keep hoping that I will discover a young Cantona! It is a dream!

As I close this letter, I would like to hope that we will have a chat, a drink, or a meal together soon. I know the club has written to you about the forthcoming dinner and I hope you will manage it, but that is not the most important thing, for me it is to remind you how good a player you were for Manchester United and how grateful I am for the service you gave me. I will never forget that and I hope you won't either.

You are always welcome here and if you just pop in unexpectedly for a cup of tea, no fanfare, just for a chat as friends, that would mean more to me than anything. Eric you know where I am if you need me and now that you are no longer one of my players, I hope you know you have a friend.

Good luck and God bless.

Yours sincerely

Alex Ferguson CBE
MANAGER

A letter acknowledging one of Manchester United's true greats.

# Celtic

14 March 2002

Celtic plc
Celtic Park
Glasgow G40 3RE
Tel: 0141 556 2611
Fax: 0141 551 8106
http://www.celticfc.co.uk

Sir Alex Ferguson
Manchester United plc
Sir Matt Busby Way
Old Trafford
MANCHESTER
M16 ORA

Dear Sir Alex

This is just a brief note to thank you for your time and attention on Wednesday, when you showed me around Carrington with Willie Haughey.

Youth development and quality training facilities have been lower on the Celtic agenda than I believe they should have been and I wish to take steps to address our shortfalls.

Your own personal insights, opinion and advice were not only welcome but very much appreciated.

Thank you very much for your time, once again, particularly at such an important time for Manchester United.

Finally, congratulations on reaching the Champions League Quarter Finals.

Kind regards,

Yours sincerely

**Ian McLeod**
**Chief Executive**

A letter from Ian McLeod, Celtic's Chief Executive, following
a visit to Carrington training ground, 2002.

the
## MANCHESTER UNITED
FOOTBALL CLUB plc
## OLD TRAFFORD
MANCHESTER M16 0RA
Registered Office: Old Trafford, Manchester, M16 0RA

Registered No. 95489 England
Telephone:
061-872 1661 (Office)
061-872 0199 (Ticket and
Match Enquiries)
061-872 3488 (Commercial
Direct Line Mgr.
Fax No. 061-873 7210
Telex: 666564 United G

| Chief Executive | Manager | Secretary | Commercial Manager |
|---|---|---|---|
| C. Martin Edwards | Alex Ferguson | Kenneth R. Merrett | D. A. McGregor |

£                    per week basic wage.

When playing in the First Team, or being nominated as a substitute for Football League Championship matches you will receive:

a.     A bonus of £100 per point.

       For the purpose of assessing the bonus payments contained in Clause 2(a), points will be awarded on the basis of 3 points for a Win and 1 point for a Draw.

b.     In addition a sum of £100,000 will be distributed among the First Team Pool of players if the Club wins the First Division Championship.

       This bonus calculation will be based on the number of League games played by each individual.

       Example:    If a player appears in all 38 matches, he will receive 1/13 of £100,000 which equals £7,692.

c.     In addition a sum of £25,000 will be distributed among the First Team Pool of players if the Club finishes in the top four of the First Division or qualifies for the UEFA Cup Competition through its final League position.    This payment will not be made in the event of the Club winning the First Division League Championship.

d.     A bonus of £100 for a Win and £50 for a Draw for First Team Friendly matches.

e.     The above payments only relate to First Division matches.    In the event of the Club being relegated then the above payments will be reduced by half.

When playing or being nominated as a substitute in the Football Association Cup Competition a win bonus will be paid as follows:

a.    
| | |
|---|---|
| Third Round: | £400. |
| Fourth Round: | £500. |
| Fifth Round: | £600. |
| Sixth Round: | £750. |
| Semi Final: | £1,500. |
| Final: | £2,500. |

b.     Any player selected or being nominated as a substitute for the Final will be paid appearance money of £1,000.

c.     In the event of any round in the Competition ending in a Draw half bonus will be paid.

d.     In addition a sum of £40,000 will be distributed among the First Team Pool of players, based on the number of appearances made by each individual, if the Club wins the Competition.

When playing or being nominated as a substitute in the Littlewoods Cup Competition, a win bonus will be paid as follows:

a.    
| | |
|---|---|
| Second Round: | £400. |
| Third Round: | £400. |
| Fourth Round: | £500. |
| Fifth Round: | £600. |
| Semi Final: | £2,000. |
| Final: | £2,500. |

b.     Any player selected or being nominated as a substitute for the Final will be paid appearance money of £1,000.

c.     In the event of any round in the Competition ending in a Draw half bonus will be paid.

d.     Where a round is played over two legs, a player playing in one game only will be paid full win bonus.

President: Sir Matt Busby CBE.
Directors: C.M. Edwards (Chairman), J.M. Edelson, R. Charlton CBE, E.M. Watkins, A.M. Al Midani, N. Burrows.

The official bonus structure for the Manchester United squad, late 1980s.

## the MANCHESTER UNITED FOOTBALL CLUB plc OLD TRAFFORD MANCHESTER M16 0RA

Registered Office: Old Trafford, Manchester, M16 0RA

Registered No. 95489 England
Telephone:
061-872 1661 (Office)
061-872 0199 (Ticket and Match Enquiries)
061-872 3488 (Commercial Direct Line Mgr.
Fax No. 061-873 7210
Telex: 666564 United G

| Chief Executive | Manager | Secretary | Commercial Manager |
|---|---|---|---|
| C. Martin Edwards | Alex Ferguson | Kenneth R. Merrett | D. A. McGregor |

e.   In addition a sum of £40,000 will be distributed among the First Team Pool of players, based on the number of appearances made by each individual, if the Club wins the Competition.

5.   When playing or being nominated as a substitute in the European Champions Cup Competition, a win bonus will be paid as follows:

   a.   First Round:      £1,000.
        Second Round:     £1,500.
        Third Round:      £2,000.
        Semi Final:       £3,000.
        Final:            £4,000..

   b.   Any player selected or being called on to play as a substitute in the Final will be paid appearance money of £1,000.

   c.   A player playing in only one-leg in any round will be paid Full Win Bonus.

   d.   In addition a sum of £40,000 will be distributed among the First Team Pool of players, based on the number of appearances made by each individual, if the Club wins the Competition.

6.   When playing or being nominated as substitute in the European Cup Winners Cup Competition, a win bonus will be paid as follows:

   a.   First Round:      £1,000.
        Second Round:     £1,250.
        Third Round:      £1,500.
        Semi Final:       £2,500.
        Final:            £3,000.

   b.   Any player selected or being called on to play as a substitute in the Final will be paid apperance money of £1,000.

   c.   A player playing only one-leg in any round will be paid Full Win Bonus.

   d.   In addition a sum of £30,000 will be distributed among the First Team Pool of players, based on the number of appearances made by each individual, if the Club wins the Competition.

7.   When playing or being nominated as substitute in the UEFA Cup Competition, a win bonus will be paid as follows:

   a.   First Round:      £1,000.
        Second Round:     £1,250.
        Third Round:      £1,500.
        Fourth Round:     £2,000.
        Semi Final:       £2,500.
        Final:            £3,000.

   b.   Any player selected or being called on to play as a substitute in the Final will be paid appearance money of £500 for each game.

   c.   A player playing in only one-leg in any round will be paid Full Win Bonus.

   d.   In addition a sum of £30,000 will be distributed among the First Team Pool of players, based on the number of appearances made by each individual, if the Club wins the Competition.

8.   If you are injured whilst playing in the First Team, you will receive your basic wage and full bonus payments for a period to be decided at the Manager's discretion.

9.   If you are not selected to play but are named on the First Team Sheet you will receive your basic wage and half of any points bonus payment made to the members of the Team for Football League games, or half bonus paid in respect of any Cup ties in Competitions organised by UEFA, The Football Association or The Football League.

10.   Other Competions:   In the event of the Club playing in any other FIRST TEAM Competition apart from those listed above, the Directors undertake to make available a sum of money, the amount to be decided at their discretion for distribution pro-rata to the number of appeatances.

11.   Friendly Matches:   A bonus of £100 for a win and £50 for a Draw for First Team Friendly matches.

12.   Reserve Team:   A bonus of £10 for a win and £5 for a Draw.

# LIVERPOOL FOOTBALL CLUB
### AND ATHLETIC GROUNDS P.L.C.
**ANFIELD ROAD, LIVERPOOL L4 0TH**
**051-263 2361/2**
Telex 627661 LFC G     Fax 051-260 8813
Registered No. 35668, England
Match Information Service Only     Match Ticket Office, Enquiries Only
051-260 9999                         051-260 8680

Official Sponsor
*Candy*

KD:SW                               29th August, 1989

Mr. Alex Ferguson,
Manchester United Football Club,
Trafford Park,
Manchester, M16 0RA.

Dear Alex,

    Just a note to thank you most sincerely, albeit belatedly, for your kindness at the time of the Disaster.  We needed all the help we could get at that time and we greatly appreciated the co-operation and kindness of you and the lads in attending Colin Ashcroft's funeral.  We know that seeing you all there was a great comfort to his family.

    Thanks again Alex to you and the lads.

    Good luck,

                          Yours sincerely,

                          Kenny Dalglish.

Registered Trade Marks

K.M. DALGLISH, M.B.E.          P.B. ROBINSON
PLAYER/TEAM MANAGER            CHIEF EXECUTIVE/GENERAL SECRETARY

A letter from Kenny Dalglish in the wake of the Hillsborough disaster.

## PLAYER ANALYSIS

| | **SQUAD** | **CURRENT** | | **YOUTH** | **TRANSFER** |
| | | **EXCESS** | | **POTENTIAL** | **TARGETS/POSSIBILITIES** |
|---|---|---|---|---|---|
| GOALKEEPERS | 3 HOWARD<br>CARROLL<br>STEELE | RICARDO | | HEATON<br>LEE | |
| DEFENDERS | 6 NEVILLE, G<br>SILVESTRE<br>BROWN<br>FERDINAND<br>O'SHEA<br>FORTUNE (1) | | | SPECTOR (3)<br>MCSHANE<br>BARDSLEY | → HEINZE (PSG)<br>MEXES (AUXERRE)<br>KOMPANY (ANDERLECHT)<br>➤ PIQUE (YOUTH - BARCELONA) |
| MIDFIELD | 9 GIGGS<br>KEANE<br>SCHOLES<br>RONALDO<br>NEVILLE, P<br>KLERBERSON<br>DJEMBA DJEMBA<br>FLETCHER<br>MILLER | (BUTT)<br>CHADWICK<br>STEWART | | RICHARDSON<br>EAGLES (4)<br>N'GALULA<br>D JONES | |
| ATTACK | 4 VAN NISTELROOY<br>SAHA<br>SOLKSJAER (2)<br>BELLION | (FORLAN) | | FANGZHOU (5)<br>TIMMS | → SMITH (LEEDS) |
| **TOTAL** | 22 | 5 | | | |

**Notes of discussion with AF:**
(1) Injury issue – may not be available until 2005
(2) Injury issue – further specialist advice being sought
(3) Possibility of promotion to 1st team squad
(4) Reviewing a season long loan option
(5) Unkown quanlity – work permit issues

Discussion document from a board meeting about squad composition, 2004.

# SIR ALEX FERGUSON

The euphoria from Tuesday's demolition of the Gunners needs to be set aside today; with City the visitors, the priority is on maintaining the momentum from last week's slick showing at the Riverside

Terrific, tremendous ...the whole place is buzzing! We're going to Rome in a bid to achieve what has never been done before – and that of course is to successfully defend our Champions League crown. The statistics tell you how difficult it is, as we know to our personal cost after failing in Europe following our victory in Barcelona 10 years ago. We are ready for another crack at it, though, after a great semi-final win against Arsenal at the Emirates on Tuesday.

We went through on the back of our first-leg 1-0 win at Old Trafford and then a dominating 3-1 success this week in London. Now we look forward to a fantastic final against Barcelona. But of course Europe is only part of our story this season. We also have a domestic title to defend, so we have to get our Premier League heads on again as we welcome Manchester City to Old Trafford today. We have to put Europe out of our minds, because although we are in a strong position in the league, we must make sure we are completely focused on our remaining games if we are to come out on top.

So enough of Europe for now, especially this afternoon, because

**Maturing nicely: Giggs marked game number 801 with another cracking strike**

4 Manchester United v Manchester City

a derby poses particular problems as we also know to our cost, especially now that Mark Hughes is in charge. I know him too well to expect anything but a full-on challenge. Mark was a warrior as a player; it's a quality still in him and one that he's trying strenuously to imbue in his players.

Management is not an easy task at the best of times, and Mark is managing City at a vital and transitional stage following the Middle East takeover that put great financial resources at their disposal.

> "Mark will be only too aware that signing players, however good they are, is only the start of the process"

They made a startling impact at the start of the season with a £32 million signing, a transfer which put down a big marker of intent. City became the centre of a media storm – in fact I can't remember a time when we were so much squeezed off the back pages!

That kind of media situation does not sit easily with Mark, whose qualities made him one of our great players, but who nevertheless was never one for over-the-top hype, either concerning himself or the team. He was always a constant and consistent trainer, but he enjoyed his family life too and wouldn't hang around before heading for home. He preferred a low-profile life, so what he is experiencing now is something new for him.

He was able to keep his head down when he was manager at Blackburn where, incidentally, he did an outstanding job with a limited budget. Now he is firmly in the media spotlight, and there is no escaping it with all manner of speculation ranging from transfers both in to and out of his club, to chatter about his own future. It's always good to be the manager of a club with money available for new players, but how you spend it is what matters. I am sure there will be all kinds of possibilities turning over in his head as we draw towards the end of the season.

A message to the fans from the official match-day programme, *United Review*, 10 May 2009, Manchester United vs. Manchester City.

The lads head for the away end at the Emirates after an imperious display

Like every manager, Mark will be only too aware that signing players, however good they are individually, is only the start of the process. Building a team is what counts, and this can take years. The nature of the media beast is not one of patience, though, and Mark has already come in for a lot of unfair and hasty criticism.

What he needs is time, and I hope the City owners are prepared to give him a fair share of that precious commodity. He will need the patience of City supporters, too, and I think the whole club must have been cheered by the recent results that suggest the Blues are going to finish the season on a high.

It's certainly something we have noted, and which adds to the challenge we meet today as we seek to maintain our momentum. I thought our 2-0 win at Middlesbrough last Sunday was a big step forward. We have had some tricky moments at the Riverside, and I was worried about having a Saturday-lunchtime start after playing in the Champions League on the Wednesday with obviously not

**"Against the Gunners there was a real maturity to the team that is going to be invaluable in Rome"**

a lot of recovery time. Happily I have a squad that enables me to make changes, and I was delighted with the way Ryan Giggs and Paul Scholes in particular returned to the starting line-up. They gave such masterly displays in midfield that we ran the game and got an excellent result.

The win topped a great week for Ryan, voted the PFA Player of the Year and then celebrating 801 appearances for Manchester United by scoring! I have run out of ways of praising his contribution in a fabulous career in a red shirt, and can only congratulate him on another fine effort!

Now we go into today's game after a decent break. Playing at Arsenal on the Tuesday gave us four clear days before taking on City. And maybe I will make another change to keep us

fresh. Certainly we are approaching it in good shape after a brilliant display against the Gunners who started extremely well, only to give us a break when their young full-back slipped at a vital moment.

Ji-sung Park scored to set the scene for two fabulous goals from Cristiano Ronaldo and a performance that I believe would have prevailed even without our fortunate opening. There was a real maturity to the team that is going to be invaluable in Rome. The only disappointment was the red card for Darren Fletcher ruling him out of the final, which made it a bitter-sweet occasion.

Now though, we must put all those issues to one side, to make sure we maintain the energy and drive that's vital if we are to get over the line for the championship.

*Alex Ferguson*

Manchester United v Manchester City 5

11-05-13

IAN SETTLE
CUNNINGHAME.

Dear Sir Alex,

I came in from work today and turned on Match Of The Day. Your speech to the crowd had me beaming, what a wonderful way to bring the curtain down. My dad was a Govan man of your fathers generation, he had connections with Sommerston Church way back, and the 129th BB, if I remember. I believe this is where he introduced me to yourself when you were at Ibrox. Lost him in 76, but know he'd have loved your journey. At 52 it's a bit late in the day to start writing to personalitys, but I dare say like others felt this was a once in a lifetime moment.

This was also a big day for my family, as it started with the birth of my third grandchild. At moments like that you think of your oldman. So to turn on the telly at the end of the day and see a Govan lad holding them all spellbound was a bit special.

All the very best for the future.
That was wonderful.

Ian Settle

A fan responds to Sir Alex Ferguson's retirement.

# INDEX

Aberdeen
    chairman 194–5, 200, 228, 229, 264
    discipline 29–30
    European Cup Winners' Cup victory (1983) 15, 30, 76–7, 138, 176, 266
    managing 179–80, 228, 256–7, 324
    players' pay 266
    pre-match lunch 288
    rivalries 306
    scouts 76
    staff 39
    workdays 165
Abramovich, Roman 156, 313, 332
AC Milan, Champions League titles 337
academy system 312–13
Adams, Tony 40, 47, 104
age composition of team 87–9
agents 276–80, 298
Agüero, Sergio 272
Airbnb 61, 351
Ajax 104, 116, 188, 245, 279, 337
Al Nahyan, Mansour bin Zayed 309

Albert, Philippe 73
alcohol 40, 316, 326–7
Allardyce, Sam 70, 234, 300
Allison, George 228
Amazon 354, 363, 370, 376, 377
Ancelotti, Carlo 39, 156, 230, 318, 332
Anderson 45, 54, 315
Anderson, Jerome 234
Anderson, Viv 258
answering 213–20
Apple 350, 351, 354, 361, 363, 370, 376, 384
Archibald, Steve 20, 324
arriving 323–8
Arsenal, owners 230
assistant managers 146, 243, 331–2
Atkinson, Ron 120, 215, 324
atmosphere 74
audacity 365
authority 23, 225, 336, 365–6, 370
Ayr United, salary at 265
Azarenka, Victoria 133

balance 87, 89
Bale, Gareth 261

Ballon d'Or 118, 137, 170

Balotelli, Mario 153

Barcelona
  Champions League final losses
    to 73–4
  Champions League titles 337
  youth development 81

Bardsley, Phil 158

Barthez, Fabien 30–1, 71

Basler, Mario 67

Batistuta, Gabriel 188–9

Bayern Munich
  Champions League titles 337
  managers 227

BBC 12, 132, 217

Bébé 245

Beckham, David
  background 44
  creativity 94–5
  drive 47
  and free kicks 69
  loyalty to 129
  making room for 89
  and number 7 shirt 98
  pursuit of 253–4
  sale 259
  winning attitude 41
  youth 78, 81

Benítez, Rafael 227

Berbatov, Dimitar 116, 232, 255, 276

Berg, Henning 234

Best, George 40, 97, 253, 313, 325

Bett, Jim 257

Bezos, Jeff 371

Bielderman, Erik 14

Bishop, Bob 253

Biver, Jean-Claude 163

Blackburn Rovers, managership 234

Blackett, Tyler 82

Blair, Tony 299

Blanc, Laurent 90, 262

bleep tests 41, 294

Blockbuster 376

Bocelli, Andrea 205

Bolton, Allardyce managership 70

bonuses 267

Bosman ruling 201, 265, 277, 311

Bosnich, Mark 31, 188

Bracewell-Smith family 230

Bradford City 314

Brin, Sergey 368, 383–4

brokers see agents

Broomloan Road Primary School 3

Brown, Bobby 190, 242

Brown, Steve 241

Brown, Wes
  background 44
  and penalties 53–4

Bruce, Steve
  and Cantona signing 14
  as captain 104, 278
  departure 262
  drive 47
  as great player 112
  injuries 154
  networking with 155
  and penalties 54
  signing 293
  and youth players 80

BSkyB 312, 313

Buchan, Martin 51

Buffett, Warren 226, 277, 362, 370

Burkinshaw, Keith 144

Busby, Matt

advice from 194
after retirement 331, 336
funeral 210
as manager 228, 325, 328
Bush, George W. 218
Butt, Nicky
background 44
as coach 152
coaching potential 66, 330
drive 47
making room for 89–90
youth 78, 81
buying 251–4

Çakir, Cüneyt 219
Calder, Bobby 253
Calvert-Toulmin, John 314
camaraderie 343
Campbell, Fraizer 260, 276
Campbell, Gordon 299
Cantona, Eric
as captain 105, 106, 314
dress code breach 31
handling 125–6
'kung-fu' kick 128, 214
loyalty to 128–9
and number 7 shirt 97
and penalties 54
retirement 131
rituals 381
signing 14, 255, 261, 314
suspensions 33–5
as world class 20, 112
and youth players 80–1
captains 102–6
goalkeepers as 105
virtues 103–4
Carbone, Benito 314

Cardiff City, managership 233–4
Caro, Robert 178
Carragher, Jamie 40–1
Carrick, Michael, signing 150
Carrington training ground,
planning 148–9
Cass, Bob 216
Čech, Petr 20, 187–8
celebrations 137–9
CEOs, role 359–61
chairman
relationship with 199–201,
229–30
*see also* owners
Champions League
1997 semi-final 338
1999 semi-final 308
1999 final 67, 105, 179, 189, 203
2002 semi-final 338
2008 semi-final 67
2008 final 54, 179
2009 final 338
2011 final 338
approach to pursuit of 116
disappointments 337–8
Chapman, Herbert 228
character clashes 98–9
charitable activities 169, 170, 175–6,
209
Charlton, Bobby
advice from 77, 145
background 264
and Beckham signing 78
club service 152
support from 195
as world class 112–13
Chelsea
managers 227

spending 309, 313
Chester, James 261
Chicharito (Javier Hernández) 315
Chrysler 350
cinema 172
Cisco Systems 378
Clark, Bobby 342
Cleverley, Tom
    loaned out 260
    technical skills 65
Clough, Brian 22, 101
coaching staff, talking to 201–2
Cobbold family 230
Coerver, Wiel 65–6
Cole, Andy
    coaching potential 330
    creativity 95
    and other players 95, 98
    signing 260
    training 65
Collina, Pierluigi 340
Collins, Tony 243
compensation 263–71, 366
complacency 132–9
compromise 366
confidence, shaken 185–6
confidentiality 297–300
confrontation, not seeking 328
consistency 122, 364, 367
control 235–8, 374
    power versus 236
conviction 49–56, 365, 369, 376–7
Cook, Tim 372
Coppell, Steve 76
correspondence 169–70, 213
Costa, Diego 279
Cowdenbeath FC 28, 342
creativity 94–6

Crerand, Paddy 151
criticism
    couching of 123–32
    dealing with 184, 191–5
Cruyff, Johan 104, 193, 240

da Silva, Fábio 45, 82, 259, 315
da Silva, Rafael 45, 82, 259, 315
Dalgarno, Les 299
Dalglish, Kenny 193–4, 318
data overload 291–7
Davies, Kevin 70
Davies, Norman 36
de Gea, David 38, 53
decision-making 242–6
defeats
    learning from 181–3
    worst 183–4
Dein, David 230
delegation 238–42, 365
Dell, Michael 376
Di Canio, Paulo 233
Di María, Ángel 279
Di Matteo, Roberto 317
Di Stéfano, Alfredo 15–16
diet 286–9
discipline 27–37, 375–6
distance-keeping 120–1, 381
distractions 167–77, 372
Djemba-Djemba, Eric 317
Djokovic, Novak 42
Doherty, Paul 218
Donald, Dick
    as Aberdeen owner/chairman
        229, 256–7
    and players' pay 264, 266
    relationship with 200, 228, 229
Downes, Wally 72

drinking  172
drive  46–9, 375–6
Drogba, Didier  20, 88, 188
Drumchapel Amateurs  28, 212
Dulles brothers  341
Dunfermline, salary at  256
durability  93
Dyche, Sean  155, 220

East Stirlingshire, managing  164,
    179, 288
eBay  363, 377
education  173
Edwards, Louis  230, 355
Edwards, Martin
    as CEO  61–2, 151, 359
    and hiring of Ferguson  30,
        257–8
    and player acquisitions  274,
        293
    and player sales  88
    relationship with  200–1, 229,
        230–1, 270
    United sale attempt  269
Elberse, Anita  2–3
Elite Coaches Forum  340
The Elizabeth Hardie Ferguson
    Charitable Trust  170
Ellison, Larry  363–4, 371
Enke, Robert  193
entrepreneurs, characteristics
    368–72
Essien, Michael  20
European Cup Winners' Cup
    1983 final/victory  15, 30, 76–7,
        138, 176, 266
    1991 final  19–20, 54–5
Evans, Jonny  260

Everton, complacency against
    (2012)  135
Evra, Patrice
    as captain  106
    language skills  315
    as older player  88
    and penalties  53
    signing  97, 259
    substituted  244–5
excellence  111–18

FA Cup, 1996 final  36
FA Youth Cup  79
Fàbregas, Cesc  82
Facebook  363, 368, 373
failing  178–91
Fallon, Sean  212, 235, 342
fellow managers, networking with
    153–5
Ferdinand, Rio
    advice from  150
    background  44
    as captain  106
    career at United  258–9
    and manager's absence  122–3
    signing  258
Ferguson, Sir Alex
    books  4, 212
    first League game  355
    fresh challenges  338–43
    lifestyle  357
    post-retirement match days
        347–9
    resilience  367
    retirement as manager  334–7,
        356–7, 385
    role as manager  359–61
Ferguson, Cathy

in Aberdeen 324
as confidante 299, 357
and Darren 101–2
and family 168–9, 173
and retirement 334–5
Ferguson, Darren 101–2, 263
Ferguson, Jason 50
Ferguson, Mark 103, 173, 210–11, 261
Ferguson, Martin 20, 192, 253, 299, 349, 357
Ferguson, Ron 342
Fidgeon, Malcolm 78, 254
Figo, Luís 261
firing 155–9, 382–3
Fletcher, Darren 80, 130, 330, 356
'floaters' 68–9
foreign-born managers 317–18
foreign players 310–17
    arrival 311–15
    physique 316
Forlán, Diego 315
Fortune, Quinton 45, 146
fraternising 119–20
Frost, David 11–12
frugality 255–63

gambling 172
Gascoigne, Paul 95–6, 251–2
Gaskell, Rita 343
Gates, Bill 368, 371, 372–3
Gates, Melinda (née French) 373
Generation Investment Management 173
Gerstner, Lou 376
Gibbons, Glenn 216, 217–18
Gibson, Darron 135

Gibson, Steve 235
Giggs, Lynne 43
Giggs, Ryan
    advice from 150
    agent 278
    as assistant manager 152, 333
    background 43
    as captain 106
    coaching potential 66, 330, 331
    compensation 268
    creativity 95
    disciplining 127
    and free kicks 69
    training at Manchester City 254
    versatility 92, 245
    as world class 112
    youth 78, 80, 312
Gill, David
    as CEO 62, 201, 241–2, 270, 339, 359, 361
    and former players 151–2
    meetings with 166
    and player acquisitions 189, 254, 272–3, 275–6
Gillespie, Keith 260
Glasgow, managers from 318
Glasgow Celtic
    rivalry with Rangers 306
    winners of five competitions (1966–67) 180
Glasgow Rangers
    managership offer 13
    player at 133, 178
    rivalry with Celtic 306
    salary at 256
    spending 309
Glazer family 201, 231–2, 270, 333
global markets 310–18

goals, setting  377–8
Goodwin, Doris Kearns  23
Google  361, 363, 368, 370, 373, 378, 383–4
Govan, growing up in  192, 256, 306
Govan High School  1, 3
Graham, George  40, 270
Grant Thornton  279–80
Grove, Andy  376, 385
Guardiola, Pep  73, 193, 332

Hansen, Alan  78
Hargreaves, Owen  275
Harrison, Eric  79, 210, 306
Harvard Business School  1–4, 340
Harvey, Joe  228
Haynes, Johnny  266
Heddergot, Karl-Heinz  19
hedge-fund managers  267
Henderson, Colin  274
Hewitt, John  253
Hewlett-Packard  385
Heysel stadium disaster  20, 193
Hill-Wood family  230
Hillsborough disaster  193–4
Hitzfeld, Ottmar  189–90
Hodgson, Roy  151, 227, 340
Hogg, Graeme  298–9
homework  67–8
honesty  98–9, 159
horse-racing  341
Houllier, Gérard  14, 193, 330, 340
Howard, Tim  44–5, 52–3, 125
Hughes, Mark
  confidence  52
  durability  93

as manager  331
at Manchester City  156, 331
sale  246
signing  274
Hughton, Chris  15
Hysén, Glenn  273

Iacocca, Lee  350
IBM  363, 376
Ibrahimović, Zlatan  279
ill-discipline  73–4
improvisation  72–3
Ince, Paul
  nerves  54–5
  and penalties  53
  sale  89, 246
  signing  153
  upbraiding  126–7
  and youth players  80
industry, virtues of  373
information, sharing  295–6
in-house development  381–2
Iniesta, Andrés  81–2, 96
injuries
  effects of many  187
  increased proneness to  93
innovation  285–91
inspiring  118–32, 380–1
Intel  354, 363, 370, 376, 385–6
Inter Milan  15, 89, 144, 262
interval training  290
interviewing  145–7
Ipswich Town  230
Irwin, Denis
  departure  262
  drive  48
  and penalties  54
  reliability  93

Jackson, Reggie 360
Januzaj, Adnan 45, 82, 260
job hunting 143–7
Jobs, Steve 350, 372, 376
Jones, Dave 150
Jones, Phil 275
Joorabchian, Kia 279
Juventus 20, 88, 127, 188, 279, 308

Kaká 261
Kanchelskis, Andrei 45, 246, 314, 338
Kean, Steve 234
Keane, Roy
    as captain 99, 105
    departure from United 157
    drive 47
    as great player 112
    and number 7 shirt 98
Keane, Will 82
Keegan, Kevin 73, 278
Kennedy, John F. 23, 246
Kenway, Jim 153
Kenwright, Bill 272
Kenyon, Peter 150, 359
Kershaw, Les 77, 157, 243
Kidd, Brian 77, 146, 235, 243
Kinzer, Stephen 341
Klopp, Jürgen 332
Kluivert, Patrick 273
Knox, Archie
    as assistant manager at United 146, 183–4
    at Aberdeen 17–18, 38, 121
    and Darren Ferguson 101
    and delegation 17–18, 240
    move to United 324

relationship with 17, 200, 299–300
    watching games with 38
    and youth players 79
Kompany, Vincent 174
Koum, Jan 368
Künnecke, Ernst 296

Laffin, Lyn 169–70
Lambert, Paul 318
Larsson, Henrik 37, 65
Laudrup, Michael 20
Lawrence, John 155–6
Lawrence, Lennie 39
Le Tissier, Matthew 68
Lea, Trevor 289
leadership, management versus 239
leaving 328–38
Leeds United 14, 22, 243, 258, 261, 273–4, 306, 318, 330
Lennon, Neil 155
Lerner, Sandy 378
Leverkusen, Bayer 182
Levy, Daniel 276
Lincoln, Abraham 23, 208
LinkedIn 351, 376
Lippi, Marcello 308
listening 11–16
Little, Jimmy 80
Liverpool
    managers 227
    rivalry with United 306, 307, 337
    talent development 62
Lombardi, Vince 21
Lowry, L. S. 178
loyalty 128–9, 357, 379, 382
lunch invitations 170

Lupescu, Ioan 340
Lyall, John 49–50, 67, 153, 156, 300

Macheda, Federico 82, 260
Macintyre, Ben 341
Mackay, Dave 147
Mackay, Malky 233
management, leadership versus 239
management succession 330–3, 384–5
managers, long-serving 227–8
Manchester City
  buying team 261
  heavy defeats to 184
  managers 227
  rivalry with United 306, 308
  spending 309–10
  talent development 62
Manchester United
  appointment at 144–5
  arrival at 324–8
  discipline 30–7
  flotation 201
  match attendances 362
  revenues 361, 375
  rivalries 306
  scouts 77
  staff 62, 119
  turnover 285
  workdays 165–6
Manchester United Foundation 175
Mancini, Roberto 317, 318
Mandela, Nelson 208
Mansour, Sheikh 62, 309
Manucho 261
Marks & Spencer 149
Martínez, Roberto 317

Matthews, Stanley 264, 313
Mayorga, Jose 314
McClair, Brian
  departure 262
  in negotiations 278
  and penalties 54
  reliability 93
  signing 258
  and team talks 202
  training 292
  and youth players 80
McClaren, Steve 63, 146, 235
McCoy, A. P. 42
McGhee, Mark 30
McGrath, Paul 88, 258
McGuinness, Wilf 120, 151, 331
McGurr, Bill 153
McIlvanney, Hugh 80, 208, 212, 216
McKinven, Ron 80
McLean, Jim 39
McLeish, Alex 264
McManaman, Steve 106
McNair, Paddy 82
McNally, Steve 296
McNeill, Billy 228, 288
McParland, Dave 144
McShane, Harry 156–7
measuring players 147
medical care 241, 287, 296
Meek, David 212
Mendes, Jorge 150, 278–9
mentors 16, 81
Messi, Lionel 81–2, 96, 111–12
Meulensteen, René 65–6, 99, 115, 147, 331–2
Microsoft 363, 368, 372–3, 384
Middlesbrough, managership 235

military history 22–3
Miller, Willie 104, 264
mission statements 379
Moore, Gordon 376
Moorhouse, Barry 315
Moran, Kevin 89
Moratti, Massimo 144
Morgan, Albert 31, 150, 255, 343,
  349
Moritz, Michael 5–6
Morrison, Ravel 45–6
Moura, Lucas 272–3
Mourinho, José 39, 189, 230, 270,
  309, 317, 330, 332
Mowat, John 28
Moyes, David 146, 272, 328, 333,
  337, 385
Müller, Thomas 112, 188
multiculturalism 315–16
multi-purpose players 92
Murdoch, Rupert 269–70
Murdock, Colin 174
Musk, Elon 371, 377
MUTV 100, 218, 285

Nani 73, 89, 185, 275, 315
Nasri, Samir 189
national team managers 117
negotiation 271–6
nepotism 100–1
Netflix 376
networking 148–55
Neville, Gary
  advice from 150
  autobiography 22
  coaching potential 66, 330
  compensation 268
  and criticism 126

drive 47–8
  long-range shooting 128
  in negotiations 278
  retirement 131
  signing 272, 277
  winning attitude 41
  and youth players 80
  youth 78, 81
Neville, Phil
  debut 78
  departure 262
  drive 47–8
  signing 272, 277
  versatility 92
New York 12, 99, 332, 358
newcomers 96–7
Neymar 112
Nixon, Richard 11–12
Noyce, Bob 376
nutrition 286–9
Nvidia 376

observation 19–20
obsession 168–9, 367, 369
O'Kane, John 55
Old Trafford, pitch size 205
O'Leary, David 330
Olsen, Jesper 88, 258, 311
optometry 287, 289–90
Oracle 354, 363, 370
organisation 61–2
O'Shea, John, 92
overseas players
  see foreign players
Owen, Michael 65, 262
owners 225–35
  see also chairman
Özil, Mesut 82

Page, Larry 371, 378, 383–4
Paisley 208–9
Paisley, Bob 333–4
Pallister, Gary
  and Cantona signing 14
  coaxing 126
  goal-scoring ploy 23
  signing 89, 258, 273, 274
Pardew, Alan 155, 220
Park, Ji-sung 20, 34–5, 152
Park, Stan 211
Parker, Paul 154
patience 364, 365, 377
Paton, John 13
PayPal 6, 351, 377
Peace, David 22
Pearson, Nigel 220
Pemberton, Joe 343
penalty kicks 53–4, 293
people, dealing with 367
PeopleSoft 355, 363–4
Pereira, Andreas 82
perfection 386
perseverance 128, 147, 364
Phelan, Mick
  advice from 204
  as assistant manager 66, 146
  club service 66
  departure 333
  free transfer 262
  as message conveyor 237
  relationship with 299, 343
  signing 89
  and sponsors 174–5
  watching games 171
Philby, Kim 341
pipeline 75–83
Piqué, Gérard 82, 259

Pirlo, Andrea 35
pitches
  improvements 286–7
  width 240
Pixar 375–6
Platini, Michel 14, 340
Platt, David 158
Player of the Year awards 118, 137, 170
players, talking to 202–6
players' contracts, expiry 16
Poborský, Karel 32
Pogba, Paul 279
Possebon, Rodrigo 82
possession, importance of 19
post-game interviews 100, 214
power, control versus 236
pre-match warm-up 180–1
pre-season preparation 70–2
preparation 62–75, 79, 364, 373
press
  dealing with 213–20
  handling after defeat 184–5
press conferences 166, 186, 214, 216, 217, 218–20
programme notes 211–12
proprietorship, long-term 365
protection of players 131
pub management 164–5
public speaking 206–11

Queen's Park
  as amateur club 256, 265
  interview at 143–4
  player at 1
Queiroz, Carlos
  and coaching 64, 67, 122
  departure 244

interview 146–7
and player acquisitions 149–50,
    275
as potential successor 330
relationship with 299

radio 172
Raiola, Mino 279
Ramsey, Aaron 150–1
Ramsey, Alf 230
Rangnick, Ralf 193
Rao family 234
reading 21–3
Real Madrid 15, 76, 88, 92, 127,
    150, 184, 189, 219, 238, 261, 266,
    279, 330, 337, 353
recruitment 353, 379
Redondo, Fernando 51
Reid, Ian 28
Reid, Jimmy 207–8
reliability 92–3
respect 103, 118, 119, 121, 194, 370,
    381
reticence 371, 373
retirement 332, 334–8, 342, 356–7,
    385
Revie, Don 243
Richardson, Kieran 158
risk, approach to 74–5
rivalries 305–10, 363
Robertson, Bridget 299, 335
Robertson, John 299, 339, 349
Robinho 62
Robson, Bobby 22, 230, 295, 300
Robson, Bryan
    agent 278
    background 44
    as captain 104, 278

as coach 152
drive 47
FA Cup final squad omission
    33–4
as great player 112
and number 7 shirt 97
and youth players 80
Rodríguez, James 261
Ronaldo (Brazilian) 188
Ronaldo, Cristiano
    agent 279
    background 44
    creative role 94
    departure 33
    and free kicks 69
    rituals 381
    sale to Real Madrid 238, 261
    self-discipline 32, 171
    signing 149–50
    technical skills 65
    and Van Nistelrooy 98
    winning attitude 41–2
    as world class 111–12
    youth 313
Rooney, Wayne
    background 44
    and free kicks 69
    injury 297
    omission against Everton 131
    and penalties 54
    signing 272
Rose, Charlie 12–13
Rossi, Giuseppe 82, 259, 260
Rougvie, Doug 264
Roxburgh, Andy 146
Rudge, John 39–40
Ryan, Jim 146, 149, 188
Ryder Cup 133–4

Saha, Louis 255–6

salesman, leader as 251–2

Sánchez, Alexis 82, 112

SAS 22–3

Savage, Robbie 158

Schmeichel, Peter
  as captain 105
  departure 262–3
  retirement 188
  signing 261, 314

Scholar, Irving 144

Scholes, Paul
  advice from 150
  background 44
  as coach 152
  coaching potential 66
  compensation 268, 279–80
  creativity 94–5
  disciplining 127
  early career 91
  limelight shunned 100, 103
  making room for 89
  return from retirement 298
  versatility 92
  as world class 112
  youth 78, 81

Schroeder, Alice 277

Scotland, managers from 318

Scott, Teddy 17, 39

scouting systems 252–3, 314–15

Seaman, Barry 350

Sequoia Capital 5–6, 350–1, 353, 354, 382

Shankly, Bill 13–14, 203, 242, 328, 333–4, 336

Shawcross, Ryan 158

Shearer, Alan 104, 188

Sheringham, Teddy 95, 98, 115

Shinawatra, Thaksin 232

shipyards 37

shirt numbers, coveting 97–8

Silicon Valley 351, 352–5, 368–74, 375–6, 378–80, 383–5

Silva, David 69

Silver, Leslie 273

Silvestre, Mikaël 342

Simeone, Diego 129

Sinclair, Tony 343

Sirrel, Jimmy 16, 168

Sivebaek, John 311

Smalling, Chris 151

Smith, Alex 39

Smith, Douglas 28, 212

Smith, Jim 154

Smith, Tommy 242

Smith, Walter 146, 200

Snapchat 368

social media 219

Solskjaer, Ole Gunnar 48–9, 95, 233–4

Souness, Graeme 309

speaking 199–211, 378–9

Spiegel, Evan 368

sponsors 174–5

Sporting Lisbon, relationship with 149–50

sports science 241, 287, 290, 295

St Johnstone
  new stadium opening 183–4
  player at 190
  training with 164

St Mirren
  criticism at 191–2
  discipline 28–9
  dismissal 177, 199–200
  expectations 113–14

managing 164–5, 179, 256, 323–4
public speaking at 208–9
staff 39
staff retention 379–80
Stam, Jaap 90, 245
Stapleton, Frank 89
Stark, Billy 244
Steele, Eric 53
Stein, Jock
advice from 15–16, 120
death 117, 166
European Cup win 15
and Sean Fallon 342
networking 154–5
and press 216
treatment by Celtic board 156, 234–5, 334
Stephenson, Gail 289–90
Stiles, Nobby 77
Stillitano, Charlie 351
stock compensation 380
Stoichkov, Hristo 20
Strachan, Gordon 77, 88, 145, 258, 273–4
Strudwick, Tony 290, 291
Struth, Bill 228
Suárez, Luis 112
successor, search for 328–33
Sullivan, Stephen 342
supporters 153
supporters' club events 169, 170
Swales, Harry 278
Swales, Peter 308
Symon, Scot 13, 155–6, 215, 228

Tampa Bay Buccaneers 231
Tan, Vincent 233–4
targets, setting 115–18

team talks 46, 130, 180, 202–3, 237
teamwork 87–102, 206
technology, advances in 286, 374–5
technology industry
failed companies 354–5
giants 354
temper, displays of 236
Terry, John 104
Tévez, Carlos
advisor 279
background 45
failure to sign 245
goal against United (2007) 136
tirelessness 73
training 292
Thatcher, Margaret 312
Thomson, Elizabeth 3
Thornley, Ben 51, 89
time 163–7
Todd, Willie 199
Torres, Fernando 256
Tottenham Hotspur
first foreign players 311
job offer 144
trade-union leaders 271
training 62–5, 290–1
transfer market, regrets 187–9
transfer windows 274–5
trust 120–1, 382
Turner, Chris 88
Twitter 385

UEFA Champions League
see Champions League
UEFA coaching 340
undersoil heating 325–6
UNICEF 170, 175

Valencia, Antonio  45, 98
Valentine, Don  351
van der Sar, Edwin  53, 188, 259
van Gaal, Louis  332, 333, 337
van Nistelrooy, Ruud
    compensation  268
    confidence  52
    and penalties  54
    and Ronaldo  98
    signing delayed by injury
        129–30
    training  292
van Persie, Robin
    failure to sign  188
    and penalties  54
    signing  232, 255, 335
Varane, Raphaël  189
Venglŏs, Josef  317
Verón, Juan Sebastián  34, 255
video analysis  241, 287, 293–5, 296
Vidić, Nemanja
    as captain  106
    language skills  315
    signing  97, 259
viruses, effects of  187

Waddell, Willie  13
wages  264–5
    maximum  265
    see also compensation
Walker, Jim  80
Wallace, Danny  89
Wallace, Jock  49–50, 155
watching  17–21
Watkins, Maurice  272, 274, 335
Webb, Neil  89
Webvan  376–7
Welbeck, Danny

    background  44
    loaned out  260
    progression to first team  260
    technical skills  65
Wembley, first final at  177
Wenger, Arsène
    games managed  227
    length of tenure  328
    players recruited  313
    Premier League winner  318
    relationship with  308
    signing of Aaron Ramsey  151
    team development  82
    work ethic  39
West Ham, 2011 relegation  7
    2–3
WhatsApp  368
White, David  119–20
Whiteside, Norman  89, 151
Wilder, Chris  155
Wilkinson, Howard  273, 318
Williams, Carol  343
Williams, Norman  153, 308
Williams, Serena  133
Wilson, Danny  43
Wilson, James  81, 82
winter breaks  63
Wolverhampton Wanderers,
    interview at  143, 144
Wooden, John  5, 21
work ethic  373
work rate  37–46
working-class backgrounds  42–6,
    264–5, 356
'world class' players  111–13
writing  211–13

Xavi  81–2, 96

Yahoo! 368, 383, 385
Yang, Jerry 368
Yeung, Carson 232
Yorke, Dwight
  coaching potential 330
  creativity 95
  signing 273, 316
youth 77–83
  emphasis on 82–3, 259–60

Zappos 377
Zickler, Alexander 67
Zidane, Zinedine 189, 261
Zola, Gianfranco 40
Zuckerberg, Mark 368, 371